AMAZING NORTHEAST

MIZORAM

AMAZING NORTHEAST

MIZORAM

Edited & Compiled by
Aribam Indubala Devi

Vij Books India Pvt. Ltd.
(Publishers, Dustributors & Importers)
4675-A, 21, Ansari Road, Darya Ganj,
New Delhi-110002

Published by
Vij Books India Pvt. Ltd.
(Publishers, Distributors & Importers)
4675-A, 21, Ansari Road, Darya Ganj,
New Delhi-110002
Phone: 91-11-65449971, 91-11-43596460
Fax: 91-11-47340674
E-mail: vijbooks@rediffmail.com

First Edition: 2010

ISBN: 978-93-80177-28-1

Contents

Preface

In India, the Northeastern region is quite charming and interesting enough to be known about. Among the eight Northeastern States, Mizoram occupies an area of great strategic importance in the northeastern corner of India. Mizoram has great natural beauty and an endless variety of landscape. It is rich in fauna and flora. The origin of the word 'Mizo' is not known. The Mizos came under the influence of the British Missionaries in 19th century. Now, most of the Mizos are Christians. Mizo language has no script of its own. The missionaries introduced Roman script for Mizo language and formal education. Literacy in the state has grown rapidly, and in Mizoram literacy at 88.8 per cent, is second highest in the country. The state government is striving hard to attain the top position in near future.

Mizoram is a mountainous region, which became the State of the Indian Union in February 1987. It was one of the districts of Assam till 1972, when it became a Union Territory. After being annexed by the British in 1891, for the first few years, Lushai Hills in north remained under Assam, while the southern half remained under Bengal. Both these parts were amalgamated in 1898 into one district, called Lushai Hills District, under the Chief Commissioner of Assam. With the implementation of the Northeastern Reorganisation Act in 1972, Mizoram bacame a Union Territory and as a sequel to the signing of the historic memorandum of settlement between the Government of India and the Mizo National Front in 1986, it was granted statehood on 20 February 1987. Mizoram is sandwiched between Myanmar in east and south and Bangladesh in west.

This small but comprehensive and compact book on this northeastern state, offers all information, within one cover. Hopefully, it would serve all those working on or interested in knowing about northeastern India, be they scholars, researchers, journalists, students or general readers. This is in fact, 'Knowledge in Nutshell'.

— *Editor*

Mizoram

An Overview

Governor	:	Lt. Gen. (Retd.) M.M. Lakhera
Chief Minister	:	Pu Lalthanhawla
Speaker	:	R. Romawia
Chief Secretary	:	Vanhela Pachnau
Capital	:	Aizawl
High Court	:	Guwahati (Bench at Aizawl)

Brief Description

Mizoram, the land of the Mizo tribe, is the southern most state in India's northeast. It is stretched between 92.15□□° to 93.29° East longitude and 21.58° to 24.35° North latitude. Spread over an area of 21,087 sq km, Mizoram constitutes 8.042 per cent of the total landmass of the entire North-East and 0.67 per cent of India as a whole. It shares its border with Myanmar in the east and south, and Bangladesh in the west, and Assam, Tripura and Manipur in the north. With Myanmar, Mizoram shares an international boundary of 404 km and with Bangladesh it has a boundary of 318 km.

Mizoram had been a district of Assam till 1972 when it became a

Facts and Figures

- *Area:* 21,087 sq km (8% of total area of North-East)

- *Geographical Location:* Situated between latitude 21° 58' to 24° 35' N & longitude 92° 15' & 93° 29' E

- *Capital:* Aizawl

- *Population:* 8,91,058 (2001 Census) (2.4% of population of North-East)

- *Principal Languages:* Mizo and English

- *Female:* 4,31,275

- *Male:* 4,59,783

Contd...

Union Territory. With the implementation of the North-Eastern Reorganisation Act in 1972, Mizoram became a Union Territory on 21 January 1973 and following the signing of the memorandum of settlement between the Government of India and the Mizo National Front (MNF) in 1986, it became the 23rd State of the Indian Union on 20 February 1987.

Aizawl, the capital of Mizoram, is located 3,715 feet above the sea level. For administrative purposes, the State is divided into eight districts, 22 blocks and 23 subdivisions. There are three Autonomous District Councils in the State, formed under the Sixth Schedule of the Indian Constitution.

The inhabitants of Mizoram are known by the generic name Mizo, which means people of the hills. The origin of the Mizos can be traced back to the great Mongoloid wave of migration from China who moved into India. Historically there has been a considerable concoction of different tribes in the State leading to three main subgroups — Lushais, Pawis and Lakhers. According to Census 2001, Mizoram has a total population of 8,91,058 with a density of 42 persons per sq km. It constitutes .09 per cent of the total population of India and 2.28 per cent of that of the North-East. Majority of the population are Christians.

Mizo language has no script of its own. The Christian missionaries introduced the Roman script for the Mizo language and literacy in the state has grown rapidly. Mizoram has a

- *Density (per sq km):* 42 (National Figure: 324)
- *Population below Poverty Line:* 19.5 % (National Figure: 27.5%)
- *Sex Ratio:* 938 females to 1,000 males (National figure: 933 females to 1,000 males)
- *Literacy Rate (2007):* 89.9% (National Figure: 67.6%)
- *Birth Rate (2006):* 17.8 (National Figure: 23.1)
- *Death Rate (2006):* 5.5 (National Figure: 7.4)
- *Infant Mortality Rate (2007):* 23 (National Figure: 55)
- *No. of Towns (as per 2001 Census):* 22
- *No. of Villages (as per 2001 Census):* 817
- *Per Capita Income (in Rs.) (2006-07):* 25,679 (National Figure: Rs. 29,901)
- *Net State Domestic Product (NSDP) (Rs. in crore) (2007-08):* 2,887 (National Figure: 38,11,441)
- *Per Capita NSDP (2007-08):* Rs. 27,501 (National Figure: Rs. 33,283)
- *Per Capita GSDP (2004-05):* Rs. 30,357 (National Figure: Rs. 25,944)
- *State Bird:* Hume's Bartailed Pheaasant (Vavu)
- *State Animal:* Serow (Saza)
- *State Flower:* Dancing Girl (Aiting)
- *Language:* Mizo, English and Hindi

Contd...

high literacy rate of 88.49 per cent, the second highest in the country.

Mizoram is primarily an agricultural state. About 59.77 per cent of the total working population are engaged in cultivation and other agricultural activities. The main pattern of agriculture is *jhum* or shifting cultivation. Of the total 2.1 million hectares of estimated land, 6,30,000 hectares of land is available for cultivation of horticulture crops. The per capita per capita Gross State Domestic Product (GSDP) in 2004-05, is rupees 30,357. Mizoram ranks 7th in the human resource development index and 14th in the poverty index in India.

- *No. of Districts:* (08) Mamit, Kolasib, Aizawl, Champhai, Serchhip, Lunglei, Lawngthai, Saiha
- *Major Towns:* Aizawl, Kolasib, Serchhip, Lunglei
- *Major Crops:* Rice, Maize
- *Major Plantations:* Tea, Rubber, Coffee, Tung Oil
- *Major Fruits, Vegetables & Spices:* Banana, Pineapple, Orange, Passion Fruit, Chillies and Ginger
- *Major Minerals:* Coal, Limestone
- *Airport:* Lengpui Airport (Aizawl)

The entire Mizoram was a notified backward area and was categorised under 'No Industry District' in mid- 1970s. With the announcement of State Industrial Policy 1989, few modern small-scale industries have come up during the past decade. No major mineral deposits of economic importance have been located so far in the state. Consequently the state's economy revolves around agriculture and traditional industries. Since the 1986 Peace Accord, Mizoram has been largely free from insurgent violence, although its has witnessed insurgency movements by the Reang and the Hmar tribes. Presence of the Chin population from Myanmar too has occasionally created societal problems.

Area, Population and Headquarters of Districts

S.No.	District	Area (sq km)	Population	Headquarters
1.	Aizawl	3,576.31	3,39,812	Aizawl
2.	Lunglei	4,538.00	1,37,155	Lunglei
3.	Chhimtuipui	1,399.90	60,823	Saiha
4.	Lawngtlai	2,557.10	73,050	Lawngtlai
5.	Champhai	3,185.85	1,01,389	Champhai
6.	Kolasib	1,282.51	60,977	Kolasib
7.	Mamit	3,025.75	62,313	Mamit
8.	Serchhip	1,421.60	55,539	Serchhip

[Based on Latest Official Data Available]

Mizoram

Outline Map

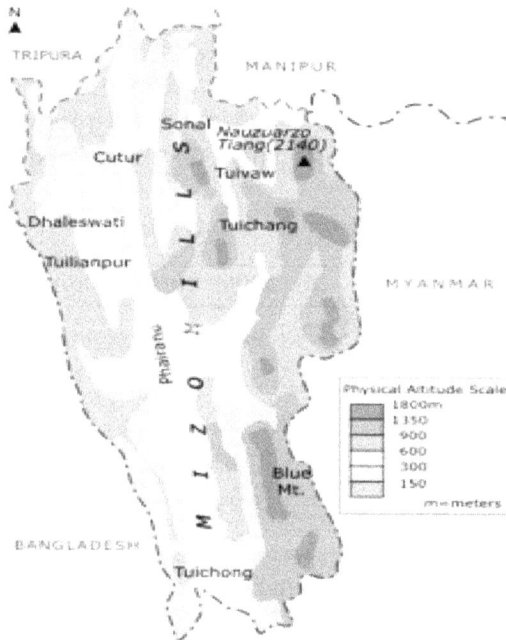

Geographical Map

Tourist Map

Districts of the State

$$\boxed{1}$$

Introduction

Mizoram is one of the Eight Sister States in Northeastern India. It shares land borders with the states of Tripura, Assam, Manipur, Bangladesh and the Chin state of Burma. Mizoram became the 23rd state of India on 20 February 1987. Its population at the 2001 census stood at 891,058. Mizoram ranks second in India with a literacy rate of 89.9 per cent. Mizoram has the most variegated hilly terrain in the eastern part of India. The hills are steep (average height 1,000 metres) and separated by rivers which flow either to the north or south creating deep gorges between the hill ranges.

The highest peak in Mizoram is the Blue Mountain with a height of 2,210 metres. Its tropical location combined with the high altitude gives it a mild climate all year round. Mizoram is rich in flora and fauna and many kinds of tropical trees and plants thrive in the area. Mizoram literally means land of the highlanders. Mizoram has a mild climate, not very warm in summer and not very cold in winter. During winter, the temperature varies from 11°C to 21°C and in summer it varies between 20°C and 29°C. The entire area is under the regular influence of monsoons. It rains heavily from May to September and the average rainfall is 254 cm per annum. The average annual rainfall in Aizawl and Lunglei are 208 centimetres and 350 centimetres, respectively. Winter in Mizoram is normally rain-free.

Historical Aspects

The origin of the Mizos, like those of many other tribes in the Northeastern India is shrouded in mystery. Generally accepted as part of a great Mongoloid wave of migration from China and later moved out to India to their present habitat. It is possible that the Mizos came from Shinlung or Chhinlungsan located on the banks of the River Yalung in China. They first settled in the Shan State and moved on to Kabaw Valley to Khampat and then to the Chin Hills in the middle of the 16th century.

The earliest Mizos who migrated to India were known as Kukis, the second batch of immigrants were called New Kukis. The Lushais were the last of the Mizo tribes migrated to India. The Mizo history in the 18th and 19th century is marked by many instances of tribal raids and retaliatory expeditions of security. Mizo Hills were formally declared as part of the British-India by a proclamation in 1895. North and south hills were united into Lushai Hills District in 1898 with Aizawl as its headquarters.

The process of the consolidation of the British administration in tribal dominated area in Assam started in 1919 when Lushai Hills along with some other hill districts was declared a Backward Tract under government of India Act. The tribal districts of Assam including Lushai Hills were declared Excluded Area in 1935.

It was during the British regime that a political awakening among the Mizos in Lushai Hills started taking shape. The first political party, the Mizo Common People's Union was formed on 9th April 1946. The Party was later renamed as Mizo Union. As the day of Independence drew nearer, the Constituent Assembly of India set up an Advisory Committee to deal with matters relating to the minorities and the tribals. A subcommittee, under the chairmanship of Gopinath Bordoloi was formed to advise the Constituent Assembly on the tribal affairs in the North-East. The Mizo Union submitted a resolution to this subcommittee demanding inclusion of all Mizo inhabited areas adjacent to Lushai Hills. However, a new party called the United Mizo Freedom Organisation (UMFO) came up to demand that Lushai Hills join Burma after Independence.

Following the Bordoloi subcommittee's suggestion, a certain amount of autonomy was accepted by the government and enshrined in the Six Schedule of the Constitution. The Lushai Hills Autonomous District Council came into being in 1952 followed by the formation of these bodies led to the abolition of chieftainship in the Mizo society. The autonomy, however, met the aspirations of the Mizos only partially. Representatives of the District Council and the Mizo Union pleaded with the States Reorganisation Commission (SRC) in 1954 for integration of the Mizo-dominated areas of Tripura and Manipur with their District Council in Assam.

The tribal leaders in the North-East were laboriously unhappy with the SRC Recommendations. They met in Aizawl in 1955 and formed a new political party, Eastern India Tribal Union (EITU) and raised demand for a separate state comprising all the hill districts of Assam. The Mizo Union split and the breakaway faction joined the EITU. By this time, the UMFO also joined the EITU and then understanding of the Hill problems by the Chuliha Ministry, the demand for a separate hill state by EITU was kept in abeyance.

Origin

The origin of the Mizos, like those of many other tribes in the Northeastern India, is shrouded in mystery. The generally accepted view is that they were part of a great wave of migration from China and later moved out to India to their present habitat. It is possible that the Mizos came from Sinlung or Chhinlungsan located on the banks of the Yalung River in China, first settled in the Shan State and moved on to the Kabaw Valley. It is also believed that Mizos originated from Mongolia, however, there is no written proof.

Facts and Legends

Folklore has an interesting tale to offer. The Mizos, so goes the legend, emerged from under a large covering rock known as *Chhinlung*. Two people of the Ralte clan, known for their loquaciousness, started talking noisily while coming out of the region. They made a great noise which made their God, called *Pathian* of the Mizos, to throw up his hands in disgust and say "enough is enough". He felt too many people had already been allowed to step out and he closed the door with the rock. History often varies from legends. But the story of the Mizos getting out into open world through a rock opening is now a part of the Mizo fable.

Chhinlung

Chhinlung, however, is taken by some as the Chinese city of Sinlung or Chhinlungsang situated close on the Sino-Burmese border. The Mizos have songs and stories about the glory of the ancient Chhinlung civilization handed down from one generation to the other. According to Mr. K. S. Latourette, there were political upheavals in China in 210 BC when the dynastic rule was abolished and the whole empire was brought under one administrative system. Rebellions broke out and chaos reigned throughout the Chinese State. Then the Mizos left China as part of one of those waves of migration.

Kabaw Valley

Then they changed settlements several times, moving from the Shan state to Kabaw Valley to Khampat in Burma. It was in the Kabaw Valley that Mizos got the opportunity to have an unhindered interaction with the local Burmese. The two cultures met and the two tribes influenced each other in the spheres of clothing, customs, music and sports. According to some, the Mizos learnt the art of cultivation from the Burmese at Kabaw. Many of their agricultural implements bore the prefix *Kawl*, which was the name given by the Mizos to the Burmese.

Shan State

It seems probable that the Mizos moved from China to Burma and then to India under forces of certain circumstances. They first settled in the Shan State after having overcome the resistance put up by the indigenous people. The Shans had already been firmly settled in their state when Mizos came there from Chhinlung around 5th century. The Shans did not welcome the new arrivals, but failed to throw the Mizos out. The Mizos had lived happily in the Shan state for about 300 years before they moved on the Kabaw Valley around the 8th century.

Khampat

The earliest Mizos who migrated to India were known as Kukis, the second batch of immigrants were called New Kukis. The Mizo history in the 18th and 19th century is marked by many instances of tribal raids and retaliatory amount of autonomy was accepted by the government and enshrined in the Six Schedule of the Indian Constitution. The Lushai Hills Autonomous District Council came into being in 1952 followed by the formation of these bodies led to the abolition of chieftainship in the Mizo society. The autonomy, however, met the aspirations of the Mizos only partially. Representatives of the District Council and the Mizo Union pleaded with the States Reorganisation Commission (SRC) in 1954 for integration of the Mizo-dominated areas of Tripura and Manipur with their District Council in Assam. The tribal leaders in the North-East were laboriously unhappy with the SRC recommendations. They met in Aizawl in 1955 and formed a new political party, Eastern India Tribal Union (EITU) and raised their demand for a separate state comprising all the hill districts of Assam. The Mizo Union split and the breakaway faction joined the EITU. By this time, the UMFO also joined the EITU and then understanding of the hill problems by the Chuliha Ministry, the demand for a separate hill state by EITU was kept in abeyance.

Chin Hills

The Mizos, in the early-14th century, settled at Chin Hills on the Indo-Burmese border. They built villages and called them by their clan names such as *Seipui*, *Saihmun* and *Bochung*. The hills and difficult terrains of Chin Hills stood in the way of the building of another central township like Khampat. The villages were scattered so unsystematically that it was not always possible for the various Mizo clans to keep in touch with each other.

Mizo Hills

The earliest Mizos who migrated to India were known as Kukis, the second batch of immigrants were called New Kukis. The Lushais were the last of the Mizo tribes migrated to the Lushai Hills. By the time they crossed the Tiau River bordering Myanmar, the descendants of Zahmuaka, who came to be known as the ruling Sailo clan, had proven their mettle as able and assertive chiefs. The traditional system of village administration, too, had been perfected. As the head of the village, the Chief or Lal allocated lands for cultivation, settled all disputes in the villages, fed and cared for the poor and offered shelter to anyone seeking refuge. The Mizo history in the 18th and 19th centuries is marked by many instances of tribal raids and retaliatory expeditions.

British Rule

Mizo Hills were formally declared as part of British India by a proclamation in 1895. North and south hills were united into Lushai Hills District in 1898 with Aizawl as its headquarters. The process of the consolidation of the British administration in tribal dominated area in Assam started in 1919 when Lushai Hills, along with some of the other hill districts, was declared a "Backward Tract" under the 1919 Government of India Act. The tribal districts of Assam including Lushai Hills were declared "Excluded Area" in 1935.

Mautam Famine

In 1959, the Mizo Hills was devastated by a great famine known in Mizo history as 'Mautam Famine'. The cause of the famine was attributed to flowering of bamboos which resulted in a boom of the rat population. After eating bamboos seeds, the rats turned towards crops and infested the huts and houses and became a plague to the villages. The havoc created by the rats was terrible and very little of the grain was harvested. For sustenance, many Mizos had to collect roots and leaves from the jungles. Still others moved to far away places, and a considerable number died of starvation. In this hour of darkness, many welfare organisations tried their best to help starving villagers. Earlier in 1955, the Mizo Cultural Society was formed with Pu Laldenga as its secretary. In March 1960, the name of the Mizo Cultural Society was changed to 'Mautam Front'. During the famine of 1959-1960, this society took the lead in demanding relief and managed to attract the attention of all sections of the people. In September 1960, the Society adopted the name of Mizo National Famine Front (MNFF). The MNFF gained considerable popularity as a large number of Mizo youth assisted in transporting rice and other essential commodities to interior villages.

Insurgency

The Mizo National Famine Front dropped the word 'famine' and a new political organisation, the Mizo National Front (MNF) was born on 22 October 1961 under the leadership of Laldenga with the specified goal of achieving sovereign independence of Greater Mizoram. Simultaneous large-scale disturbances broke out on 28 February 1966 in government installations at Aizawl, Lunglei, Chawngte, Chhimluang and other places. The Government of India bombed the city of Aizawl with 'Toofani' and 'Hunter' jet fighters. This was the first time that India had used its air force to quell a movement of any kind among its citizens. In the afternoon of March 4, 1966, a flock of jet fighters hovered over Aizawl and dropped bombs leaving a number of houses in flames.

The next day, a more excessive bombing took place for several hours which left most houses in Dawrpui and Chhingaveng area in ashes, recollected 62-year-old Rothangpuia in Aizawl. The search for a political solution to the problems facing the hill regions in Assam continued. The Mizo National Front was outlawed in 1967. The demand for statehood gained fresh momentum. A Mizo District Council delegation, which met Prime Minister Indira Gandhi in May 1971 demanded full-fledged statehood for the Mizos. The union government on its own offered the proposal of turning Mizo Hills into a Union Territory (UT) in July 1971. The Mizo leaders were ready to accept the offer on the condition that the status of UT would be upgraded to statehood sooner rather than later.

The Union Territory of Mizoram came into being on 21 January 1972. Mizoram has two seats in Parliament, one each in the Lok Sabha and in the Rajya Sabha.

Birth of Mizoram State

Rajiv Gandhi's election to power following his mother's death signalled the beginning of a new era in Indian politics. Laldenga met the Prime Minister on 15 February 1985. Some contentious issues which could not be resolved during previous talks were referred to him for his advice. With Pakistan having lost control of Bangladesh and no support from Pakistan, the Mizo National Front used the opportunity that had now presented itself. New Delhi felt that the Mizo problem had been dragging on for a long time, while the Mizo National Front was convinced that disarming, to live as respectable Indian citizens, was the only way of achieving peace and development. Statehood was a prerequisite to the implementation of the accord signed between the Mizo National Front and the Union Government on 30 June 1986. The document was signed by Pu Laldenga on behalf of the Mizo National Front, and the Union Home Secretary R. D. Pradhan on behalf of the government. Lalkhama, Chief Secretary of Mizoram, also signed the agreement. The formalisation of the state of Mizoram took place on 20 February 1987. Chief Secretary Lalkhama read out the proclamation of statehood at a public meeting organised at Aizawl's parade ground. Prime Minister Rajiv Gandhi flew in to Aizawl to inaugurate the new state. Hiteshwar Saikia was appointed as Governor of Mizoram.

Geographical Aspects

Mizoram geography includes the climate of the area, the flora and fauna of the state, the lakes, rivers and the general topography of the region. The state is blessed with many natural resources. Adorned with lush green mountains and free flowing rivers, Mizoram takes a paradaisical look. The region receives heavy rainfall and enjoys a very pleasing climate throughout the year. The presence of some major rivers like Tlau, Tlawng, Tuirini, Serlui and Mat and some picturesque lakes is also a highpoint of Mizoram's geography.

The Land

Mizoram is a mountainous region which became the 23rd State of the Union in February 1987. It was one of the districts of Assam till 1972 when it became Union Territory. Sandwiched between Myanmar in the east and south and Bangladesh in the west, Mizoram occupies an area of great strategic importance in the northeastern corner of India. It has a total of 630 miles boundary with Myanmar and Bangladesh. Mizoram has the most variegated hilly terrain in the eastern part of India. The hills are steep and are separated by rivers which flow either to the north or the south creating deep gorges between the hill ranges. The average height of the hills is about 900 metres. The highest peak in Mizoram is the Phawngpui (Blue Mountain) with a height of 2,210 metres. Mizoram has a pleasant climate. It is generally cool in summer and not very cold in winter.

During winter, the temperature varies from 11 to 21°C and in the summer it varies between 20 and 29°C. The entire area is under the direct influence of the monsoon. It rains heavily from May to September and the average rainfall in Aizawl is 208 cm. Winter in Mizoram is wonderfully blue, and in the enchanting view of wide stretches of a vast lake of cloud. Mizoram has great natural beauty and endless variety of landscape and is very rich in flora and fauna. Almost all kinds of tropical trees and plants thrive in Mizoram. The hills are marvellously green.

Climate

The upper part of the hills are, predictably cold, cool during the summer, while the lower reaches are relatively warm and humid. Storms break out during March-April, just before or around the summer. The maximum average temperature in the summer is 30°C while in the winter the minimum average temperature is around 11°C. The four months between November and February are winter in Mizoram which is followed by the spring. The storms come in the middle of April to herald the beginning of the summer. The mercury starts rising and the hills come under the cover of a haze. The three months from June to August are known as the rainy season. The climate is at its moderate best in the two autumnal months, September and October, when the temperature moves between 19 and 24°C. Taken all in all, Mizoram is made up of wooded hills, swift flowing rivers quicksilver streams and still lakes, the combination of all this is a rarity. And it is the combination of these physical features that has given Mizoram its own charm and fascination.

Topography

The topography of Mizoram is not very different from its other Northeastern neighbours. Mizoram topography is conspicuous with the presence of hills and mountain ranges. The tall green hills are moated with free flowing rivers. The eastern side of the state is situated at a higher altitude than the western side of the state.

The average height of the Mizoram hills is approximately 900 metres. The tallest among the hills is the Phawngpui (Blue Mountain) with a height of 2,210 metres. The picturesque valleys and flat lands of Cachar, Mat, Champhai, Chamdur and Tlabung are blessed with very fertile soil and natural resources suitable for excellent agricultural and horticultural productions. The geographical location of Mizoram lies between East Longitude 92°15' to 93°29' and North Latitude 21°58' to 24°35'. Covering a total area of 21,081 square kilometres, the state is blessed with rich forest resources and beautiful lakes.

Flora and Fauna

The lush green vegetations and forests infested with many type of animals signify the rich Mizoram Flora and Fauna. The excellent flora and fauna of Mizoram is a strong reason behind its popularity among the tourists.

The abundance of bamboo forests is one high point of Mizoram's flora. The hills of Mizoram have dense deciduous vegetations. The valleys and the mountain peaks are blessed with many known and unknown orchids. The ever admirable rhododendron is seen in abundance in these areas. The Blue Mountain (Phawangpui) is one such place where the Veitchiunum and Arboretum species of Rhododendron are found in plenty.

The presence of thick forests and good climate facilitated the fauna of Mizoram. The animal kingdom of Mizoram comprises several rare and endangered species. Some of the animals found in the Mizoram forests, wildlife sanctuaries and national parks are:

- Bear,
- Tiger,
- Hoolock Gibbon,
- Leopard,
- Porcupine,
- Mongoose,
- Claw-less Otter, and
- Chinese Pangolin.

The forest areas and the lakes of Mizoram attract large number of migratory birds besides the local birds. Several species of pheasants, hawks, eagles, bulbuls, herons and egrets are sighted in Mizoram. Numerous species of butterflies, moths and many colourful insects are also found in these regions.

Hills

Mizoram is a land of rolling hills, rivers and lakes. As many as 21 major hills ranges or peaks of different heights run through the length and breadth of the state, with plains scattered here and there. The average height of the hills to the west of the state are about 1,000 metres. These gradually rise up to 1,300 metres to the east. Some areas, however, have higher ranges which go up to a height of over 2,000 metres. Phawngpui, or the Blue Mountain, situated in the southeastern part of the state, is the highest peak in Mizoram.

Rivers

The biggest river in Mizoram is the River Kaladan also known as Chhimtuipui Lui in local Mizo language. It originates from Chin State in Burma and passes through Saiha and Lawngtlai districts in southern tip of Mizoram and goes back to Burma's Rakhine state, finally it enters Bay of Bengal at Akyab, a very popular port in Sittwe, Burma. Indian Government has invested millions of rupees to set up inland water ways along this river to trade with Burma. The project name is known as Kaladan Multi-purpose Project.

Although many more rivers and streams drain the hill ranges, the most important and useful rivers are the Tlawng (also known as Dhaleswari or Katakhal), Tut (Gutur), Tuirial (Sonai) and Tuivawl which flow through the northern territory and eventually join the Barak River in Cachar District.

The Koldoyne (Chhimtuipui) which originates in Burma, is an important river in the south of Mizoram. It has four tributaries and the river is in patches. The western part is drained by Karnaphuli (Khawthlang tuipui) and its tributaries. A number of important towns, including Chittagong in Bangladesh, are situated at the mouth of the river. Before Independence, access to other parts of the country was only possible through the river routes via Cachar in the north, and via Chittagong in the south. Entry through the latter was cut-off when the subcontinent was partitioned and ceded to East Pakistan (now Bangladesh) in 1947.

Lakes

Lakes are scattered all over the state, but the most important among these are Palakdil (Pala Tipo), Tamdil, Rungdil, and Rengdil. The Palak Lake, the biggest lake in Mizoram is situated in Mara Autonomous District Council (MADC) within Saiha District which is part of southern Mizoram and covers an area of 30 hectares. It is believed that the lake was created as a result of an earthquake or a flood. The local people believe that a village which was submerged still remains intact deep under the waters. The Tamdil Lake is a natural lake situated 110/85 km from Aizawl. Legend has it that a huge mustard plant once stood in this place. When the plant was cut down, jets of water sprayed from the plant and created a pool of water, thus the lake was named '*Tamdil*' which means of 'Lake of Mustard Plant'. Today, the lake is an important tourist attraction and a holiday resort.

However, the most significant lake in Mizo history Rihdil is ironically located in Burma, a few kilometres from the India-Burma border. It was believed that the departed souls pass through this lake before making their way to "Pialral" or heaven.

Social Aspects

The Mizos are impregnable society with no class difference and no discrimination on the grounds of sex. Ninety per cent of the total society are into cultivation and the village seems like a big family. Birth of a child, marriage in the village and death of a person in the village or a community feast organised by a member of the village are prime events in which the whole village takes part.

Social Life

The fabric of social life in the Mizo society has undergone tremendous change over the last few years. Before the British arrived in these hills, for all practical purposes, the village and the clan formed units of Mizo society. The Mizo code of ethics or dharma focused on *"Tlawmngaihna"*, an untranslatable term meaning that it was the obligation of all members of society to be hospitable, kind, unselfish, and helpful to others.

Tlawmngaihna to a Mizo stands for that compelling moral force which finds expression in self-sacrifice for the service of others. The old belief, *Pathian*, is still used to mean God. Many Mizos have embraced their new-found faith of Christianity. Their sense of values have also undergone a drastic change and are largely being guided (directly and indirectly) by the Christian church organisations.

Clothing

The original garment of the Mizos is known as *puan*. They were used by men and women more or less in the same fashion. One has to see them to believe the intricate traditional designs woven by the Mizo women, born weavers who produce what can only be described as art on their looms. The Mizo have held on to certain patterns and mottos that have come down through the ages. These designs have become deep rooted in their tribal consciousness and become a part of the Mizo heritage.

The unique value of Mizo *puan* comes from the personal involvement of the weaver, who with great labour weaves her dreams into each work and weft until every design has a story to tell. These traditional hand woven apparels are of different shades and designs without exquisite play of colour combination and intricate weaving patterns has been evolved. Some of the common clothing or *puan* are:

- *Puanchei:* It is by far the most colourful costume and is used by every Mizo lady.

- *Kawrchei:* A distinctive blouse of the ladies.

- *Ngotekherh:* This traditional *puan* is won round the waist originally it was a men's *puan* but now it is worn by men and women alike.

- *Hmar am:* Originally this was a small hand woven cloth of handspun cotton and indigo dye.

- *Cyhna hno:* It is a beautiful embroidered silk *puan* of the Mara's. It is used by both men and women.

Custom

Although Christianity brought about a near — total transformation in the Mizo lifestyle and outlook some customary laws have stayed on. The efforts of the Missionaries, so it seems, were not directed at changing the basic customs of the Mizo society presumably because they saw nothing much wrong with them. The customs and traditions which they found meaningless and harmful were abolished by persistent preaching. Thus, tea replaced ZU as a popular drink among the Mizos. Zawlbuk (Bachelor's dormitories) had been replaced by modern education. Animal sacrifices on ceremonial occasions, which were once an integral part of Mizo religious system, are now considered anathema. But such traditions as the payment of bride price are still continued and so are some other customs and community traditions.

Bride Price: The Mizos are not alone in putting a price on a bride. This custom is prevalent in a few other Indian communities as well. When a Mizo boy approaches his fiancee's parents for permission to get married, the first thing he has to do is to settle the bride price. If the price among other things, demanded by him, is acceptable to the parents, the boy and the girl are allowed to get married. Thus, the settlement of the bride price to be paid by the bridegroom is an essential prerequisite to a Mizo marriage.

It so generally happens that part of the bride price which may be paid on the eve of the wedding, while the part of bride price called 'Thutphah' is held back over the years as a sort of security of paying off the debts fall on the next generation. In case of the death of a husband, his son is obliged to pay the bride price.

The principal bride price is known as Manpui. Besides, there are subsidiary bride prices like sumhmahruai and sumfang. These prices are to be paid to the bride's father or brother. Pusum is payable to the nearest relation on the side of the bride's mother who most often than not turns out to be the maternal uncle of the bride. An equivalent amount, known as Ni-ar, is paid to the bride's paternal aunt as well.

The elder sister or sisters of the bride are entitled to Naupuakpuan, which is the price received by them for having given the bride their clothes to wear or taken of the bride in her childhood. In the event of the bride being the eldest daughter take or an only child, this price is received by other female relations. A sum also goes to the Palal who acts as the bride's foster father and takes on the responsibility of safeguarding her interests throughout her married life. The bride's maid also get a price known as *thianman*. There are some optional payments as well. Taken together, the bride price adds up to a considerable figure which is often impossible for the bridegroom to pay at one time.

However, it would be a mistake to continue bride price with sale or dowry. For all those who get a share of it come under a special obligation to look after the welfare and interest of the bride.

Wedding: A Mizo marriage is proceeded by courtship and engagement. The boy and girl are allowed to mix freely during the engagement period. But an engagement may be broken-off midway through if the couple fails who get on with each other.

As the majority of the Mizos are now Christians, marriages are solemnised in Church. Both bride and the bridegroom wear wedding dresses in the latest Western Style. But sometimes the bride is also decked in puanchei, a traditional Mizo costume, and white blouse.

The bride bring along to her husband a traditional rug called *Puandum* in which his body is to be wrapped during burial. This is an integral part of the Mizo marriage and failure to bring the cloth entails punishment leading to a reduction in the bride price.

There are other types of marriages as well. In the Makpa chhungkhung type of wedding the bridegroom does not pay bride price but goes to his wife's house to live with her. This type of marriage happens in families where there are no male heirs. Consequently, it becomes the duty of the son-in-law to care for his wife's parents.

Another type of Mizo marriage, as Luhkhung, is performed without a social ceremony. If a girl becomes pregnant, she start living quietly with the boy responsible for her condition in his house. However, the marriage of a pregnant girl is sometimes performed in the vestry instead of the main hall of a church. Tlandun is yet another kind of marriage in which a couple runs away from home to get married.

Inheritance: The Mizos being patriarchal, property is inherited by men rather than women. The family property usually goes to the youngest son although the father may leave shares to other sons, if he desires. If a man has no sons, his property is inherited by the next kin on the male side.

If a man dies leaving a widow and minor children, a male relation (who usually happens to be a brother of the deceased) takes charge of the family and looks after the property until one of the sons comes of age. If no such male relative is around, then the widow acts as a trustee of her husband's property until such times as his son or sons are old enough to inherit it.

However, although the youngest son of the family is the natural or formal heir to his father under the Mizo customary laws, in actuality the paternal property is generally divided among all sons. The youngest of them gets a preferential treatment in that he would get the first choice of the articles, and he would get two shares of the cash in case of one each for the other brothers.

A daughter or a wife can inherit property only if the deceased has no heir on the male side. Women, however, are entitled to their own property, the dowry, called *thuam* — she gets during the marriage from her parents is exclusively her own property. However, a written 'will' formally executed may now confer woman the right to inherit the family property. This is a happy amendment to the traditional customary laws.

People

Historians believe that the Mizos are a part of the great wave of the Mongolian race spilling over into the eastern and southern India, centuries ago. Their sojourn in Western Burma, into which they eventually came around seventh century, is estimated to last about two centuries. They came under the influence of the British Missionaries in the 9th century, and now most of the Mizos are Christians. One of the beneficial result of Missionary activities was the spread of education. The Missionaries introduced the Roman script for the Mizo language and formal education. The cumulative result is high percentage 95 per cent (as per National Sample Survey, 1997-98) which is considered to be highest in India. The Mizos area distinct community and the social unit was the village, around it revolved the life of a Mizo. Mizo Village is usually set on the top of a hill with the chief's house at the centre and the bachelor's dormitory called *Zawlbuk*, prominently. In a way, the focal point in the village was the Zawlbuk where all young bachelors of the village slept. Zawlbuk was the training ground, and indeed, the cradle wherein the Mizo youth was shaped into a responsibility adult member of the society.

Demographics

The great majority of Mizoram's population is several ethnic tribes who are either culturally or linguistically linked. These myriad ethnic groups are collectively known as the Lushais/Lusais (people who play with heads) /Luseis (long-headed people) or otherwise called Mizos (Mi = People, Zo = Hill) both of which are umbrella terms. These days, there is an increasing importance of unity among all the Mizo tribes living in different parts of the Northeastern States of India, Burma and Bangladesh. The Mizos are divided into numerous tribes, the largest of which is possibly the Lushais, which comprises almost two-thirds of the state's population. Other Mizo tribes include Hmar, Mara, Paite, Lai, Ralte. The Riang, a subtribe of Tripuri and the Chakma of Arakanese origin, are a non-Mizo tribe living in Mizoram.

Political Aspects

As in other Indian states, the ceremonial head of the State Government is a governor appointed by the Union Government. His/her appointment is largely ceremonial, and his/her main role is to oversee the swearing in of the Chief Minister. The Chief Minister, who holds the real executive powers, is the head of the party or coalition garnering the largest majority in the state elections. The governor also appoints the Cabinet ministers on the advice of the Chief Minister. Mizoram has a unicameral legislature like most other Indian states. Mizoram has one seat in the Lok Sabha and one in the Rajya Sabha. The Lais, Maras and Chakmas have separate autonomous District Councils.

Administration

After the 1986 signing of the Historic Memorandum of Settlement between the Government of India and the Mizo National Front, Mizoram was granted Statehood on February 20, 1987 (as per the Statehood Act of 1986). Mizoram became the 23rd State of the Indian Union.

The capital of Mizoram is Aizawl. The Mizoram State Legislative Assembly has 40 seats. Mizoram has witnessed vast constitutional, political and administrative changes in recent years. The traditional chieftainship was abolished and the District and Regional Councils (created under the Sixth Schedule of the Constitution of India) gave a substantial measure of local control. Today, the Lais, Maras, and the Chakmas have separate Autonomous District Councils. The Village Councils are the grass roots of democracy in Mizoram.

Mizoram is divided into 8 districts:

S.No.	District	Area (sq km)	Population	Headquarters
1.	Aizawl	3,576.31	3,39,812	Aizawl
2.	Lunglei	4,538.00	1,37,155	Lunglei
3.	Chhimtuipui	1,399.90	60,823	Saiha
4.	Lawngtlai	2,557.10	73,050	Lawngtlai
5.	Champhai	3,185.85	1,01,389	Champhai
6.	Kolasib	1,282.51	60,977	Kolasib
7.	Mamit	3,025.75	62,313	Mamit
8.	Serchhip	1,421.60	55,539	Serchhip

There are three Autonomous District Councils (ADC) for ethnic tribes in Mizoram, namely Chakma Autonomous District Council (CADC) for ethnic Chakmas in southwestern Mizoram bordering Bangladesh, Mara Autonomous District Council (MADC) for Mara people in the southernmost corner and Lai Autonomous District Council (LADC) for Lai people in southeastern part of the state.

Economic Aspects

In terms of economic development, Mizoram lags behind in comparison to the rest of the country. Cottage industry and other small-scale industries play an important role in its current economy. The people of Mizoram have not taken a keen responsibility for the development of industry due to the lack of market raw materials. The industry is wanting but lately there is a much wider chance for the development of forest products. The 9th Five Year Plan (1997-2002) gives much priority to the "agro-based industry" as nearly 70 per cent of the population is engaged in agriculture.

Sister Organisations of Industry Department:

- Zoram Industrial Development Corporation, (ZIDCO).
- Mizoram Khadi and Village Industry Board, (MKVIB).
- Zoram Handloom and Handicraft Corporation Limited, (ZOHANCO).
- Mizoram Food and Allied Industries Corporation Limited, (MIFCO).
- Zoram Electronics Development Corporation, (ZENICS).

Macroeconomic Trends

Below is a chart of trends in gross state product of Mizoram at market prices estimated by Ministry of Statistics and Programme Implementation with figures in millions of Indian rupees.

Year	Gross State Domestic Product
1980	680
1985	1,810
1990	3,410
1995	9,370
2000	17,690

Mizoram's gross domestic state product for 2004 was estimated at $685 million at current prices.

Agriculture

Agriculture is the mainstay of the people of Mizoram. More than 70 per cent of the total population is engaged in some form of agriculture. The age-old practice of *Jhum* cultivation is carried out annually by a large number of people living in rural areas. The climatic conditions of the state, its location in the tropic and temperate zones, and its various soil types along with well-distributed rainfall of 1,900 mm to 3,000 mm spread over eight to ten months in the year, have all contributed to a wide spectrum of rich and varied flora and fauna in Mizoram. These natural features and resources also offer opportunities for growing a variety of horticultural crops.

Bamboo

Thirty per cent of Mizoram is covered with wild bamboo forests, many of which are largely unexploited. Mizoram harvests 40 per cent of India's 80 million-ton annual bamboo crop. The current state administration wishes to increase revenue streams from bamboo and aside from uses as a substitute for timber, there is research underway to utilise bamboo more widely such as using bamboo chippings for paper mills, bamboo charcoal for fuel, and a type of "bamboo vinegar" which was introduced by Japanese Scientist Mr. Hitoshi Yokota, and used as a fertilizer.

Food Processing

The agro-climatic conditions of Mizoram are conducive to agricultural and horticultural crops. As this is the case, a strong and effective food processing sector should play a significant supportive role in the economy. The total production of fruits, vegetables, and spices will be increasing year by year as the number of farmers are weaned away from *Jhum* cultivation and are taking up diversification towards cash crops. Recently, Godrej Agrovet Limited has entered for a new venture wherein Oil Palm and Jatropha cultivation is their main theme in Mizoram.

Mines and Minerals

The present main mineral of Mizoram is a hard rock of tertiary period formation. This is mainly utilised as building material and for road construction work. However, several reports (both from Geological Survey of India and State Geology and Mining Wing of Industries Department) revealed the availability of minor mineral in different places.

Handlooms and Handicrafts

Mizo women typically use a handloom to make clothing and other handicrafts, such as a type of bag called *Pawnpui* and blankets. The Mizo rarely did much craft work until the British first came to Mizoram in 1889 when a demand for their crafts was created with the exposure to foreign markets. Currently, the production of handlooms is also being increased, as the market has been widening within and outside Mizoram.

Energy Sector

Despite having a rich potential in hydropower, Mizoram does not have its own power generation operation worth mentioning. At present, there are 22 isolated Diesel Power Stations scattered about the state and 9 Mini/Micro Hydel Stations in operation. The total installed capacity of the Diesel Power Stations is 26.14 MW and the Mini/Micro Hydel Stations is 8.25 MW. As per the 16th Electric Power Survey of India under CEA, Government of India, the restricted peak load demand of the state during the 2002-2003 year was 102 MW. Against this, an effective capacity of about 16 MW from Diesel Power Stations and 6 MW from the Mini/Micro Hydel Stations was available from local generation at present.

Medicinal Sector

The socio-economic life of the rural people depends on their local vegetation from where they derive all their material requirements — timber, food, fuel wood, medicinal plants, etc. About 95 per cent of the interior population depends on herbal medicine and nearly 98 per cent of raw materials are harvested from the wild plant resources without replenishing the growing stocks. The villages' herbal preparations include uprooting of the plants, which is detrimental to both the plants themselves and the growing area. As a result of this practice, many commonly used and effective medicinal plants have become rare and endangered species. Some are on the verge of extinction unless conservation measures are taken up for revival.

Media and Communication

Mizoram's media is growing quickly. Internet access is average, and private cable channels are quite popular — the big players in the cable market being Skylinks, LPS (Laldailova Pachuau & Sons) and Zonet from Aizawl and smaller operators are JB cable Networks, LDF Cable, Eldo Zenith Links from Lunglei. Other major media players are the press, All India Radio, Doordarshan and local cable TV operators. A Broadband Internet is also available.

Tourism

With its abundant scenic beauty and a pleasant climate, Mizoram hopes to develop its tourist-related industries. Specific tourist projects can be developed to put Mizoram on the "tourist map" of India. With the development of Reiek resort centre and a number of other resort centres in and around Aizawl, as well as establishment of tourist's huts across the entire state, tourism has been much developed. The ever smiling faces of the Mizos is an experience to cherish, and gives new meaning to life. Tourists require a special permit for visits.

Capital of the State: Aizawl

Aizawl (population 339,812) is the largest city as well as the capital of the state of Mizoram in India.

Geography

Aizawl is located north of the Tropic of Cancer in the northern part of Mizoram. It is situated on a ridge 1,132 metres (3,715 feet) above sea level, with the Tlawng River valley to its west and the Tuirial River valley to its east. In the summer the temperature ranges from 20-30°C, and in the winter 11-21°C.

Education

The department of Mizoram education is looked after by a council minister and the Education Directorate, who work under the Minister of Education. Initially, before this place was declared a union territory in the year 1987, the educational system of Mizoram was looked after by the missionaries of the state.

The Education Directorate was created in the year 1973. The important positions of this directorate are the education director, three deputy education directors and a joint education director. The system of education at Mizoram follows the 10+2 pattern. This state offers a number of schools, colleges and a major university, which cater to the different types of educational needs of the society of Mizoram.

The schools of the state form an important part of the educational system at Mizoram. There are quite a few schools in this state, which provide the basic school education to the children of the region. Some of the most well-known schools of Mizoram are Mizoram Institute of Comprehensive Education, Jawahar Navodaya Vidyalaya of Thenzawal, Kendriya Vidhyalaya and Jawahar Navodaya Vidhyalaya of Chhimtuipui.

There are quite a few colleges in Mizoram, which offer a variety of courses on different subjects. The Mizoram colleges include Engineering colleges, Pharmacy colleges, Nursing colleges, Hotel Management colleges, Veterinary colleges, Computer institutes, Polytechnic colleges and Law colleges.

The Mizoram University, a significant part of Mizoram education, provides research facilities and regular courses in a variety of departments like natural sciences, humanities, physical sciences, forestry, social sciences and many others.

All the above educational institutes of Mizoram are quite popular throughout the entire northwestern region of India.

Schools

There are a number of Mizoram schools, which provide the basic education to the children of the state. These schools are quite well known not only in the state but in the whole northeastern part of the state. The total number of primary schools in the state is 1,280 while the total middle schools are 770.

The Mizoram Institute of Comprehensive Education is one of the most well-known schools. This school does not put immense pressure on the young minds and impart good-quality education.

One of the most popular schools of Mizoram is called the Kendriya Vidyalaya. This school is often preferred by the parents over the other schools of the state as it offers the basic school education in a very simple way.

The Jawahar Navodaya Vidyalaya of Thenzawl and the Jawahar Navodaya Vidyalaya of Chhimtuipui also offer all the basic amenities that the parents may expect in a good-quality school. The Jawahar Navodaya Vidyalaya of Hrangchalkhawn is well reputed in the educational field of the state. The teachers of the Jawahar Navodaya Vidyalaya of Thenzawal give personalised attention to the students and offer the basic school-level information.

All the above Mizoram schools provide almost all the facilities that are necessary to impart good-quality school education. The school infrastructure of this state is well equipped to train the young minds to strengthen the future of the state.

Colleges

There are quite a few Mizoram colleges, which form a very important part of the total education system of the state. The colleges offer educational courses in a number of different streams.

The various types of colleges that one can avail of in the state are Engineering colleges, Polytechnic colleges, Nursing colleges, Hotel Management colleges, Pharmacy colleges, Law colleges, Veterinary colleges and Computer institutes.

There is one major Engineering college. It is called the Mizoram Engineering College. There are quite a few polytechnic colleges in Mizoram. The Regional Paramedical and

Nursing Training Institute, the Government Polytechnic, the College of Veterinary Sciences and Animal Husbandry and the Women's Polytechnic are the main polytechnic institutes.

The College of Nursing — Regional Paramedical and Nursing Institute is the leading nursing college of the state. There are two hotel management institutes in the region, namely, Lunglei Government Aizwal College and IGNOU Study Centre.

The main pharmacy college of Mizoram is Regional Institute of Para Medical and Nursing. The chief law college of Mizoram is Aizwal Law College. The College of Veterinary Sciences and Animal Husbandry, one of the popular colleges offers quality education on the subject of veterinary.

There are three major computer institutes in the area. The names of these institutes are the DOEACC Centre, the Academy of Computer and the Golden Republic Information Technology Centre. All the above Mizoram colleges impart high-quality education to the youth of the state and hence are quite popular among them as well as the students of the remaining parts of Northeastern India.

University

Mizoram University was founded on 2nd July, 2001, under the provision laid down by Mizoram University Act. Mizoram University aims at disseminating knowledge and providing research facilities in natural and physical sciences, humanities, social sciences and other allied disciplines.

The permanent campus of the university is built on 978 acres of land, which is leased at Tanhril by the Government of Mizoram. Mizoram University gives affiliation to about 27 undergraduate colleges. Two professional institutions are also affiliated under the Mizoram University. At present, the total number of students enrolled in the university is around 8,279 students.

It is noteworthy that Mizoram University has received a grant of Rs. 43.50 crores (approximately) from UGC. As a result, the university has taken adequate steps for its development, so that it can work at par with the other universities in India.

Transportation

Aizawl is connected with Silchar and Shillong by road and there are daily flights from Aizawl to Kolkata and Guwahati.

Salient Features

- -

Historical and Geographical Aspects

Mizoram is a mountainous region which became the 23rd state of the Indian Union in February 1987. It was one of the districts of Assam till 1972 when it became a Union Territory.

After being annexed by the British in 1891, for the first few years, Lushai Hills in the north remained under Assam while the southern half remained under Bengal. Both these parts were amalgamated in 1898 into one district called Lushai Hills district under the Chief Commissioner of Assam. With the implementation of the Northeastern Reorganisation Act in 1972, Mizoram became a Union Territory and as a sequel to the signing of the historic memorandum of settlement between the Government of India and the Mizo National Front in 1986, it was granted statehood on 20 February 1987. Sandwitched between Myanmar in the east and the south and Bangladesh in the west, Mizoram occupies an area of great strategic importance in the northeastern corner of India. Mizoram has great natural beauty and an endless variety of landscape. It is rich in fauna and flora. The origin of the word 'Mizo' is not known. The Mizos came under the influence of the British Missioneries in the 19th century. Now most of the Mizos are Christians. Mizo language has no script of its own. The Missionaries introduced the Roman script for Mizo language and formal education.

Mizoram is a mountainous region which became the 23rd state of Indian Union in February 1987. It was one of the districts of Assam till 1972 when it became a union territory. After being annexed by the British in 1891, for first few years, Lushai Hills in the north remained under Assam while the southern half remained under Bengal. Both these parts were amalgamated in 1898 into one district called Lushai Hill district under the Chief Commissioner of Assam. With the implementation of the Northeastern Reorganisation Act in 1972, Mizoram became a union territory and as a sequel to the signing of the historic memorandum of settlement between Government of India and the Mizo National Front in 1986, it was granted statehood on 20 February, 1987.

Sandwiched between Burma in east and south and Bangladesh in west, Mizoram occupies an area of great strategic importance in northeastern corner of India. Hills in Mizoram run from north to south with a tendency to be higher in east to the territory and tapering in north and south. Average height of hills is about 900 metre, the highest peak being Blue Mountain (Phawngpui) rising to 2,210 metre. Mizoram has great natural beauty and an endless variety of landscape and it is rich in fauna and flora.

The world 'Mizo' is a generic term and is used to mean hillmen or high landers. They came under the influence of British missionaries in the 19th century and now most of the Mizos are Christians. One of the beneficial results of missionary activities was the spread of education. Mizo language has no script of its own. The missionaries introduced the Roman script for Mizo language and formal education.

Religious Features

Some 87 per cent of the population (including all ethnic Mizos) is Christian. Other faiths include Hindus who form a small minority in the state, at 3.6 per cent of the population following the religion. Muslims also form a small minority with 1.1 per cent of the population following the faith. People who believe in this faith are from other state but living in Mizoram.

Christianity

The major Christian denominations are the Presbyterian. The Mizoram Presbyterian Church was established by a Welsh Missionary named Rev. D. E. Jones. The Mizoram Presbyterian Church is one of the constituted bodies of the General Assembly of the Presbyterian Church of India, which has its headquarters at Shillong in Meghalaya. The administrative set up of the Mizoram Presbyterian Church Synod is highly centralised. The Synod, having its headquarters at Aizawl, the Capital of Mizoram State, is the highest decision-making body of the church. The financial operation, the personnel matters, the administration, management and the execution of works of the church are directly or indirectly supervised and controlled by the Synod Headquarters. Other churches are Baptist Church of Mizoram, Evangelical Church of Maraland, Salvation Army, Seventh-day Adventist Church, Roman Catholic, Lairam Jesus Christ Baptist Church (LIKBK), and the Pentecostals.

Judaism

In recent decades, a number of South East Asian-looking people from Mizoram, Assam, and Manipur have claimed to be Jewish. This group is known collectively as the

Bnei Menashe, and include Chin, Kuki, and Mizo. Several hundred have formally converted to Orthodox Judaism and many openly practise an Orthodox type of Judaism. The Bnei Menashe do not see themselves as converts, but believe themselves to be ethnically Jewish, descendants of one of the Lost Tribes of Israel.

Tribal

The pre-Christian spirituality of the Mizos was animism. There are certain tribes that still practice the traditional animism. Roma Bradnock writes, "The mainly nomadic Chakmas along the western border practise a religion which combines Hinduism, Buddhism and animism." The Khans are also very much influenced by Hinduism. Suhas Chatterjee writes, "The Khan culture is very likely the influence of the Puys of ancient Srikshetra, the Hindu Kingdom in Burma."

Educational Features

Under Mizoram University, there are 29 undergraduate colleges including 2 professional institutions affiliated with the university. The total enrolment in these institutions is approximately 5,200 students.

The College of Veterinary Sciences and Animal Husbandry, Selesih, Aizawl, is the premier institute of Veterinary Medicine catering the needs of Mizoram.

IT Features

Preamble

Information Technology (IT) is the world's fastest growing economic activity. It is transforming resource-based economies to knowledge-based economies. IT has become the greatest agent of change and promises to play this role even more dramatically in future. IT changes every aspect of human life, apart from impacting changes in the field of communications, trade, manufacturing, services, culture, entertainment, education, research and national security. IT breaks old barriers and is building new interconnections in the emerging concept of a single global village. It has also become one of the critical indicators of the progress of nations, communities and individuals. The advent of IT offers opportunities to overcome historical disabilities. IT is a tool that will enable Mizoram to achieve the goal of becoming a strong, prosperous and self-confident state. IT promises to compress the time it would otherwise take for Mizoram to advance rapidly in its march towards faster development and in occupying a position as a progressive and self-sufficient state.

Mizoram recognises IT as the fastest and the most advanced vehicle of change for all-round progress and development of the state. In view of the potential of IT, the State Government advocates widespread proliferation of IT in the state and adopts the following policy supports for promotion of IT in the fields of *e*-Governance, empowerment of the people and the society, education, industry, health, rural development, agriculture, tourism, IT for masses, and IT enabled services.

The Policy shall come into effect from the date of notification of this policy, till such time, the government may consider the necessity of modification. The government also reserves the right to make any amendments in the policy.

Vision

To make Mizoram the most IT literate state in the country and a global centre of excellence in IT education, training, research, and development. This vision translates into a mission. The vision objectives are:

- employment generation.
- creation of wealth.
- IT led economic growth.

To accomplish its vision, the Government of Mizoram will play the role of proactive facilitator, proactive motivator, proactive promoter, in order to spread IT to the masses speedily, and to ensure speedy IT led economic development.

Objectives

The following are the objectives of Mizoram IT Policy:

- Promotion of IT industry, IT software, IT products, and IT Services within the state.
- Promoting IT for the masses.
- Setting up a goal of achieving total computer literacy in Mizoram by the year 2010.
- Improvement of efficiency and productivity in governance.
- Improvement of transparency and responsive-attitude in governance.
- Generation of IT-skilled manpower and IT capacity-building in the state.
- Promotion of IT skills and IT know-how among the youth of Mizoram enabling them to engage in gainful self-employment and in IT related activities.
- Propelling growth of IT and IT related activities.
- Providing of people-friendly interfacing between government and citizen.
- Providing better information and interactive services to tourists, businessmen and entrepreneurs.
- Dissemination of knowledge to farmers, agriculturists and rural population of Mizoram.

- Improvement of revenue assessment and collection mechanism.

- Improvement of general employment opportunity and employment generation.

- Widespread use of IT in educational Institutions.

- Development of capabilities of Governance as a catalyst for economic development by collaborative action and learning.

- Proliferation of Internet, *e*-Governance, *e*-Commerce and *e*-Education.

Cultural Features

The culture of Mizoram reflects the quintessential lifestyle and traditional heritage of the inhabitants of the Mizoram, popularly known as the 'Songbird of the North-East'. The people are collectively known as the Mizo. Etymologically, the term Mizo can be bifurcated into 'Mi' meaning 'people' and 'Zo' that signifies the 'hill'. Thus, the very nomenclature of the tribal community illustrates the fact that they hail from the highland.

The residents of Mizoram are very proud of their cultural legacy and go great lengths to preserve it despite considerable foreign intrusion. With changing times, Mizoram too is moving towards modernisation but the State Government has ensured that every bucolic hamlet in the state, irrespective of its remote location, is endowed with an YMA (Young Mizo Association). This body has been designed with the sole aim to leave a distinct tincture of the traditional societal values and customs among the state's youth. This is reflected in the state's cultural extravaganzas and numerous fairs and festivals and music and dance that have been passed down through the generations.

It is rather interesting to note the indelible impact of Christianity on the state's culture. At the advent of the 19th century Christian missionaries considerably enriched the state's culture. Not only was a new and formal writing script was developed, but also the strong impact of Christianity have resulted in the Mizo inhabitants emerging some of the finest choir singers in the Indian subcontinent.

Festivals

Modern Mizos are fast giving up their old customs and adopting the new ways of life which are greatly influenced by western cultures. Music is a passion for the Mizos, and the youth especially have become quite enamoured of western music.

Mim Kut: The *Mim Kut* festival is usually celebrated during the months of August and September, after the harvest of maize. *Mim Kut* is celebrated with great fanfare by drinking rice-beer, singing, dancing, and feasting. Samples of the year's harvests are consecrated to the departed souls of the community. Mizos practise "slash and burn" (*Jhum*) cultivation. They clear areas, the jungle, burn the stumps and leaves of the downed trees, and then cultivate the land. All their other activities revolve around the Jhum operation and their festivals are all connected with such agricultural operation.

Chapchar Kut: Chapchar Kut is another festival celebrated during March after completion of their most arduous task of Jhum operation, i.e., jungle-clearing (clearing of remainings of burnt area). This is a spring festival celebrated with great fervour and gaiety.

Pawl Kut: Pawl means "Straw" hence pawl kut means held soon after the harvest. *Pawl Kut* is a festival celebrated in December to commemorate the end of harvest season. It is perhaps the greatest Mizo festival.

Arts and Crafts

There are various kinds of art and crafts in Mizoram, which form an important sector of the industrial market of the state. The main art and crafts of Mizoram are textiles, bamboo and cane works and basketry.

The textile industry is one of the main art and crafts of Mizoram. Generally, the Mizo women are engaged in weaving which constitutes a major sector of Mizoram cultural life. The people of Mizoram produce a wide range of textile products. Some of the most popular textile products of this part of India are puanspuon dum, puon pie, thangou puon, puon laisen, jawl puon, thangsuo puon, hmarm and zakuolaisen.

The bamboo and cane works constitute one of the well-known art and crafts in Mizoram. The state is quite advanced in this craft and has a big role to play in the economic growth of the state. It is the domain of the Mizo men. The major bamboo and cane works of the state are hats, animal and fish trapscones, different types of baskets, japis, wide range of jewellery and circular boxes.

The basketry industry is a prominent segment of Mizoram art and crafts. Some of the popular products of the basketry industry of Mizoram are paiem, dawrawn, paikawng, tlamen, emsin, fawng-te-laivel, fawng and thul. The people of the state exhibit a great deal of expertise in all the above art and crafts of the region.

Music

Mizoram is a region in India. Its folk music is based around the drum and gong, though there is also a long history of flute-playing which is now defunct. The drums are made from a hollow tree trunk and the gongs, made of brass, are very similar to those found in Myanmar.

The origin of Mizo Music is a mystery. It is therefore, difficult to trace the origin, and to arrange the chronological sequences of the heritage of Mizo Music. However, we have seen some couplets are developed during the settlement of Thantlang in Burma estimated between 1300-1400 AD. As recorded by B. Lalthangliana, the folk songs developed during this period were dar hla (songs on gong); Bawh hla (War chants), Hla do (Chants of hunting); Nauawih hla (Cradle songs). A greater development of songs can be seen from the settlement of Lentlang in Burma, estimated between late-15th to17th century AD. The

Mizo occupied the present Mizoram from late-17th century. The pre-colonial period, that is from 18th to 19th century AD was another important era in the history of Mizo folk literature. Prior to the annexation by the British Government, the Mizo occupied the present Mizoram for two centuries. In comparison with the folk songs of Thantlang and Lentlang settlement, the songs of this period are more developed in its number, form and contents. The languages are more polished and the flows also better. Most of the songs of this period are named after the composers.

The Mizo's are fortunate enough in having traditional way of classification of their folk songs. A study of their folk songs on the basis of the indigenous system of classification shows that the Mizo's are having about one hundred different types of folk songs. But it can broadly be classified into ten as follows.

Bawh hla: This is the chant or cry raised by the warriors when returning from successful raid. The warriors chant Bawh Hla to show his superiority over the enemy, and in order to let his people know that a successful raid has taken place. No other members of the warriors except the killer of the enemy can chant Bawh Hla.

Hlado: This is the chant or cry raised by the hunters when a successful hunting has taken place. Chanting Hlado can be done on the spot, or on the way home, or just before entering the village, or on the celebration. Anyone who witnesses his success can chant Hlado at any time and place.

Thiam hla and Dawi hla: These two verse forms are chanted by the Priests and the witch while performing ceremonies.

Dar hla: These are named after musical instruments. These songs are not sung by human voice, it is meant for musical instruments. Dar hla means 'song for gong'. There are several songs named after the instruments; but Dar hla is the most popular and greatest in number. So, it is commonly known as Dar hla. It has three musical notes.

Puipun hla: These are songs named after merry and festive occasions. These songs are the most popular among the folk songs. People sung together with dancing at the time of merry and festive occasions.

Lengzem Zai: These are love songs. It has no distinctive form but it was named after the theme.

Songs Named after Tribes: Some verse forms are named after the particular tribe such as sailo zai, saivate zai, etc.

Songs Named after Villages: A few songs are named after the village such as lumtui zai, dar lung zai, etc.

Songs Named after Modulation of the Voice: A few song are named after modulation of the voice or sound such as kawrnu zai, zai nem, vai zawi zai, puma zai, etc. For example, Kawrnu is a kind of Cicada whose voice is gentle and low. So the tune of new song resembling to the tune of kawrnu is called kawrnu zai.

Songs Named after Individuals: A great number of Mizo folk songs are named after individual. Most of them are named after the original composer of the music as well as the verse tunes. But some of the songs are named after a beautiful women or the hero of the tribe. The first six have their own common name while the last four have no such common name.

Musical Instruments

From time immemorial, the Mizo have been using different musical instruments. Even though we cannot date the origin, the "Mizo of Kabaw valley during late-10th to 13th century AD had developed their music as nearly as they have done today". The traditional Mizo musical instruments are very simple and crude in comparison to other Indian musical instruments and very outdated to modern musical instruments. They can broadly be divided into three: beating or striking instruments; wind instruments and string instruments.

Striking Instruments: Most of the Mizo musical instruments used at the time of festivals and dances are striking instruments such as different types of Khuang and Dar, Bengbung, Seki, Talhkhuang.

Khuang (Drum): It is Mizo indigenous instrument which occupies a very significant place in Mizo social and religious life. Khuang is a must on all occasions. It is made of hollow tree, wrapped on both sides with animal skin. The Mizo gives different names according to its size and length. The big sized one is call *Khuangpui* (big drum), the middle one is called *Khuanglai*; and the small sized, Khuangte (little drum). If it is longish, they called it *Kawlkhuang.* As far as the history of Mizo is concerned it is commonly concluded that the Mizo ancestors started using drum as far back as when they sung and composed song. Lianhmingthanga believes that the Mizo had received drum from Chinese civilization through cultural diffusion. The process of that cultural diffusion might have passed through the Burmese with whom the Mizo had a close cultural contact which took place from the middle of the 9th century AD until the end of Pagan period at the close of 13th century AD. Khuang is the only Mizo traditional musical instrument that is popularly used in the 20th and 21st century. In the olden days, Khuang has no role in the religious functions; but today the use of drum is a must in every church service.

Dar (Gong): Another popular musical instruments are various sizes of brass-gongs, viz., Darkhuang, Darbu and Darmang.

Darkhuang: Darkhuang is the biggest type. Darkhuang is very costly and is one of their most valuable possessions. In the olden times, it was sometimes used as a means of exchange; and sometimes the parent of a bride demanded Darkhuang for the price of their daughter. In one of the oldest folk songs we have the following lines: Chawngvungi her price so high I gave necklace hut they refused, I gave a gong and they refused. They demanded our sacred gong, Chawngvungi, her price unsurpassed.

But this song (dar hla) is played with Darhu. Darkhuang is played on all occasions.

Darbu: Darbu is a set of three different sizes of brass-gongs, producing three musical notes. Darhu is usually played by three experts. Some experts played individually by tying the two gongs, one on each sides of his body with rope and hung one gong by his left hand, produce three distinct, rhythmic notes by simultaneous beating. Darbu is meaningfully used on certain occasions like Khuallam and other traditional group dances.

Darmang: Darmang is the smallest type of gong. It has no effect without other gongs or instruments, but it is used in the traditional dances to keep timing. All these gongs appear to be Burmese in origin, and therefore, it is tempting to conclude that Mizo got them from the Burmese while they were living in the Kabaw Valley during 9th to 13th century AD.

Bengbung: Benghung is another Mizo indigenous instrument which has some similarity with xylophone. It is a musical instrument consisting of a series of flat wooden bars, producing three musical notes. Bengbung is usually played by girls in their leisure.

Talhkhuang: The process of making Talhkhuang is almost the same with that of Bengbung but Talhkhuang is much bigger than that of Bengbung. It is made of three wooden pieces which are curved out, the depth of the curves being made vary so that the sound produced when beaten are different in notes. It is played with a wooden hammer. The Mizo would never take Talhkhuang to their houses or anywhere wise except to Lungdawh, the great platform at the entrance of the village. It has played when a chief or the village erected memorial stones.

Seki: Seki is the domesticated mithun's horn. The two hollow horns are beaten to lead or to keep timing for the other musical band like Darbu, etc. It was commonly used at the time of group dances are performed.

Wind Instruments: The Mizo have six varieties of wind-instruments such as Rawchhem, Tumphit, Mautawtawrawl, Phenglawng, Buhchangkuang, Hnahtum.

Rawchhem: It is a kind of Scottish "Bagpiper" or Chinese "Snag". Nine small Bamboo pipes or hollow reeds, Having different sizes and lengths are inserted to the dried gourd. One of the pipes serves as a mouthpiece. Small portions of the pipes are struck out so that it can produce sound when the instrument is blown. The Musician blows in to the mouthpiece, and by controlling the holes with his fingers, he can produced various musical notes.

Tumphit: Tumphit is made of three small bamboos having different sizes and length. The types are tied and plated in a row with caves or strings. The upper ends are cut open at different length so that each tube has different notes. The players put the open tube against his lower lip and then blows down. This musical instrument was used during ritual ceremonies and particularly on the occasion of a ceremony called *Rallulam* and *chawng* festival, the use of this music was a must.

Mantawtawrawl: This is a bamboo trumpet. Different sizes of bamboo tubes are cut-off. The smaller tube is inserted to the bigger tube and so on. Many bamboo tubes are joined one after another till the last tube happens to be the size of a forefinger from where the trumpet is to be blown. A dry empty gourd, the bottom part is cut-off and joined with bigger end of the bamboo tubes. The whole length can be more than five feet.

Phenglawng: It is the Mizo flute made of bamboo. Originally, Phenglawng had only three holes producing three different sounds. Flute is popular among the other Indians.

Buhchangkuang: This is another flute made of reed or a paddy stalk. This simple instrument was usually played by girls.

Hnahtum: The Mizo boys can skilfully turn leaves of many trees into simple but indigenous musical instruments. They can produce interesting sound by blowing deftly folded leaves. This is called Hnahtum.

Stringed Instruments: The Mizo have only three kinds of stringed-instruments such as Tingtang; Lemlawi and Tuiumdar:

Tingtang: This is Mizo guitar. Mizo tingtang is a kind of fiddle or violin having only one string. A piece of bamboo shaft is fixed in the gourd to carry the string made of Thangtung, the fibre of the Malay Sago palm. The hollow gourd is cut open and covered with a dry bladder of animal.

Lemlawi: Lemlawi is the family of Jew's harp but the shape and size are different. It is made of small pieces of bamboo. From the piece of bamboo, the craftsman took out a small portion with knife for its string. The sound it produces is controlled by the mouth.

Tuiumdar: This simple musical instrument is also made of bamboo having three strings producing three different notes. From the outer covering of the bamboo, three pieces of cane like strings are curved out. The strings are then raised up by inserting two pieces of bamboo. It is played like a guitar.

Artistes

Popular female Artiste include Daduhi, Liandingpuii, Zoramchhani Spi and Mami Varte among the current generation and Vanhlupuii, Vanlalruati and C. luri among the more senior artiste. Among the Male Artiste, the more popular one include Vanlalsailova, Michael M. Sailo, Mama Chawngthu among the many other artiste.

Dances

Cheraw: The most colourful and distinctive dance of the Mizo is called *Cheraw*. Long bamboo staves are a feature of this dance and it is known to many as the Bamboo Dance. Originally, the dance was performed to wish a safe passage and victorious entry into the abode of the dead (*Pialral*) for the soul of a mother who had died during childbirth. To dance *Cheraw* takes great skill and alertness.

Khuallam: *Khuallam* was originally a dance performed by honoured invitees while entering into the arena where a community feast was held. To attain a position of distinction, a Mizo had to go through a series of ceremonies where friends from nearby villages were invited and *Khuallam* was the dance for the visitors or guests. *Khuallam* is performed by a group of dancers, the more the merrier, in colourful profiles to the tune of gongs and drums.

Chheih Lam: *Chheih Lam* is the dance done over a round of rice-beer in the cool of the evening. The lyrics in triplets are usually spontaneous compositions, recounting their heroic deeds and escapades and also praising the honoured guests present in their midst.

High Seat of Learning

1. Mizoram University, P. B. 341, H. Q. Lumami, Kohima.

Economic Features

Agriculture

About 60 per cent of the people of Mizoram are engaged in agricultural pursuits. The main pattern of agriculture followed is *jhum* or shifting cultivation. Out of the estimated potential available area of 4.4 lakh hectares for horticulture, the area put under plantation is around 25,000 hectares only. The main horticulture crops are oranges, lemon, *kagzi* lime, passion fruits, *hatkora, jamir,* pineapple and papaya. Other crops are sugarcane, tapioca and cotton. People have started extensive cultivation of ginger and fruit crops.

About 60 per cent of the people of Mizoram are engaged in agricultural pursuits. The main pattern of agriculture followed is Jhum or shifting cultivation. Out of the estimated potential available area of 4 lakh hectare for horticulture the area put under plantation is around 25,000 hectare only. The main horticulture crops are citrus like oranges, lemon, Kagzi lime, passion fruits, Hatkora, Jamir, pineapple and papaya. Other crops are sugarcane, tapioca and cotton. With the processing unit coming up such as Ginger Dehydration Plant at Sairang and fruit juice concentration plants people had already started extensive cultivation of ginger and fruit crops. Out of potential flat land of 50,000 hectare only about 16,000 hectare have been put under cultivation so far. Fertilizer consumption has gone up from 16 kg/hectare in 1989 to 25 kg per hectare in 1992.

Irrigation

The ultimate surface irrigation potential is estimated at 70,000 hectares of which 45,000 hectares is under flow and 25,000 hectares for river lift irrigation. The irrigated area has now gone up to 7,260 hectares by constructing and completing 70 *pucca* minor irrigation projects and six lift irrigation projects for raising double and triple crops in a year.

The ultimate surface irrigation potential is estimated at 70,000 hectare. Of which 45,000 hectare is under flow and 25,000 hectare for river lift irrigation. The irrigated area has now gone up to 7,260 hectare by constructing and completing 30 pucca minor irrigation projects for raising double and tripple crops in a year. Another area of 2,250 hectare is expected to be under irrigation after the completion of ongoing 14 minor irrigation projects.

Industry

The entire Mizoram is a Notified Backward Area and is categorised under 'No Industry District". However, concerted efforts were made in the last decade to accelerate the growth of industries in Mizoram. For the development of industries in the state, Government framed industrial policy in 1989. In the policy resolution priority industries identified are: agro and forest-based industries, followed by handloom and handicrafts, electronics, consumer industries. Sericulture is operating at Aizawl with two wings, viz., handloom and handicrafts wing and geology and mining wing.

The completed projects of fruit preservation factory at Vairengte, Mizo Milling Plant at Khawzawl and Fruit Juice Concentrate Plant at Chhingchhip were transferred to the incorporated Mizoram Food and Allied Industries Corporation (MIFCO) for commercial operation. Maize Milling Plant also has been completed and commissioned by MIFCO. Development of tea industry/gardens and raising of Tooklai approved varieties of ten seedlings has been taken up by the government around Biate areas.

Entire Mizoram is a Notified Backward Area and is categorised under 'No Industry District'. However, concerted efforts were made to accelerate the growth of industries in Mizoram, For the development of industries in the state, the Mizoram government framed the industrial policy of Mizoram in 1989. In the policy resolution, priority industries have been identified. These are: Agro and forest-based industries followed by handloom and handicrafts, electronics, consumer industries. Sericultures is operating at Aizawl with two full-fledged wings, viz., handloom and handicrafts wing and geology and mining wing. The completed projects of Ginger Oil and Oleoresin Plant and Ginger Dehydration Plant at Sairang and Fruit Preservation Factory at Vairengte and the projects under implementation, namely, Maize Processing Unit (renamed Maize Milling Plant) at Khawzawl and Fruit Juice Concentrated Plant at Chhingchhip were transferred to the newly incorporated Mizoram Food and Allied Industries Corporation (MIFCO) for Commercial Operation. Maize Milling Plant also has been completed and commissioned by MIFCO.

Power

Construction of Tuirial hydel project capable of generating 60 MW is in progress. DPR of Kolodyne Phase-I having a capacity of 120 MW has been handed over to the State

Government by Brahmaputra Board and CWC. A 3 MW Teirei hydel project was commissioned and 23 diesel power houses have been functioning. A total of 691 villages have been electrified and 588 km of 132 KV line and 165 KV of 66 KV line completed. DPR for Bairabi hydel project capable of generating 80 MW has been handed over to the State Government by the Brahmaputra Board on 18 April 2000.

Government is giving utmost importance to rural electrification, many villages have been electrified and part of its power demand is met through mini and micro-hydel projects. Construction of 132 KV lines have been taken up to connect all the important load centres in the state so that grid power could be supplied throughout the state. Construction of Serlui 'B' Hydel Projects had already been started. The state is making efforts to obtain early clearance for the 60 MW Tuirial Hydroelectric Project and investigation of Tuivai 210 MW Hydel Project. The proposed Chhimtuipui Hydel Project is also under active consideration.

Transport

Total road length in the state is 4,001.53 km. Rail link in the state has been established at Bairabi. Aizawl is connected by air. State PWD has completed metalling and black topping of 4,531 km of primary road and 2,277 km of secondary road.

Total road length 4,787 km. National highway number 54 links Tuipang the southern-most district of Mizoram to Silchar town in Assam in the border of Mizoram. Rail link in the state had been established at Bairabi. Aizawl, the capital town of the state, is airlinked by daily Vayudoot service. Mizoram State Transport, besides running passenger services in 33 routes including two inter-state services to Silchar in Assam and Shillong, also provides goods carriages at hire and also functions as 'Railway Out Agency' for Silchar railway station in Cachar district of Assam.

Festivals

Mizos are basically agriculturists. All their activities centre round *jhum* cultivation and their festivals are linked with such agricultural operations. *Kut* is the Mizo word for festivals. Mizos have three major festivals called *Chapchar Kut, Mim Kut* and *Pawl Kut.*

Mizos are basically agriculturist. All their activities centre round Jhum cultivation and their festivals are with such agricultural operations. KUT is the Mizo word for festival. Mizos have three major festivals called Chapchar Kut, Mim Kut and Pawl Kut.

Tourist Centres

Aizawl located at nearly 4,000 feet above sea-level, is a religious and cultural centre of Mizoram. Champhai is a beautiful resort on the Myanmar border. Tamdil a natural lake with virgin forest is 85 km from Aizawl and 7 km from tourist resort of Saitual.

Vantawng falls, five km from hill station Thenzawl, are the highest and most beautiful waterfalls in Mizoram. The Department of Tourism has opened Tourist Lodges at Aizawl, Lunglei, Champhai and wayside restaurants at Thingdawl, Hnahthial, recreational centre at Beraw Tlang and Alpine picnic hut at district park near Zobawk.

Aizawl hilly city located at nearly 4,000 feet above sea-level is a religious and cultural centre of Mizo where indigenous handicrafts are also available. Champhai is a beautiful resort on the Burma border. Tamdil is a natural lake with Virgin Forest around 60 km from Aizawl and 10 km from the beautiful tourist resort of ritual where modern picnic facilities are being developed. Vantawng Fall is the highest and most beautiful waterfall in Mizoram. It is 5 km from the hill station of Thenzawl.

3

History

The ancient history of Mizoram is shrouded in mystery. According to the popular beliefs, Mizoram among all the Northeastern States has a more recent history. Moreover the historical researches have not indicated so far the trace of any aborigines in the state who were anterior to the present tribes of the land.

Prior to the inhabitation of the present race of people, the land must have afforded a passage to the preceding tribes who crossed from east to west and who later on, were dispersed to Tripura, Chittagong and other places. There are the clues to the fact that Mizoram was occupied more recently, than were the northern parts of the northeast which have afforded a passage or have cradled the diverse tribes now diffused in Arunachal Pradesh, Nagaland, Assam and Meghalaya.

Ethnic Backdrop

Language is very important for determining the cognate, ethnological and cultural relations with the other tribal groups with whom the Mizos were intimately related. Language is a very important clue to the factors which centre on the origin and particularly the homogeneous character of the people.

The Mizo language has been classed with a Tibeto-Burman super-stock. They have been ascribed under the Sino-Tibetan family of that super-stock. This family consists mainly of the Kuki, the Lushai (Mizo) and the Meitei groups. This family is distinct to the Kuki, the Chin and the Mizo as almost homogenous.

The near homogeneity than heterogeneity in this regard is most essential for our consideration. These groups along with the other Sino-Tibetan speeches (Kuki or Chin mainly) in Tripura should be attributed to these groups of the family which lie most southward in the northeast. The Sino-Tibetan family of speeches have their important position lying contiguous to the major languages known as *Tai* or *Karen*, Bodo or Boric, Kachin or Singpho and Austric. Mizo languages also occupy a position very close to Bengali spoken in Cachar and Tripura plains.

Obviously the groups of tribes speaking the Sino-Tibetan speeches of Kuki-Mizo-Chin branch must have had shared a common history in the remote past and were diffused, from some great river valleys through the different streams of migration. But different stories are told how the tribes under the different channels of migration when migrating downward, had encamped themselves at the lower flanks of the snowy mountains before emerging through the hills and valleys to the middle reaches of the river Chindwin in Burma and finally coming down to the Chin hills.

That is why the Chin hills are believed to be another great centre before the dispersal of the tribes to Manipur, Tripura, North Cachar and Mizoram had taken place. In fact the Mizos themselves besides inhabiting Mizoram had stayed in their lesser numerical strength in various places in the neighbouring States. The renowned linguists have classed the southern Sino-Tibetan speeches as follows:

Kuki-Lushai Meitei:

- Old Kuki — Hrangkul, Halan, Chaw, Langrong, etc.
- Kuki Chin Meitei, Old Kuki Chin,
- Northern Chin Group — Thado, Sukte, Ralte, Paite, etc.
- Central Chin Group — Lushai, Lakher and others.

These views seem to have been corroborated by the first English administrators who made their first contacts. They had been treated as one race of people during the first decade of the British regime in spite of the fact that some customary and cultural variations are found among them. It would indicate that hordes of immigrants of tribesmen stemming from the same home and batch after batch, had taken themselves to wandering away because, they wanted to maintain their original culture, customs and institutions.

The period of this exodus seems to have been very near to the age after Buddhism had started to gain momentum in that part of the world bordering China and Burma. A few ethnologists such as C. A. Soppitts might hold this view. Otherwise their tradition recounts that they fled away, to escape certain havocs caused upon their habitation.

But the oneness of this race has already been transcended by the administrative divisions created from time to time. These divisions had been super-imposed among themselves and reimposed by the English administrators to suit with their administrative interest. Batch after batch poured down the mountains and valleys. But the most powerful tribe would assert their authority over the others leading to the vacation of the land by the weaker tribes or a system of assimilation over them was imposed.

The Mizos headed by the powerful Sailo families who made their final arrival arbitrated the destiny of their land. The pre-Mizo inhabitants, all Kuki and close Kindreds of their own, were left to their fate. The situation coupled with the tensions brought about, caused an eruption. It caused an exodus of the first tribesmen from Mizoram to other places in Assam, Nagaland, Manipur and Tripura.

Yet there were other tribesmen of the other clans who preferred to stay with the Mizos. The struggle for supremacy centred also on the institutionalisation of the powerful chiefdom which vested in the strong families. This misnomer of Kuki, Lushai tribes and clans must at one time have created confusion to outsiders. The British administration had considerably assisted to regularise the tribal nomenclatures in the region where the tribes were settled.

It is probable on these grounds Soppitt holds that the word Lushai (a British nomenclature of Mizoram) is derived from Lua or Luhai over whom a Lua King governed them. The oneness of the Kukis with Rangkols, co-tribe Bete (Biate), Jansens, co-tribe Tadoi (Thado), O Poeys (Pawi) and the Lushais demonstrated by Soppitt beyond doubt.

In spite of their being so integrated, these tribes were taking themselves to battles for authority and for Maiming their rights over the lands which would be subservient to their interest. The explosive situation had paused the separation of tribes to the tear and far-flung places.

Inter-clanish or tribal feuds in many instances of tribal history had become inevitable. We can attribute certain reasons for the growth of such circumstances. Obviously these feuds were raging on because they were the possible means to curtail the explosion of population at the cost of others. The feuds also took their turn to subside when a situation of normalcy was restored.

Again, considering this hectic situation, the cause of this turmoil is attributed by the earliest ethnologists that tribal lands in the areas stated, had no defined demarcations, a sort of a loose division existed and casual intrusions were not so binding. Shakespeare further suggest that strong linguistic agglutination was in force so that in a short pan of time, some minor dialects were driven to disappearance.

In this context, the tradition is clear that the Rangkols and the Biates were the oldest inhabitants in the land; they made a league among themselves with regard to allocating their respective spheres of jurisdiction. They had settled there for sometime when they were superseded by the Thado; the Thado had already agreed with the Jansen Kukis to live with each other as neighbours and decide their respective spheres. The Jansen subsequently became a strong tribe. Beyond doubt, the Lushais come last. They made the power felt that the Jansen and Thado were compelled to forsake the land.

However, the southern tract was occupied by the tribes who were not essentially in every respect Lushai but it seems that an understanding was reached with them for settling with their respective jurisdictions. The word Mizo now coined for Lushai Hills suggests that there are non-Lushai clans residing in Mizoram. Considering the situation as whole with regards to the events taking place, we are inclined to accept that the modern history of Mizoram started contemporaneously with the growth of British power in Eastern India.

Ancient History

The origin of the history of Mizos is mysterious. Their history is marked by a series of raids and expeditions. It is said that the Mizos came from Shinlung or Chhinlungsang, which is believed to be the Chinese city situated close on the Sino-Burmese border. They first settled in the Shan area and lived there for about 300 years and then moved to the Kabaw Valley around 8th century. It was here that the Mizos got an opportunity to interact with the local Burmese. The two cultures met and influenced each other in the fields of clothing, sports and music. It is said that from here the Mizos learnt the art of cultivation. From Kabaw they came to Khampat. The areas they claimed here were encircled by a clay wall and was divided into several parts. It is said that, they planted a banyan tree before they left Khampat as a sign that town was made by them. In the 14th century the Mizos settled at the Chin Hills on the Indo-Burmese border. They built villages and called them by their clan names such as Seipui, Saihmun and Bochung. The hill and difficult terrain of Chin Hills stood in the way of the building of another central township like Khampat. The villages were scattered that it was not possible for the various Mizo clans to keep in touch with one another. They finally moved across the river Tiau to India in the Middle of the 16th century.

Medieval History

The Mizos who earlier migrated to India were known by the name Kukis. The last of the Mizo tribes to migrate to India were the Lushais. The Mizo Hills were declared as part of British India in 1895. The areas including Lushai Hills were declared as backward tracts. It was during the British rule that there was a political awakening among the Mizo and as a result in 9th April 1946, the first political party, the Mizo Common People's Union was shaped. The party was later renamed as Mizo Union. The Constituent Assembly started an Advisory Committee to deal with the problems of the minorities and the tribals. A subcommittee was formed to advice the Constituent Assembly on the tribal affairs. The Mizo The Mizo Union submitted a declaration demanding the inclusion of all Mizo inhabited areas adjacent to Lushai Hills. Nevertheless, a new party called the United Mizo Freedom (UMFO) came up demanding that Lushai Hills be joined Burma after Independence. The Government under the suggestion of the Bordoloi Sub-Committee allowed a certain amount of Independence. This suggestion was enshrined in the sixth schedule of the Constitution.

In 1952, The Lushai Hills Autonomous District Council was formed which lead to the abolition of chieftainship in Mizo society. The autonomy met the objectives of the Mizos only partially. In 1954, the representatives of the District Council and the Mizo Union appealed with the States Reorganisation Commission (SRC) in for integrating the Mizo-dominated areas of Tripura and Manipur with their District Council in Assam. The tribal leaders were unhappy with the suggestions of the SRC. As a result they met in Aizwal and formed a new political party called the Eastern India Union (EITU) and raised the demand for a separate state.

The tribal leaders in the North East were laboriously unhappy with the SRC suggestions. They met in Aizawl in 1955 and formed a new political party, Eastern India Union (EITU) and raised demand for a separate state comprising of all the hill districts of Assam. The Mizo Union split and the separated faction joined with the EITU. By this time, the UMFO also joined the EITU and they demanded for a separate Hill state. Therefore, it seems that the Mizos moved from China to Burma and then to India under forces of circumstances. According to K. S. Latourette, there were political turmoil's in China in 210 BC and when the dynastic rule was abolished and the whole empire was brought under one administrative system. Rebellions broke out and the Mizos left China as part of one of those waves of migration.

Territorial Distribution

The territorial distribution of the tribes can be conceived with reference to Six tribes connected with Mizoram who were Rangkol and Biate, Jansen and Thado, Lushai and Pawi. But even as Pawi' and Lushai were settled as one tribe and in spite of being closely related and also differing among themselves (in some points) were sometimes fighting among themselves. This situation continued until the coming of British administration into the Lushai Hills.

Evidently many Kuki and Lushai words have a broad based area of phonetic agreement and the several numbers of cognate words are seen. They agree orthographically, numerically and even syntactic. However, the long separation had resulted in the number of deviations as well. This was due to the fact that the environmental surroundings had caused such the changing concepts in the language spoken also.

They had stemmed from a simultaneous origin and had been separated to different places and had been exposed to different conditions. In making adaptations and adjustments broadly to the new civic, social and techno-economic concepts, a system of alteration had become unavoidable. It had affected the language structure also.

The evidence of the cognate relations, however, cannot be ruled out. We have already classed Lushai as belonging to the Central Chin group. Biate and Thado to the northern

Chin group, and Hrangkul to the Old Kuki group. Shakespeare suggests that all the Lushai-Kuki Clans resemble each other very closely in appearance and the Mongolian type of countenance prevails. The term Lushai .... covers a great many clans under various chiefs of Thangur family, who came into prominence in the eighteen century and who was responsible for the eruption into Cachar of old Kukis at the end of that century and of the new Kukis half a century later.

Even many of the 'non-Lushai clans' living in Mizoram slowly were absorbed by the Lushais under the Thangur-Sailo chiefs, "the clans which live among the Lushais under the rule of Thangur chiefs have become practically assimilated by them". This view however is controversial as some people may feel that Lushai is a different language and does not bear relations with Kuki. I am personally confident that Lushai was originally one of the dominant Kuki Sub-tribes formed of the union of conspicuous clans and that Lushai and Mizo are only the early 20th and the modern nomenclature of a tribe.

On the above antecedental grounds, we are prone to accept that Lushai and the Cognate tribes or Sub-tribes identified with Mizo were the latest group of the Kuki tribe who stemmed out from their abode in Chin Hills and who sent the powerful hordes of immigrants to the present Mizoram through two or three routes as the situation had become inevitable. Each group consisted of a few influential clans claiming descent from a powerful clans chieftain who enforced his authority in administration as an autocrat.

However, in matters concerning the common affairs, the view of the other leaders was taken to confidence. In whatever circumstances, during the migratory or pre-settled stages of habitation, the, matters resting with policy decisions vested with the Chief and the other patriarchs. The Chief held a great deal of power with regard to the distribution of lands, allocation of portfolios, exploitation of the natural resources, maintenance of trade and such vital public affairs. He also maintained his judicial authority.

A Chief maintaining his authority over a small entity covering a small number of villages likewise was to be assisted by other chiefs who exercised their power under his jurisdiction. These chiefs also controlled their respective systems of slaves since the system of slaves existed, the slaves were either captives, kidnapped or taken off but some of them may have voluntarily enlisted themselves to the services of their masters since slavery was never reduced to a system of absolute serfdom and subsequently saves would be entitled to the status of subjects or citizens. The system of assimilation is reckoned as the important factor in the formation of cognate tribalisation. The opinion is controversial since in a few reports, we find that slaves were treated cruelly and many were killed in cold blood.

In a crucial system and considering the situation as a whole, the system of chiefdom must have been consistently resorted to. That is why during the British regime, we hear that the ruling power vested in the powerful chiefs and when the system of constitutional democracy was worked out by the Government of India Act, 1935, the concept for democracy, became widely acknowledged. The chiefs were vested sometimes with the unlimited authority. Struggle for chiefship went on incessantly until the English administration introduced a settled administration in Lushai Hills.

Although Lushai is a clan name yet, it strikes us that its nomenclature, is a mixture of the Lushai clans along with the other Kuki groups such as the Biate, Vaiphe and others who were the remnants of their predecessors who had migrated from the Chin Hills to Mizoram held up there and others then on a circuitous route moved to Cachar Hills. I remember a Biate in North Cachar remarked that their forefathers once stayed in Mizoram; his forefathers due to the scarcity of lands were compelled to leave their home and they left their other place name which remain to this day in Mizoram.

Land and Tribes

The tradition in Mizoram recounts that decades ago, the forefathers of the present tribes had migrated from a place called *Siang,* on the north and came southward, during a long journey. Siang' their homeland, is even now cherished with a great reverent memory. A tradition, I have heard in North Cachar Hills about two decades ago, recounts in a parabolical saying that they came through a great distance to the Chin hills, to plant the arum and start cultivating the land while the other tradition says that they came to escape a great deluge or a natural havoc which swept their ancient land.

In all probability a great famine had driven them through in search of another homeland and during their wandering, came to the Chin hills where they halted for sometime and later on, hordes of their immigrants pushed themselves on to Mizoram and the neighbouring places in Assam, Tripura and Manipur. Chin hills are still remembered as their ancient homeland where the forefathers of the Lushai - Kuki race of people were sheltered and where they found their sufficient means to settle on and most probably for a longer period of time.

Power Struggle among Tribes

On settling in Mizoram, there was a great struggle amongst the tribesmen for power and supremacy and an effective system of Chiefdom was instituted. It is also seen that the different tribesmen took possessions of lands where they created their spheres of influence.

On comparing the traditions, it would appear that the settlement of the tribes in the land had already started, prior to the rise of the British power in Bengal.

The views of the local writers may now be assessed. According to Liangkhaia, the Mizos have settled in their land for about 200 years while Van Chungnga goes further in suggesting that they have been there for a period between 300 and 400 years. Their forefathers had made haltages during a long journey from the Tao valley in northwest China, then moving to Kakaung valley through the reaches of the Chindwin river and then pressed to the Kalbaw valley. They had left the trace of their migration and were confined on the Than range in the confine of Chindwin river. Then they left, came to the Len range. Finally they crossed the Tiau or Tau river and embarked an their journey to Mizoram.

British Period

Anglo-Burmese War

The First Anglo-Burmese war fought up-till 1826 had its great incursion all over the northeast and it was probable that the war opened up the first more known contacts with the Kuki-Lakher-Lushai tribes hither isolated. The war had occurred during the stormy events which occurred in Mizoram which had its impacts in the neighbouring territories as well. The stories of migrations poured from Burma and struggles among the tries occurred contemporaneously.

The groups of tribes made of different lineages traced descent from a conspicuous parental ancestry and in which many cases, chiefdom was determined by a family descent from father to son. Coming to the more recent times, the powerful Sailo and Thangur chiefs who formed a dominant Sub-tribe had laid down the civic and social system distinct on its own. But even the Sailo chiefs had to fight against the Zadengs who were finally constrained. The institution of strong chiefships for reasons stated, became unavoidable.

The powerful chiefs established their respective entities or principalities in many cases, forming groups of villages. The dispersal of the earlies Kukis made the Mizo dominant. In course of time, many non-Mizo clan, probably the Lakher and Pawi, entered protection under the Lushais, spread to the southern tract and other groups established themselves independently outside the Sailos' domination. For instance ROREHLOVA of Fanai family who owned allegiance to the Zahaos another dominant clan or a subgroup when establishing himself with a small following of 70 households, near the Lunglei, he had been able to achieve so much due to the protection he had received from the Lushai chiefs and had extended his domination near CHAMPHAL.

He broke off allegiance to Zahao and exercised his authority under Lushai tutelege. The Raltes also once exercised their ruling power broadly under the Lushai protectorate but later on were reduced to subjection by the successors of the previous chiefs. Chiefdom was based on a single system of clannage or a combined model of clans.

The reciprocal relations among the Lushai and other chiefs gave history its turn immediately before the Anglo-Mizo relations had started to develop. This had made Vuite as well to receive some assistance from a Thangur chief against the oppression meted out by the SUKTE and Falam. Thangur later on became cruel to them. The Vuites now vacated the Thangur area and were prepared to fight against them.

The political considerations for ousting any dominant group and making way for a weaker group appears to have had its impact in Mizoram as in the other tribal entities. The system of adjustment seems to have rested on the principle of a compromising attitude but when it failed, it produced certain adverse effects.

The Lushai inroad was a very decisive factor although the Kukis are known as the strong tribe who on having been ousted, they set fresh inroads to Cachar Hills, Naga Hills, Tripura, Manipur and greatly disturbed the stability of the region. They also established themselves at the cost of the weaker tribes. The administrative reports give us ample instances on these trends. The tribe diffused on the northeast later sent depredations of raids to the bordering Assam valley, Barak valley and parts of modern Bangladesh.

Due to their strength they occupied in North Cachar Hills clore to Zeliangrong Nagas. The Lushai, Kuki as well as almost all the tribes were known for their notoriety in sending out such depredations. This was one of the most important causes which led to the British advent and penetration into the inaccessibly rugged and steepish terrain of the region. It was in these circumstances that the nomadic Kukis from Manipur made inroads into southern Nagaland and established themselves even until about 1918-19.

The situation became chaotic so that Dr. J. H. Hutton, the Naga Hills Deputy Commissioner an ethnologist and administrator of great repute, led an expedition from Kohima to settle down the matter across the Manipur border in Chakhesang area, and it was at the great cost that the situation was normalised. Hutton subdued a Kuki Chieftain there.

British Paramountcy

In course of time, the gradual establishment of the British administration in the Assam and Barak valley, had also opened a series of contacts with Kuki and Mizo tribes who inhabited the neighbouring places. Frequent tribal raids it is well known, were frequently conducted among the tribes themselves and sometimes upon the plains which lay within the British boundary. Their recurrences had considerably upset the British administration. Therefore, the sending of the frequent punitive expeditions to punish the marauders was necessary. This led to the gradual extension of the British control.

Primarily the government was intended to exert moral exercise upon the tribe to restraint them from taking themselves to raids towards creating such onslaughts and devastations to the people upon where the raid was affected. Each punitive expedition entered the hills even at the great cost of men and energy and exacted lessons upon the perpetrators of raids, the expeditions had certain results upon winning over some of the western Lushai chiefs who complied with Government and who, made worthwhile attempts to normalise their own relations with the government authorities and, at the same time maintaining regular trade with the plains. They also acted as the buffer watch and ward agencies against their own turbulent kith and kin from the highlands.

As with Mizoram, it had taken several decades to establish the British administration. It was almost after fifty years or so that Government was established fully.

The strained Anglo-Kuki (Lusei) relations had dated since those days when the first Anglo-Burmese war was fought and that war ended in 1826 since the Chittagong hill tract, had since been exposed to raids and had caused several adverse consequences to the administration and the inhabitants alike who had been, little protected in those days of turmoil. Moreover, the long warfare fought among the tribes on the highlands, had these effects. In fact the punitive expeditions embarked upon by Government started in 1844. The administration even with the strength they had rallied, was compelled to take over the help of the Rajas of Manipur. Tipperah and of the Chakmas to assist in dealing effectively with the raids.

The creation of strong buffer posts was enforced. The neighbouring areas, however, were frequently devastated due to these raids, harassments and assaults. Each was followed by the taking of several heads and taking off prisoners to the hills. The Government sent several punitive expenditions having employed competent persons to head them such as Col. F. G. Lister who undertook it in 1849; as also the expedition led by Nuthall which followed in 1869 and there was another expedition undertaken in 1871-72. The expeditions undertaken sporadically could hardly check the raids which during all these years went unabated.

Lushai Depredation

The course of events may be briefly serialised. There was a Lushai depredation of raid in 1847 affected upon the Kuki settlement in nearby plain district causing a great havoc where about 150 persons were killed. It was followed by another, yet the more vigorous raid which brought onslaughts upon a mixed community, affecting many Kukis where several persons were taken off as captives and many were killed. Then followed another raid in January 1850 with yet, many devastating effects caused upon the villages subject to raid. The Government despatched a punitive expedition which completely ravaged Sentlang, a village in the interior hills where about 1,000 houses were burnt and reduced to ashes.

The Lushais, it was learnt, had a very strong system of settlement, containing contentments and arsenals capably maintained by the military rank of trust and responsibility under the Sordars which screened the defendent villages where, the riots most of them the cultitors and servants of the chiefs, stayed. The Government had embarked upon, some plans, some of them successfully carried out, to screen that side of the boundary with the help of the Lushai and Kuki levies loyal to them.

Colonel F. G. Lister, twice wounded in the war with the Khasi tribe in 1829 and 1836 and with his vast experience in taking with the hillmen's tactics of guerrilla warfare was placed in command of this arrangement. Later on we find that experienced administrators of Naga hills such as A. Porteous and McCabe were deputed to storm the Lushai, Lakher and Chin Strongholds at the commencement of the formation of Lushai Hill Frontier Districts. Many powerful chiefs had in their service, the ranks and files known as Mantris, Sardars and other hierarchal terms.

The recurrence of raids in future was sought to be effectively curtailed. The border posts instituted were to keep vigilance as much possible as could be. Government during a decade sought to procrastinate their military operations and rallied instead upon the policy of compromise with the belligerent chieftains.

It appears in consequence of a disastrous raid perpetrated by Suakpuilala and Vanpuilala believed to have been implicated in the latest state of insurgency and the raid which had its repercussion on a line of villages known as Adampore, upon a series of negotiations conducted, the Lushai envoys, who came to meet the then administrators in the plain districts, agreed to some terms imposed on them, with due regard to respecting the Sardar's territory and receiving annual compensations on condition, that each of them rendered an annual nominal tribute to the administration. Earlier Major Ravan inflicted punishment upon the villages concerned in affecting raids at that time.

Ruton Puia Raid

The next raid believed to have been affected by ROTIIANGPUIA or Ruton Puia gave an impetus for effectively dealing with the situation and subduing that chief fully. Herein we find that a drift from the so called policy of compromise also called Non-Intervention was made. An exploration expedition yeas undertaken by Lt. Coll. Thomas H. Lewin right into the interior of the hills for bringing that chief to terms. Lewin in company of an improvised force covered the journey in several marches; in part of the foothills, he had sailed in boats and canoes and then made, a hazardous accent to the hills.

The endeavour was a success because it served as one of the real first explorations and because it acquainted the team with the knowledge of the land and the people. He was given reception by ROTHANGPUIA but failed to recover the captives taken off as some had been waylaid and others in turn were carried off by the southern tribe. The tribes besides using spears had in their possession several flint locks with different barrels so antiquated, which looked like the old flint-locks of King George III's time.

These raids were repeated in 1868 and 1869. The expedition set out from Dhaleswari, commanded by Major Stevenson and J. W. Edgar, District Commissioner of Cachar. The expedition, however, delayed to 1869, did not succeed to detect the criminal. It was, therefore, repeated in January 1871 in which a chieftain named Suapuilala was sought to be brought to terms.

The raid perpetrated on 23 January 1871 at Cacharipunjee Cansel widespread havoc in which one English tea planter, Mr. Winchester was killed and his daughter, Mary was taken off. According to a District Gazetteer," "The raiders were eventually driven off, but not before they had succeeded in killing twenty seven persons in addition to those already mentioned, seven of whom were sepoys sent to protect the outlying gardens. Raids were also made on Sylhet, Hill Tippera and Manipur.

Such violent and ferocious forays called for vigorous measures of repression and in the cold season of 1871-72 two columns were sent into the hills, one from Chittagong, the other from Cachar. This expedition was completely successful, and the peace of the Assam frontier remained undisturbed for the next twenty years". Mary, only a small girl changed beyond doubt, was restored.

Until the British occupation, "the people form a mingling of clans, who are known to us by various names Kookies, Lushais, Pois, Shendus, Chins, etc." About the system of Chiefship, it is recorded that "almost every village has its own chief, who generally, however, owes some sort of allegiance to the most powerful chief of the group of villages to which he belongs, for convenience sake, is known as the leader of his clan. From time to time the chief of some subordinate village gets powers and throws off his allegiance to his former head, and found a new clan for himself, which gets known sometimes by his name, sometimes by the name of the hill on which the chief's village is situated and sometimes by a variation of the original clan's name.

The people of these chiefs, change about from time to time, leaving a declining or feeble chief to settle under some one more able and energetic. Nothing does more to establish, a chief and bring him followers and influence them success in raids upon weaker chiefs, upon the villages of Manipur Hill, Tipperah or Upper Burma or upon our villages and outposts and tea gardens. The last are the most attractive of all, for there are more plunders and heads to be got there, with much less risk than elsewhere". The record further has it as follows:

> "In addition to the constant changes in the relative position of individual chiefs, a general movement would seem to take place from time to time amongst these people, apparently as if swarms were thrown off from the more crowded villages in the higher central hills, such swarms forming new communities all round the outer fringe of the tract and in doing so driving before them the villages which had previously inhabited the fringe: The inhabitants then are compelled, in consequence of the pressure to take refuge in our territory or in Tipperah or Manipur, where they are often followed, themselves killed, or taken captive and their villages plundered by the new comers. This seems to have been the origin of what is called the great Kooki rising of 1849 and 1850, as it certainly was of the great series of rains in 1860-61".

Government was alive to these problems. The administrators were prompted with a great desire to protect their subjects as well as the inhabitants within the British protectorate. It was envisaged also that the frequent raids had affected the Cachar District, modern Tripura and Chittagong hill tract and even Manipur. It was essential in course of time that the local administration would have to concert and coordinate joint action to subdue the marauding tribes on all fronts. Government further was greatly concerned with protecting the tea gardens located on nearby plains tract.

The raids frequently committed had affected the collection of hill tract revenue, there was a fall in tolls on hill produce year by year. At the height of this development, the situation was aggravated when two raids were committed in February 1888 by a group of Shendoos or Pois near Saichul range and Chema valley. At the first raid which occurred on 3rd February, Capt. J. R. Stewart, two other British soldiers and one Sepoy while, conducting a survey within the British boundary, were killed.

In a later raid which took place on the 15th February, 6 persons were killed, 2 wounded and 23 prisoners taken off. On 13th December, 1888 occurred a raid in a village close to Semagiri on pakuma Rani's village in which the Rani and 21 men were killed, moreover the captors took 13 heads and carried off 15 captive. For these reasons the Chief Commissioner of Assam, the Chief Secretary of Bengal and the Chief Commissioner of Burma were to be implicated in affecting a concerted punishment of the raiders who had created these depredations. These circumstances led to the Chin - Lushai expedition which occurred in 1889-90 and subsequently the establishment of the administration followed in the hills.

Elaborate plans to concentrate operations were made for which the task was entrusted to a team of competent persons. A viable military strength would be equipped. The expedition would entail huge expenditure and would be fully exposed to several risks and hazards especially in committing themselves to establishing posts in the hills. The futility in delaying to send the well concentrated expedition for securing peace on the frontier can also be envisaged follows:

> "Our inaction would be misunderstood by the trans frontier tribes; we should have to expect fresh raids; the frontier police must be strengthened at ice, a telegraph line between Demagiri and Rangamati being indispensable as well as from the letter place to Chitagong; while revenue would suffer owing apprehension among the tribes within the frontier"... "we cannot permit the continuance in our midst of head taking savages without responsible chiefs, without organisations, and not amenable to political control who yet from their geographical position are enabled to commit outrages with practical impunity upon territory on all sides of them; while we are put to great and constantly increasing expense to maintain lines of defence which prove effectual to protect our peaceful people".

The coordination with Assam, Bengal and Burma would be secured by all means for which, several correspondences had been transmitted among these Governments. There was a great need to maintain the established relations with Burma. The successful expedition would be most helpful to open out the communication in this hitherto unexplored tract. The integration with the rest of the country would automatically result in.

Murray Expedition

In these circumstances, an expedition consisting of more than 1,000 men under Murray and Shakespeare visited the villages implicated in the recent raids. At villages near Lungleh as in fact, the Lakher tribesmen had also posed such problems in causing raids in the British territory. In February and March 1889, the perpetrators excepting Howsata who had already died were brought to books. Now, then time had matured to establish a post at Lungleh in the occupation of a garrison of 212 men under a British officer following the part of road construction that had completed."

The situation elsewhere had deteriorated owing to feuds among the tribesmen themselves for the possession of lands lying in Chengri valley. On the 8th January, 1889, a party of perpetrators under Lianphunga descended to Rangamati and created a great devastation having murdered about 100 persons and carrying off almost that number and having destroyed 24 villages. Many kukis were victims to the havoc.

The account furnished by Sir Robert Reid, Governor of Assam from 1937 to 1942 is found interesting. A condensed analysis of the events for our purpose will serve the purpose. When pressed to release the captives, Lianphunga refused to accept the mandate as the price demanded of him was too heavy in lieu of the absence of any compensation that he could get. Now the number of captives he had held would have been dwindling on. Now the securing of the adamant chiefs would have been the object of a largely organised expedition which visited the Lushai, Lakher and Chin Hills in the already well known Lushai-Chin expedition of 1889-1900.

The objects further are serialised below:

"to reduce the Shendoos to submission, to recover the remainder of the arms, and the heads taken when Lt. Stewart was killed, and also to release captives taken in 1883 from the village of the Lushai chief, Lalsiva main scheme of operation should be devoted to the release of captives taken away in the raids on the village of Pakuma Rani and those in the Chengri valley, and to the infliction such punishment on the perpetrators of those atrocious outrages as may suffice to prevent the commission of similar raids in future". The objects were further rectified as follows:

"To punitively visit certain tribes that have raided and committed depredations in British territory and have declined to make amends or to come to terms, secondly to subjugate tribes as yet neutral, but now by force of circumstances brought within the sphere of British dominion; thirdly to explore and open out as much as can be done on the time, then, as yet only partly known, country between Burma and Chittagong; and lastly, if the necessity arises, to establish semi-permanent posts in the region visited so as to ensure complete pacification and recognition of British power".

The operation was jointly affected from three fronts; a Bengal force of 3,400 men strong based on Demagiri, a Burma force also of formidable strength and a smaller Assam force based on Silchar, each recruited from several military and police detachments, now moved to the hills to quell the marauders implicated in the latest raids.

They were destined to accept the challenge across the hitherto impenetrable and inhospitable terrain; the second object of the expedition was the opening of suitable posts and lines of communication across the hills presumably for giving access to Cachar and Chittagong and in parts of the hills, a telegraph line, with the number of equipments and provisions they had brought, were needed to be installed. The Silchar force faced less resistance and in January-February, 1990, they had established themselves on the Aijal range where a stockade was built. Although Lengpunga or Lianphunga had sent in his captives about 70 persons, yet he had not come in person to tender his submission.

Therefore, a detachment of the force stationed at Aizawl set on to his village in the vicinity of Aijal; he came out, had an interview with an English man, the Commander of the force but the advance of a detachment of the Bengal force to Aijal, then and there, thwarted his intention to surrender. Meanwhile a post was established at Aijal while, the Lungleh fort was renovated, and south of Lungleh, another fort was constructed. The policy of a gradual consolidation was pursued. These events led to the appointment of a political officer in April-May 1890, Capt. H. R.

Brown as a Political Officer

Brown being the first political officer who assumed charge of the northern Lushai Hills: preliminarily he was provided with 300 men of the Frontier Police; from Aijal his headquarter, he was destined to conduct the relations with the chiefs and extend the system of political control; moreover he was bound to conduct relations as well with officers who represented the Bengal and Burma Governments at fort Lungleh, fort Jregear, Haka and fort White. Revenue paid by the chiefs was to be accepted; in fact payment of revenue or tribute was to be made binding to all chiefs, a condition which should be consistently fulfilled. He was moreover bound to open markets in the frontier, and explore the possibility for providing better communications to link up Cachar and Lushai. A conference of Chiefs was held where some of these conditions were announced. A regular route to Burma was envisaged.

Permanent Occupation and Local Chiefs

The permanent occupation of the hills was never desired by the local chiefs. They were opposed also to paying the annual revenue and the surrender of Lianphungo. These were the reasons why Brown was murdered on 9th September, 1890 while approaching Chengsil. He and three of his men were killed. Another survey party consisting of coolies and sepoys was also assaulted when 11 of them, at another direction perished on the same day itself. Aijal and Chengsil fell a prey to the tribesmen immediately.

The British defence, however, was stout; it was Lt. H. W. G. Cole who showed considerably ability to defend before a relief force immediately responded from Silchar covering the marches rapidly and with their presence, both Aijal and Chengsil were relieved. However, one English officer Lt. R. R. Swinton perished in the fight which occurred on 26th September; on the 4th October, Aijal capably held by Dr. Melville for its defence, was also relieved. The pacification soon prevailed, Mr. R. B. M. McCabe reached in time to consolidate the tract almost lost away 'to the marauders. Fifteen ring leaders were found implicated but the most capricious were Khalkham, Lengpunga and Thangula who were exiled and jailed first at Tezpur, then they were removed to Hazaribarg where in its jail, Khalkham and Lengpunga committed suicide.

A promenade under McCabe was sea-it in 1891 to demonstrate the British power in the western hills. Although a success, it met a resistance from the chiefs named as Lalburha and a few other groups called *Pawibawia* or *Poiboi* (probably Pai of Pawi) and Bungteva or Buangthevva which led to a skirmish on 29 February, 1892 and a battle was fought. The attacks were repeated till April.

A raid to confound the British position was affected into a tea estate of Hailakandi in which several persons were killed and carried off. McCabe was relieved finally by Colonel R. H. F. Rennick. It was the last of the great battles fought among the Mizos and the English. The expedition with enough men and provisions could reduce the recalcitrant villages, Poiboi, Bungteya, Lalbura and Maite only towards the end of May. However Kairuma, showed his sway of resistance and it had become necessary to offer a joint operation against him by both the North Lushai and South Lushai parties. It took long to subdue him. It was till December 1895 that he was finally subdued. The pacification of the hills was finally secured.

The northern hills having been almost pacified, the more stringent terms and conditions binding the southern chieftains were now sought to be stipulated in these agreements. The total prohibition of raids, the opening of villages for free passages to facilitate Government transport and undertakings, involving them in providing labour to be paid for, due and punctual collection of taxes, poll tax or any other tax whatsoever, and holding the annual conferences of the chiefs were the basic conditions stipulated therein.

It was felt in the interest of maintaining peace and security that 'the present administration by chiefs be absolutely left to as it is and that we should not interfere with the village administration of criminal, civil and social matters' within a framework to leaving other matters to the chief. The feasibility of separating the Lushai land from the Chittagong Hill tract for giving the present Mizoram a separate charge was envisaged.

The administration would be headed by a Superintendent or political officer and a sufficient police strength be manned at his disposal. The officer so designated in-charge of a district would be empowered to settle disputes "between chief and chief, village and village, tribe and tribe and prevent all raiding and public breaches of peace". We find that Capt. J. Shakespeare and later on Mr. R. H. Sney Hutchison had served in the capacities of Superintendents, South Lushai Hills during the first decade of its inception (1891-98).

However, a tremendous spade work was done for consolidating part of that rugged terrain, in as much as the administration were concerned with conducting the relations with chiefs, improving the constructions and buildings, laying the decisive administration bases and subduing the refractory chiefs.

The South Lushai Hills placed first under the Deputy Commissioner tagged from the administration point of view to Chittagong Hills tract and administered through the Superintendent, was consolidated in the new Lushai Hills district, the North Cachar Hills having already been placed in the charge of a superintendent or political officer stationed at Aijal. Lungleh became a new subdivision under the Subdivisional Officers, Mr. F. C. T. Halliday being the first SDO stationed from 1889-1899. Over 17 Subdivisional Officers had served the subdivision till 1942.

After Capt. Brown, the first political officer, or Deputy Commissioner, at Aizawl, there were 4 political officers who served at Aijal from 1890 to 1898. Over 23 Deputy Commissioners or Superintendents (to use the official designation) had served the Lushai Hills District till 1942. The most competent men fit for the post with considerable experience in frontier administration was installed.

The Lungleh subdivision was inaugurated by Shakespeare at a Conference of Clans held near Lungleh and it was attended by representatives from every tribe. "Shakespear addressed them on the subject of the permanency of our occupation; and the punishment they would suffer if they carried on feuds with each other". All of them swore amical relations with each other, 'the only one concerned in:he subsequent troubles was the petty chief Morpunga Hmawngphunga (of the Howlong clan). Five clans were represented, Howlong, Thangluah, Molienpui, Lakher or Longshen and Poi.

In these circumstances, the consolidated Mizo Hills broke off from their age old isolation with all the pathos of horror due to the internecine warfare coupled with the problem of its migratory character, unstable administration end population pressures which had also disturbed the peace and tranquillity of the adjacent settled districts in the three regions. The policy to civilizing the war-like tribes of Mizoram and of India's northeast as well had been consistently followed by the administration during those decades of consolidation which occurred exactly a century ago.

The refractory attitude of the atrocious tribesmen in Mizoram had indeed posed a great challenge to Government as feuds, killings and raids continued unabated and that was, too, after many years that a settled administration was launched. It had hindered considerably the pace of political and administrative consolidation for ensuring public peace, safety and tranquillity.

Other notable events worthy of our attention may briefly be touched. There was first a meeting amongst McCabe, Superintendent of North Lushai and Shakespeare of South Lushai Hills where a preliminary demarcation of their respective district boundaries was worked out. For the convenience of chieftains, the principle of accepting the annual tribute in rice was accepted.

"The question of enforced labour is discussed in para 10 of the report. Shakespeare considered that the labour should be paid and suggested 4 annas a day. The Commissioner considered it should be 8 annas". The question of tagging Mizoram in trade routes to Burma and Bengal was also raised. The introduction of some British laws apart from the customary laws enforceable through the administrative orders and regulations was also considered and accepted.

The headquarter establishments needed further development with respect to drawing competent personnel, technical, medical or otherwise. The demarcation of a tripartite bounding laying within the spheres of Burma, Bengal and Assam was discussed among the top administrators in many rounds. A conference held at Calcutta in January, 1892 adapted a resolution reading in the matters concerned as follows:

Administrative Readjustment

The territory referred to is at present under three distinct civil administrations in three distinct military commands. The northern Lushais are under the Chief Commissioner of Assam and the General Officer Commanding the Assam district, the southern Lushais are under the Bengal Government and the General Officer Commanding the Presidency district, and the Chins are under the Chief Commissioner of Burma and the General Officer Commanding in that Province.

It has been recognised for some time past, both by the Government of India and by Her Majesty's Secretary of State, that this tripartite division of authority is open to objections, and the main question laid before the conference was what remedies would be practicable".

The final recommendations of the Conference are stated in these words:

> "The majority of the conference are of opinion that it is very desirable that
> the whole tract of country known as the Chin-Lushai Hills should be brought

under one administrative head as soon as this can be done. They also consider it advisable that the new administration should be subordinate the Chief Commissioner of Assam ....

The conference is agreed that North and South Lushai, with such portions of the Aracan Hill Tracts as any hereafter be determined, should be placed under Assam at once on condition that:

- Complete transport and commissariat equipment for supplies from Chittagong to South Lushai, and from Cachar to North Lushai are provided;

- Funds are granted for roads and telegraphs from Aijal to Lungleh".

The conclusions at which the Governor General in Council had arrived at in respect of the proposals of the Conference were as follows:

"The whole of the Lushai country should be under the Chief Commissioner of Assam and the transfer of the Southern Lushais from Bengal to Assam should be made as early as possible ....

"The Northern Arakan Hill Tracts should be transferred from Burma to Assam ......

Until 1906-07, Zawngling remaining 7 miles south of the boundary was still classed unadministered area and the outrages committed in that year, prompted the government to intervene and again, a punitive expedition set forth and meted out the punishment to instigators to the late atrocity. Immediately a meeting with the Burmese officials at Lakhi South of Zawngling brought about a fresh demarcation of the boundary and the transfer of an uncontrolled territory to Arakan Hills Tract, Burma.

In 1924-25, the adjustment of boundary with Chin Hills made it inevitable the establishment of a demarcation in which the hitherto unadministered area laying southward, still was decided to be tagged into the district for following a uniform pattern of administration. A meeting among the Deputy Commissioner, Lushai Hills and the Deputy Commissioner Arakan, decided upon the issue which was accepted by Government. The demarcation of the western body including Chittagong was undertake early as 1911.

Among other things, the system of circle administration, splitting the Aijal District into 12 circles and Lungleh subdivision in 6 circles introduced in 1901-02 was found to work out well with regard to shaping the administrative integration. It was coupled with a system of giving out a suitable interpretation of Government rules, measures and enforceable usages through the services of interpreters.

Coupled with these, the system of holding annual durbars of chiefs was found to be very successful in promoting administration, sorting out differences amongst them and settling them out, realisation of revenue and enforcement of development schemes. A network of road communications and buildings across the land, resumption of new trades and business and opening of school system due to the advent of Christian Missions had initially laid the system of social transformation. They had promoted the ties of oneness among themselves.

The problem of food scarcity which occurred not almost frequently and rat infection due to bamboo flowering was sought to be suitably coped with, both by the administration and the people themselves.

As regards cottage industries, the job of turning out of rugs and blankets to the local cotton was recorded from 1936-37. Major McCall took the initiative to promote this industry. The traditional system of weaving, however, had persisted through the ages. Considerable measures were adopted to introduce a permanent system of rice terracing cultivation in the hills. The permanent system of cultivation actually was practised in the lower hill and plain area of the modern State although on a meagre quantity.

As regards health and health care practices, measures were also introduced as feasible to system of training. Major McCall is known to have taken considerable measures, and Miss M. Dunn the first ever woman minister in the Province in-charge of Department of Health and Medical, had boosted considerable measures during the last war to that effect. McCall further had initiated the formation of "local village consultive machinery capable of being adopted to any electoral needs might bring and with the intention also that such a system might strengthen the relationship between the chiefs and their subjects".

Revolt against British

Along with these events of far-reaching consequences, we note also some landmarks in freedom struggle. The efforts constantly made by the refractory Lushai, Lakher, Pawi and other chieftains to overthrow the British power are the clear instances. The reasons for launching the long warfare were inevitably political, economic, strategic and others. As regards the headhunting propensities, they were there in the tribal blood. They had become inherently tagged with the aboriginal customs.

The raids for plunder, massacre and looting had occurred on numerous occasions. There were the factors that impelled the British administration to push up themselves stage by stage into the interior hills leading, finally to their occupation over the entire frontier. The British occupation was resisted by the freedom loving people. The occupation of Chengsil, Lungleh and Aijal was hindered which led to the long, tedious warfare and which adversely affected the resources of the belligerent on both side.

It was a contest for mastery among them, more so when the warring chiefs were looked upon as notorious and mischievous chiefs who had confounded greatly the situation. Government, therefore, had to rely upon the use of a great force drawn from the various contingencies. The use of the joint operations and expeditions in which the Burma, Bengal and Assam Governments were involved in the embarrassing skirmishes and assaults testified to the wonderful spirit of patriotism which pervaded the whole atmosphere. The British relying upon the use of a potential force, however, came out finally. The support which the chiefs mustered from their supporters was an instance that patriotism had its strong hold.

The renowned freedom fighters were Kalkham who hailed from Setlang near Aijal, a veteran freedom fighter. He had organised a resistance movement against the British advance. He actively conducted a raid on the British headquarter at Chengsil in September 1890 in which Capt. Brown the first ever political officer was killed. Lianphunga the son of Sukpilal, the enemy of the English, was another hero who sponsored the Chengsil raid with Kalkhama. They were both renowned for their daring exploits in the situation. On being captured both were exiled and carried off first to Tezpur thence to Hazirabarg where they ended themselves by committing suicide in September 1891.

Ropuilieni Rani was another architect of Mizo freedom movement. She was the daughter of Zonolel and wife of Zandula, a chieftain. She had been known for taking active part in the freedom movement since 1872. She was captured by Shakespeare in 1883. Her son Lalthuma was also captured and both were imprisoned in the Chittagong jail. She died when very old in January 1895 in the jail. The other leaders were Vansanga or Vanchanga, Jaduna and his sons, Kapleya, Japoca, Dacola, Kairuma and a few others who showed a considerable sway of resistence even after the administration was established.

The Lushai hills during the last war, saw a series of preparation being chalked out for the defence of the border land. The war knocked very near to Mizoram because many battles were fought in Burma between Britain and Japan. In fact the Chin Hills and Arakan were also affected. The Government, however, had secured the considerable support of the Lushai chiefs at the great conferences held with the district administrators for the maintenance of the defence of the hills.

The district administration had already secured improvement of Silchar-Aizawl road, part of which had become motorable. New traffic passed up and down. Most probably they wanted to make Lushai Hills, should the Naga, Tirap and Manipur defence failed, a second defence line and diverting the Japanese strength to the isolated Lushai hills. Already the neighbourhood on all fronts had experienced the brunts of the heavy world war fought in the desolate valley and hills. Fortunately, Lushai hills escaped the bomb bursts, bullets, firing and many more stormy events.

The Lushai themselves had immensely contributed to the defence; they provided persons for the labour corps; many had served in various army and defence contingencies; many had served as scouts, volunteers and organisers in other capacities. The war on its culmination had left its drastic effect but had not altered the map of the region yet.

The war ushered in a series of transformation in society; it projected the strategic situation of the frontier and the ethnic composition. The war having been over, India now was prepared for the attainment of independence. The constitutional adjustment with regard to the tribes, therefore, had taxed the attention of the public.

The tribe out of their working in running the church councils or bodies under the first principal denominations, and out of their involvement in working out community welfare services, had now become more and more democratic minded. The upsurge of a new consciousness indeed had taken place. In these circumstances the Mizo Union was formed in 1946 which pressed for introducing the principles of democracy in working out the new village councils then almost emerging. Till then and during the interim period, the existing district system of administration was allowed to continue under the Deputy Commissioner who was responsible to the government.

Under the Government of India Act, the present Mizoram by virtue of its being an excluded territory, was barred from sending the elected representatives to the erstwhile Provincial Legislative Assembly. On the other hand, the present Constitution has provided for the universal suffrage which entitles each and every citizen to vote for and elect the members of the State Assembly and Parliament also. When the Constitution was enforced, the tribes of the Hills which till 1947 were classed as excluded, for the first time were entitled to vote for the constitution of the Parliament and the Assam State Assembly as well, that was in 1952.

Role of Mizo Union

The Mizo Union played a decisive role in affecting a legislation for curtailing the power of the chiefs and removing thereto the ancient privileges and benefits, they had been used to. The movement pivoted by the Union rallied considerable strength. At the same time, the sixth schedule had been contemplated by the then constitutional framers which would give the tribes a considerable amount of protection over their lands, forests, customs, village chiefships and enabling the tribes in the Hill districts to initiate certain institutions or projects which would benefit the society through the autonomous system of administration.

Therefore, the District Councils had been provided for the Hill districts under the Assam State Government. The District Councils are empowered also to initiate trade and communication projects. In these and the issues so stated, the jurisdiction of the District Councils would not overlap with the powers already held by the government through their departments and other undertakings over them.

The most important provision relates to the maintenance of primary education by the District Councils. There were other provisions relating to the enforcement of laws. In a nutshell, only a few provisions have been highly needed. The Mizo Union perhaps had reiterated the greatest need to introduce sweeping reforms in the system of chiefdom for making the necessary adjustment under the new constitutional set-up. The District Council would entitle the tribes a dual system of Government the bulk of seats in the Council would be filled by the Councillors elected on universal franchise by the people themselves whereas a marginal number should be filled by nominated members.

The Mizos besides sending their elected members to the State Assembly would also be entitled to elect the members to their District Council. The inauguration of the Mizo District Council was held in 1952 leaving its jurisdiction over the total area of 6,743 sq miles whereas the Pawi-Lakher District Council when inaugurated in 1953, comprised the remaining area of 1,400 sq miles. The inauguration of the District Council courts of the two District Councils occurred at a subsequent date.'

Mizo Union had spearheaded the movement with regard to limiting the power, privileges and other immunities held by the Chiefs. They were opposed to giving the chiefs a share from the spoils of hunt, surrendering tributes in the shape of paddy and even adjudicating the disputes by the chiefs and entitling the other privileges to them.

The Union put forward that the village administration should rest fully with the elected village Council. Unless these conditions were complied with, the sixth schedule would not become successful in implementing fully the clauses contained therein. The responsive attitude of the Assam State Government to tackling this burning issue in time brought about a solution to the problem and the abolition of the power and privileges of chiefs was worked out from 1948.

The formation of new Village Councils prior to the inauguration of District Council was one of the most important events in Mizoram. The abolition of chiefs affecting 259 Mizo chiefs and 50 Pawi-Lakher chiefs was enforced through the Assam Lushai Hills District (acquisition of chiefs' rites) Act, 1954. It was to take effect in April 1954, first in the area lying within the Mizo District Councils' jurisdiction and shortly after, in the Pawi-Lakher regional Councils' jurisdiction.

On chiefship, there is a system of hierarchy in which various writers have formed different opinions on this issue. Another question that poses us is that in spite of a hierarchal system, to the society more than once is said to be egalitarian.

British Policy after Revolt

The British administrators on consolidating the territory and immediately after enforcing administration, they had never interfered in the internal system of the administration and they had prescribed the judicial and administrative powers of the several chiefs especially which would stabilise their relations with the villagers in a system which subsisted from the past. Other powers with regard to the administration of justice and other issues were held by the court and the Deputy Commissioner and Subdivisional Officer, that was the powers that did not lay within the competence of the chiefs. Later the situations had impelled the need to introduce the democratic elements in the constitution and functions of the new village Councils being restituted. This impelled a new approach in this perspective.

The village chief held almost the unlimited power in the administration. He was entitled such powers, interest and privilege because he or his son would be qualified to do the job in instituting and concerting such vital issue in village organisation, administration and judiciary. Land belonged to the community but it was he, who held a portfolio in distributing and allocating plots of land to families, for cultivation and other purposes. He initiated several policies for execution and solicited support from them. However, advice by a Council consisting of well chosen Councillors and other ranks and files with different titles would be binding and some would be subject to his discretion for exercise. Later on he was the vital person in a District Conference held by district administration. On these considerations, we will try to define now his social status.

The chief on account of his qualification and functional role was held in great respect. He was to follow a prescribed etiquette or tradition to execute his function. He was like a feudal Lord on condition that his people rendered him a nominal tribute. The kind of tribute we have noted did not amount to the heavy term of exploitation as was the case with the riots in a Zamindari.

There were constraints to his usurpation of undue powers. These nominal tributes enabled him to act as a benevolent village chief and the tradition maintains that he was the nearest benefactor of his people. His dwelling was crowded with expatriates, disabled and helpless persons in which out of his resources, he sheltered and fostered them. Of course he was incumbent to exact services according to their abilities. Actually these grades of helpless and shelterless persons were sometimes called slaves but practically all of them were not slaves and were as good as other citizens.

Actually an expatriate guilty and driven away, would be given protection provided he assured a good behaviour and was amenable to the discipline within the chief's confine. In this way the chief saved starving and other miserable people. Only the war prisoners were graded initially with bondsmen but the situation in course of time would relax, and they would be treated as equal with the other inhabitants. These grades of persons were not slaves but were protected persons. The chiefs were endowed with a system of trust and responsibility and had many liaisons. Some of these chiefs were called Rajas who requisitioned the services of Mantries and Sirdars most probably the usage used by their neighbours.

Democratic Phase

The democratic elements had now become necessary. Hence, the abolition of chiefship had affected. Their place now was taken by the Village Council; it performs duties now under the District Council or district Administration.

In a hierarchy we find mention of priests and sacrifices who performed their manifold religious duties for giving spiritual guidance to their people; beseeching the help of spirits and seeking by religious means to avert crisis. They offer sacrifices and are adept in consisting the omens in the system of invocation and appreciation.

The warriors, especially those who had accomplished victories in warfare were greatly honoured as those who had accomplished marvellous feats for the safety and prestige of their land. They were given rousing receptions and were offered symbolic presents as the mark of honour.

Various implements for cultivation, forestry, construction, husbandry and hunting were needed and implements were moulded accordingly. Artisanship in this was provided by the blacksmithy attached to chiefs. It appears that they use bellows made of inside bored poles or hallowed bamboo lengthwise which when swung from their handles by the blowers directed the air for supply of fire to the furnace for the purpose of moulding, splitting, welding for making out-turns of tools and implements needed by the village folk. They must have used some anvils most essential, stone or iron for the purpose of hitting and hammering.

They must have used schist, tongues, pincers and other tools. They also catered with supplying arms and weapons. Evidently flintlocks were repaired, renovated or their parts overhauled and ammunitions for the purpose were to be manufactured at some villages which abounded with such potentials. As such blacksmiths catered to the needs of wood cutters, craftmen, cultivators, hunters and other grades of workers. The villages depended on the blacksmiths for making their implements.

The crier served summons and acted like messengers, announcers and relayers which helped to promote liaisons to the village in many respect.

A condensed quotation from the Gazetteer of Bengal and North-East India is relevant:

> "The people lived in villages, each of which is ruled by a chief who is entirely independent. The chief is supreme. He settles all disputes, decides where the village is to cultivate and when and where it shall be moved. His house is the poor house of the community and orphans and indigent people live there and get food in return for labour. The other officials are Upa or Councillors, the crier, the blacksmith, and the Puithian or Sorcerer".

There were other deputies, hereditary of non-hereditary representing respectable families who formed a Council which advised and assisted the chiefs. These dignitaries enjoyed certain concession in lands or tributes in kind and later on in kind or cash. Earlier there could have been persons of rank who served as military leaders. Some chiefs were powerful and exercised jurisdiction over an entity for which, certain inter-village relations, judicially, administrative or otherwise were stabilised. The office of chief was hereditary and passed from father to his eldest son.

According to the Assam Act XXI of 1954, the rights and interests of a chief in Ram (which designated a tract or tracts of land within a Ram Ri Lekha or a field boundary), stood transferred to invest them in the state (free from all encumbrances), since the enforcement of the Act.

It empowered the District Council or Regional Council to take over charge of any Rams, and it had hitherto required that the right and interest of the chief as such would vest in the state. Further the said Act provided that the Ram since taken away was to be administered by the District or the Regional Council "for the time being enforced in the Lushai Hills district".

Under the provisions, the compensation officer appointed for the purpose would work out a scheme to determine the total number of households within the Ram and fix the amount of compensation due to be paid "to such chiefs and the other persons whose interests are affected". It required that the payment would be made either in cash or in kind; it would decide if payment was to be made in lumpsum or in instalments, and to take note of any other particulars worth considering.

When drawing up the compensation statement, making over of payment would have to be determined so much so in accordance with certain rules to be framed. The criteria are laid down below:

- "The compensation payable to a chief shall be as follows for the period every year with effect from the date of vesting:
  - three tins of paddy per year per household up to a limit of one hundred households in his Ram; and
  - two tins of paddy per year per household for every additional household in the Ram beyond the limit of one hundred households mentioned in (i) above.

- For the purpose of Clause (a):
  - Whether the chief has more than one Ram in his jurisdictions, all Rams shall be treated as one Ram and the total number of households shall be computed accordingly.
  - The actual number of household within the Ram of a chief shall be regarded as those paying Fathang to the chief immediately preceding the commencement of this Act, and shall include those exempted from the payment from all by virtue of profession, trade, calling, employment or all the recognition of other services.

- The amount of compensation shall, as and when paid in cash, be calculated according to the market price of paddy prevailing at the time in the locality where the Ram concerned is suited.

The compensation shall, in the first instance, be determined for the Ram as a whole and in separately for each of the co-sharers or interest from any.

The compensation officer shall then apportion the share of compensation payable to a co-sharers or any persons having interests in the Ram and if, in doing so any question involving matters of civil nature arises, he shall dispose of the matter in the prescribed manner".

Now we drift to the historical antecedents and we find that the next important thing related to use of nomenclature for the district where the Lushai district was retitled Mizo District by the Act of Parliament in 1954 after a broad consensus of opinion was obtained to adopt this title, desired by the people. The enforcement to it was made by the Lushai Hills district (change of name) Act (18 of 1954).

Prior to the formation of District Council we are told that "by voluntary labour, the Lushais who prefer to be known as Mizos, have so far built over 90 miles of road, a remarkable feat by any standard". They had completed two-thirds of a 128 mile long road with its crest width of 14 feet via Aijal to Lungleh. There were difficulties faced in building culverts and portions of road at landslide affected areas. The opening of the road nearly complete, was held on the first Republic Day, coinciding with the enforcement of the Constitution.

During the visit of the State's Reorganisation Commission, in 1954-55, the United Mizo Freedom Organisation born in 1947 submitted their memorandum to the commission in favour of carving out a Hill State in which the erstwhile Lushai Hills would be included by separating them from Assam.

The Mizo Union also presented the memorandum insisting upon the enhancement of the powers provided for under the sixth scheduled of the Constitution.

For the time being, there had been several exchanges of opinion among the hill leaders for the formation of Hill State. There has been some understanding among the United Mizo Freedom Organisation leaders with the Tribal Union (subsequently known as Eastern Tribal Union) which won many seats, for the tribal districts in the Assembly in 1957. The proposed introduction of the Assam language bill consequently led to the birth of the All Party Hill Leaders Conference in 1960 in which the United Mizo Freedom Organisation was one of their constituents.

Independent Era

Post-independence Scenario

After Independence, the two main parties were Mizo Union and United Mizo Freedom Organisation. During the first election held in 1952, Mizo Union bagged all the three Assembly seats entitled to Mizo in Assam Legislature and almost 92 per cent of seats in Mizo District Council. In 1957, United Mizo Freedom Organisation had mustered considerable strength; they captured two Assembly seats against Mizo Union one.

In fact in that year one of their MLAs was appointed Parliamentary Secretary. It was in July 1960 that the All Party Hill Leaders Conference (APHLC) was formed which was opposed to the enforcement of the Official Language Bill which recognised Assamese as the official language. In spite of the opposition mounting up, the Bill was passed in 1961. This led to the resignation of the Hill MLAs from Government positions allotted to them. Other developments quickly followed.

In the election held in early 1962, the Mizo Union and Eastern Tribal Union won two and one Assembly seats respectively. In October 1962, due to the passage as the language bill and in conformity with the decision of the APHLC, both the Mizo Unionist MLAs resigned from the Assam Assembly. In the 1962, bye-election held to fill up the two vacant seats two Mizo National Front candidates were returned. The sitting MLA soon opted to serve as member of Assam Public Service Commission and resigned and, in the bye-election, held in 1964, the Mizo Union candidate was returned.

Some relations had been cultivated among the Mizo, the Khasi and other tribal leaders in those years for conceiving some broad-based common approaches for securing better protection to their rights, interests and other obligations. When the Assam language bill was proposed to be tabled in the Assembly, the Mizo Union and other Hill parties withdrew cooperation with the Assam Government. In these circumstances the APHLC was formed and the Mizo leaders were among leaders who were vocal in the formation of the Hill State. Conceiving a hill State with so vast and extensive its jurisdiction to comprise Mizoram, 'Tripura, parts of Cachar and the other existing Hills under Assam, appear to have been impracticable.

The Mizo National Front the more radical party insisted on carving a separate entity for Mizoram. Therefore, the Assam language act adopted in 1960 and the other movements which had rallied great strength had directly or indirectly resulted to the reorganisation of the region which had taken effect from 1972. There was also a joint conference of Executive Councils of District Councils held in June 1954 at Tura which had played considerable role in forging a sense of unity among the Hill Leaders of Assam.

The modern history reveals also the occurrences of many formative and decisive events in Mizoram. Experimentation in working out the District Councils proved certain inherent defeats in the system and the District Councils in Mizo hills as in the other hill districts would not be able to satisfy the public urges for providing a successful system of administration and sorting out some differences of opinion among the tribes. A brief analysis of these historical events may be found interesting.

Insurgency in the State

Another important event was that the Mizo National Front had followed a radical policy and came into conflict with the administration. As regards the state of insurgency and the adverse impacts it had exerted in the land, this event is well known; it is still remembered by many persons.

It was an armed revolt and upsurge in which almost all the tribes or sub-tribes participated. We need not go into detail with regard to the event, information can also be had from other sources. Mizoram was subject to the heavy operations conducted by the forces.

The system of village grouping and resettlement which had posed great difficulties was conducted to cut-off the peaceful inhabitants from the bellicose factions. Although difficult and strenuous, the efforts were crowned with success.

The resumption of negotiations for the cessation of hostilities paved the way for working out a reorganisation of the Mizo hills and the conduct of relations in a new set-up was sought to be defined. In these circumstances the Union Territory of Mizoram was constituted and worked out from 1972. A unicameral legislature was provided for the territory under which there would be thirty elected and three nominated members.

At the election held the Mizo Union returned with a comfortable majority securing 21 seats against 6 Congress members elected, 3 Independent and 3 nominated. The party took office in May 1972; it was the first ever Ministry which pivoted the Mizo affairs. However, it lasted for only two years" as in fact a Coalition Ministry with the Congress and Mizo Union was constituted in 1974. As such the Mizo Union was superseded by a Coalition Ministry formed of Congress and themselves. The newly formed Coalition Ministry remained for five years. This coalition Ministry in spite of several hurdles created by the complicated conditions owing to the confrontation, remained in power for a few years.

The situation soon became disastrous due to a sort of insurgency launched by the underground wing of the MNF. The latter had created a chaotic situation which sought to paralyse the functioning of the Central Government establishments. Consequently President's rule was imposed in Mizoram which lasted for nearly a year. The situation now led to the birth of new party called the People's Conference which started organising itself from 1975. The party assumed considerable importance subsequently.

The withdrawal of the President's rule brought about a normal situation and the Conference won the Parliamentary election in 1977 and in the next general State Assembly election, the Conference returned 23 members against 4 Congress (I), 1 Mizoram Janata and 2 Independent. That was in May 1978. The Ministry was installed in June 1978 but after five months only, the Assembly was dissolved and President's rule was imposed which lasted for a few months. At the next general election held in April 1979, it won a sweeping victory with its 22 members" returned against 5 Congress and 1 Independent. It held office for a full term till 1984.

The Assembly most probably since the inception of a territory could not function smoothly in the face of the harassment launched by the underground party. During the next election, a sweeping change followed as the Conference commanded only 8 seats against Congress (I) 19, Independent 1 and Mizo Convention 1. The situation considerably improved as the party in power tried by all means to secure pacifism.

The MNF becoming more and more amicable had paved the way for the resumption of negotiations, it was at this stage that Laldenga now returned from Britain was committed himself to work out a fresh agreement for the future restitution of the said territory. From October 1984, a declaration of a unilateral cease fire with the belligerent was announced. Many rounds of negotiation was undertaken. Meanwhile the Cabinet headed by Mr. Laldenga took up the rein of administration from August, 1986.

It was preceded by the Constitution Fifty Third Amendment Bill adopted by the Parliament and passed into an Act on 7th August 1986 which conferred full Statehood on Mizoram. In the ensuring elections held in February 1987, Mizo National Front with 24 members was returned against 13 Congress (I) and 3 members of the Conference. Mr. Laldenga President of the Mizo National Front soon was sworn in as the first Chief Minister of Mizoram, now having the status of a full State.

According to the provisions the Legislative Assembly shall consist of 40 elected members and an assurance was pledged that no Act of Parliament shall have effect upon the following:

- Religious or social Practices of the Mizos;
- Mizo customary law or procedure;
- Administration of civil and criminal justice involving decisions according to Mizo customary law;
- Ownership and transfer of land, shall apply to the state of Mizoram unless the Legislative Assembly of Mizoram by a resolution so decides:

   Provided that nothing in this clause shall apply to any Central Act in force in Mizoram immediately before the appointed day".

It was stipulated also that:

- In keeping with the change in status from a territory to State, the Centre shall transfer resource; to the new Government which will include resources "to cover a revenue gap for the year".
- "That Central assistance for plan will be fixed taking note of any residuary gap in resources so as to sustain the approved plan outlay and the pattern of assistance will be as in the case of special category stage".

It was agreed that the Inner line Regulations now in force shall not be subject to repletion or amendment without consulting the State Government. It was also agreed that border trade in the local agricultural commodities, may be allowed under a scheme to be chalked out by the Centre "subject to international arrangements with neighbouring countries".

The agreement agrees to:

> Preserve and protect the rights and privileges of the minorities in the state and ensure their social and economic advancement.

Government under the terms laid down may review the unification of Mizo inhabited areas in other State within one framework of administration, "the Constitution of India prescribes the procedure in this regard but .... Government cannot make any commitment in this respect".

Provisions have been made that the state will be free to adopt any one or more of the languages as the language to be used "for all or any of the official purposes of the state". The provisions also provide for the establishment of a separate university and the setting up of a High Court coinciding with the readiness of the state to accept the responsibility.

Under the conditions laid down, Mizo National Front would take necessary steps to end all underground activities, bring out their underground personnel "with their arms, ammunition and equipment to ensure their return to civil life, to abjure violence and generally to help in the process of restoration of normalcy".

The Central Government is committed to "take steps for the resettlement and rehabilitation of underground MNF personnel coming over ground". Of course after considering the modalities necessary to that scheme.

The MNF henceforth will stop to extend any support to Tripura TNV and Manipur PLA and "any other such groups, by way of training, supply of arms or providing protection or in any other matter".

It was agreed also to work out an existing scheme for payment of ex-gratia amount to heirs/dependents of persons who were killed during disturbances in 1966 and thereafter in the Union Territory of Mizoram. Effective measures to that extent will be taken to expeditiously disburse payment to those eligible persons who had already applied. Payment of compensation in respect of damage to crops, buildings destroyed/damaged during the action in Mizoram and rental charges of buildings and lands occupied by the security forces shall be made on the proper verification obtained.

Chakma Problem

The State during those years was confronted also with the Chakma problems. The Chakma area since time immemorial was like a buffer between the present confines of Mizoram and Chittagong. A considerable section of the population was confined at Demagiri now situated within the Mizo Boundary, recently remained Tlabung" The place had provided one of the important bases for the access of British into Mizoram. Several groups of Chakma expatriates were resettled under the previous administrative arrangement in Mizo villages, they have been fairly distributed, although Buddhists using a Bengali medium in education, they had been given shelter by the Mizo Chiefs.

From newspapers we know that Chakma expatriation into Tripura, parts of Mizoram and as far as Arunachal Pradesh, had continued anabated since the late sixties. The influx of Chakma refugees had posed problems of population explosion in Tripura and had posed considerable difficulties with regard to their resettlement. The analysis of the situation shows that the Chakmas received protection with regard to the realisation of their rights in Mizoram. It also appears that the swarms of movements of the Chakmas into the Indian territory had occurred and some of them had recently been pushed back to maintain the balance of population.

When the Lushai Hills District Council and the Lushai regional Council (Pawi-Lakher) were inaugurated in 1953, the elected Chakma members also set at the Councils which for the first time, with a coordinated approach, pivoted the affairs of the District. When the reorganisation of the region took place, the minorities were assured protection with regard to their rights, privileges and obligations and under the Act, three District Councils were constituted, they were the Lakher District Council, the Pawi District Council and the Chakma District Council.

The Constitution recognises the principle of election, however, a few seats were filled by nomination. The Executive Council is manned by the Chief Executive member and a few executive members returned by the Council. The adjustment with the Chakmas was worked out in the constitutional arrangement which governed the reorganisation of the region by virtue of the Act passed; negotiations also were carried over towards working out the accord which conferred Statehood on Mizoram.

When Lushai Hills was tagged with Assam, the District sent three elected members to the State Legislature during the first election held in 1952. It continued to send the same number of legislators during the elections held in 1957, 1962 and the subsequent bye-election 1963. As a Union Territory, the Legislative Assembly of Mizoram consisted of 30 elected members. The name of the constituencies is provided in the chart furnished below. As a State, the Legislative Assembly now consisted of 40 legislative members.

Constituency

Tripang, Sangau, Saiha, Chawngte, Demagiri, Duarpur, Lunglei, Tawipui, Hnahthial, An. Vanlaiphai, Khawbung, Champhai, Khawhai, Saitual, Ngopa, Suangpuilawn, Ratu, Kawnpuri, Kolasib, Kawnthah, Sairang, Phuldungsei, Sateek, Serchhip, Lungpho, Tlungvel, Aizawl-North, Aizawl-East, Aizawl-West, Aizawl-South.

Under the Union Territory, three Districts were Constituted named Aizawl, Lunglei and Chhimpui (with headquarter at Saiha).

There was a bye-election held in May 1982 consequent to the resignation of four members of the Assembly who were frustrated with the long delay since caused, to bring a reapproachment with the Mizo National front. And the verdict of the election was that three Conference candidates and one Mizo Union member were returned. This perhaps was one of the antecedents that had considerably helped to re-open the negotiations with MNF towards the conferring of Statehood to Mizoram.

It was auspicious that P.U. Ch. Saprawnga at the first session of the Assam Legislative Assembly constituted shortly after the enforcement of the constitution addressed the Assam Assembly in March 1952 in the following extract quoted from his speech:

> "Today we need more food and money. But what we need most is an entire change in our mental outlook. How that change has to be affected is more than my humble-self can say. But one thing is clear - the salvation of the country lies in this change of outlook. So long this change does not take place in our society the evils of corruption, cheating and criminal offences would always be eating the very bones of our national interest and progress; and so long this change does not take place no complicated problem could effectively be solved by any Government, however, powerful that Government might be.
>
> There are talks about corruption and nepotism all around us. Those in the government appear to have hesitated to admit the truth of these talks. But I think we must face the facts squarely and boldly. There is no doubt that there are corruptions around us in one form or the other. The remedy does not lie in trying to conceal the facts. Rather it only helps increasing the evil. There should be strong and firm measures, and such measures should be carried out courageously regardless of the consequences. The offenders should be regarded as public enemies and should be punished publicly. Then only we can expect improvement in this respect."

4

Geography

Mizoram is a gorgeous land of hills, rivers and lakes. 21 hills of different heights run through the length and breadth of the state. The highest peak, 'Phawngpui' (Blue Mountain) towers 2,065 metres above the sea level. Mizoram is the most multicoloured topography among all hilly areas in the country.

Although there are many rivers and streams the most important rivers are Tlawng, Tut (Gutur), Tuirial (Sonai) and Tuivawl. These rivers flow through the northern territory and eventually join river Barak in Cachar. The Koldoyne (Chhimtuipui), which originates in Myanmar, is an important river in the south Mizoram. It has four tributaries and the river is in patches. The Western part is drained by Karnaphuli (Khawthlang tuipui) and its tributaries. A number of important towns are situated at the mouth of the river. Lakes are scattered all over the state. The most lakes are Palak, Tamdil, Rungdil; and Rengdil.

Mizoram gets an average rainfall of about 3,000 mm with Aizawal town having 2,380 mm and Lunglei 3,178 mm. During rains the climate in the lower hills is humid. Rainfall is evenly distributed. Heavy rains start in June and continue up to August. The crops hardly ever suffer from drought. In the lower areas malarial fever is a common feature after rains. Even during the hot season, it is cool and pleasant on the higher hills. The special feature of the climate here is the occurrence of violent storms during March-April. Heavy storms sweep the hills in the entire state.

Temperature in the state varies from about 12°C in winter to about 30°C in summer. Winter is from November to February and during this season there is no rain or very little rain. Winter is followed by springwhich starts at the end of February and continues till the middle of April. In April, storms occur and the summer starts. In April and May temperature usually goes up to 30°C.

A mist covers the hills. September and October are the autumn months and the temperature is usually between 19°C and 25°C.

Climate

The general climate of Mizoram is one of the most pleasing one in the country. With moderate temperatures throughout the year, the Mizoram climate is loved by the tourists and visitors.

The summers are not very hot as the temperature remains between 20° to 30° Centigrade. The winters are very pleasing and cool with temperatures ranging from 21° to 11° Centigrade. Mizoram witnesses heavy rainfall in all parts of the state during the rainy season. Monsoon starts from June and lasts till the month of August. An annual average rainfall of 3,000 millimetres is recorded in the state. During the months of March to April, heavy storms occur in most parts of the state.

A report of a normal day during the summer will give a rough idea of the usual weather of Mizoram.

- Maximum Temperature — 26° Centigrade.
- Minimum Temperature — 16° Centigrade.

Topography

The topography of Mizoram is not very different from its other north eastern neighbours. Mizoram topography is conspicuous with the presence of hills and mountain ranges. The tall green hills are moated with free flowing rivers. The eastern side of the state is situated at a higher altitude than the western side of the state.

The average height of the Mizoram hills is approximately 900 metres. The tallest among the hills is the Phawngpui-Blue Mountain with a height of 2210 Metres. The picturesque valleys and flat lands of Cachar, Mat, Champhai, Chamdur and Tlabung are blessed with very fertile soil and natural resources suitable for excellent agricultural and horticultural productions.

The geographical location of Mizoram lies between East longitude 92°15' to 93°29' and North Latitude 21°58' to 24°35'. Covering a total area of 21,087 square kilometres, the state is blessed with rich forest resources and beautiful lakes.

Landscape

The land area is mostly hilly intertwined with several rivers and gentle streams. The average height of the hills is about 900 m. The hill ranges run in north-south direction with an average height of 920 m above mean sea level. As such the rivers also flow either from north to south or south to north. The eastern sector is higher than the western part.

The airport site is located on an elevation of 150 m above the mean sea level. The site is covered with vegetation comprising mostly of bamboo and grasses.

Landuse and Landcover

Drastic changes in landuse in Mizoram, caused by both increasing population and shifting cultivation have been noticed recently. Population pressure in upland areas and the hills has led to the expansion of agricultural areas inside evergreen forests and mixed forests dominated by bamboo. Bamboo grows everywhere with varying intensity of growth depending upon when the *jhum* was last practiced. Slope cultivation or *jhum* cultivation is the principal landuse. Mixed cropping of maize, rice, vegetables, chillies, cotton and tobacco is practiced.

Hydrology

Medium to steep slopes characterise the topography of the area. Run-off has eroded surface drainage due to unconsolidated nature of the formations over which they flow. As a result of these features the drainage pattern is well developed. Well defined narrow stream channels of all orders drain the area. The project site is located in the catchment of river Twang. Gutur, Lunghmur and Dialdawk are the major perennial rivers that flow through the study area. Few wetlands and small ponds are other sources of water. The water table at the airport site is between shallow and very deep due to steep rolling terrain of hills, small peaks and valleys. The rivers flowing through the forest areas have some fish population and form vital breeding places for them.

Rivers

The rivers of Mizoram constitute a major part of the topography of Mizoram. Aided by heavy rainfall during the rainy seasons and occasional rainfall throughout the year, most of the Mizoram rivers are perennial in nature.

Some of the rivers flowing through Mizoram are:

- Tlawng or Dhaleshwari.
- Tiak.
- Teirei.
- Tuirini.
- Serlui.
- Chhimtuipui or Kolodyne.
- Khawthlangturipui or Karnaphuli.
- Tuichang.

- Tuirial or Sonai.
- Tuichawng.
- Mat.
- Tuipui or Khawchhak.
- Tuivawl.

The northern part of the state comprises of some important rivers like the Tlawng or Dhaleshwari, Tuirial or Sonai and some other rivers. Rivers like Mat, Tyao, Tuichang, and Tuipui fall in the southern part of Mizoram. The rivers of Mizoram are the main source of water for the people of the state. The perennial rivers of the state feed the lush green vegetation of Mizoram.

Lakes

The picturesque Lakes of Mizoram have emerged as popular tourism destinations of the state. Mizoram's lakes are the venues of a lot of activities like boating, fishing, camping and trekking. Some of the important lakes in Mizoram are:

- Palak Lake.
- Tamdil Lake.
- Rengdil Lake.
- Rungdil Lake.

The Tamdil Lake has an interesting legend attached with its creation. Situated in Aizwal district, the Tamdil Lake is 110 kilometres away from the capital city. One of the most beautiful lakes of the state of Mizoram, the Palak Lake lies in the Lakher region. The oval shaped lake is bordered with stretches of deciduous and tropical evergreen forests. The lake is visited by numerous migratory birds making the place a haven for the bird watchers. The Rendil Lake is an artificial lake in Aizawl. It has emerged as one of the prime tourist attractions of the state. The Rungdil Lake covers an area of 2.5 hectares. The lake is divided into two parts and surrounded by long stretches of forests.

Tamdil

Tamdil is one of the few natural lakes of Mizoram. Located in the Aizwal district of the state, the Tamdil Lake lies at a distance of 110 kilometres from the capital city. The Saitual village is the closest locality, located at a distance of 7 kilometres from the lake.

As per legendary beliefs, the Tamdil Lake was created when a huge mustard plant was brought down. Water sprinkled out of the stems of the plant and created the lake giving the name of Tamdil, which means a lake of mustard plant.

The serene atmosphere of the Tamdil Lake of Mizoram goes in sync with the picturesque landscapes, blessed with imposing hills and green forests. Anglers have a gala time here and so do the campers. The tourists can enjoy boating in the waters of the Tamdil Lake. It has indeed emerged as one of the popular picnic and tourist spots in Mizoram.

Palak Lake

Palak Lake is one of the biggest natural lakes of Mizoram. The Palak Lake lies in the southern part of the state in the Lakher region. Located only 5 kilometres from the Pahu village, the Palak Lake of Mizoram falls in the Chhimtuipui district. The oval shaped lake has a width of 150 metres and a length of almost 200 metres. According to the local beliefs, the Palak Lake was created by a flood, which engulfed an entire village. Bordered by deciduous and tropical evergreen forests, the Palak Lake in Mizoram is one of the most beautiful lakes of the state. The Palak Lake is a paradise for bird watchers and fishing freaks. The serene ambiance, the crystal clear water and the presence of rich flora around the lake attract local and migratory birds. Various species of wild ducks and other aquatic birds are seen in abundance. No wonder it is one of the main tourism attractions of the state. The unpolluted water of the lake is the home to many rare species of fish, crabs and other creatures of the aqua kingdom. The forest area near Palak is full of animals like bear, dear, tiger and boar, making it a must visit place for the wildlife buffs and nature lovers.

Rungdil

Rungdil is one of the most significant natural lakes of Mizoram. Located at a distance of 14 kilometres from Saungpuilawn Village, Aizwal, the Rungdil Lake is one of the tourist attractions in Mizoram.

The Rungdil Lake has earned its name from the Rungdil birds. The lake was once the habitat of thousands of Rungdils — a species of partridges. The Rungdil Lake in Mizoram has a very interesting shape. The lake is actually divided into two parts by a single strip of land but with subterranean link.

The Rungdil Lake of Mizoram covers an area of 2.5 hectares and is surrounded by vast stretches of deciduous and tropical evergreen forests. The place is a must visit for the nature lovers. The area also serves as a lovely picnic spot. The adjoining forest is infested with animals like bear, deer, tiger, wild boar, etc. and can be a much admired destination for wildlife freaks. The crystal clear water of the lake is home to many known and unknown fish, making it an angler's paradise.

Hill Ranges

Approximately three-fourths of the state is covered by oblong and sturdy ranges of hills which project themselves like a huge mass of the precipitous terrain. They look also like a panorama of the blueish walls of hills radiating in all directions with slow bending alignments projecting themselves with sharp brows and summits. The greater portion evidently is dominated by the, hill chains which protrude from Burma. The ranges, however, slope gently in the west and northwest and open out into the western and northern bordering plains. However, the existence of the Chittagong hill tract at a lower attitude which lies west beyond the border, appear to have branched off from the lower flanks which run from Mizoram.

Also some of the minor hill chains from the state are merged with those lying in Tripura. On the northeastern side the hills are merged in the irregular plateau which opens out into the Manipur Valley. In this regard it is safe to assume that northward from the state, on the eastern frontier, the Barail mountain the northern Manipur, Cachar Hills and Nagaland while yet, more northwardly, the Patkoi system of mountains dominate the Tirap district of Arunachal Pradesh, the only part of that which lies south of the river Brahmaputra.

The convergence of these ranges, distinct from the Himalayas which lies north of that river, has accounted for the mountainous character of the region. This formidable mountain system dominates the entire eastern frontier.

Spur after spur of these ranges are seen in Mizoram as in the other neighbouring Hill States. They are seen changing directions from north to south. At places they form the chaostic mountain scenes, the ranges running in alternate successions and with their greatly captivating heights. They form mostly the formidable plateaux leaving the narrow glens and sometimes the petty river basins at their bases.

The region is believed at one time to have submerged under the sea. We can think that parts of Mizoram, the Arakan and the adjoining Cachar and Sylhet districts to have formed a coastland which once bordered a gulf or bay of the ocean subsequently an explosion was caused in the crust. That was how that a land mass had emerged which covered and enveloped the region which has given Mizoram, its present intricate or compressed mountainous character.

It is also known that several interior places had been hitherto inaccessible through the long ages of history. In fact Mizoram had been more isolated during the pre-British ages, the situation has now improved. The means of communications are no longer poor. A network of roads built across the length and breadth of the land, have made their considerable impact in making Mizoram more accessible to the outside world. It has helped to build and expand trade, business and also the educational interest. It has fostered on a larger scale, the sense of inter-State social integration. The age-old isolation has become the thing of the past.

The topographical character also has mixed its results. The length of the hills, sturdy and formidable as they are, has certain constraints to constructional and road making works. They entail more time and energy with regard to executing such works. Travels in the hills make greater distance as roads are curved and do not run straight ward making a series of descents and accents, following, inevitably the directions of the hills.

As a rule, soil erosions on the entire length of the eastern frontier are known to have their high incidences and land slides are frequent especially during the rainy season. They also hinder constructional and even agricultural works and make the maintenance of roads difficult. Top soils in certain places are easily eroded, washed off by heavy rains. This is a characteristic feature of a vast terrain of the eastern borderland which includes Mizoram. These depressions are due to the fact that the soft clays are prevalent in parts of the hills.

Mizoram is one of the eastern Frontier States and as such, abounds in the ranges running alternately, converging and protruding among themselves. It makes an impression of the oblong plateau. It abounds in many kinds of vegetation, herbage and foliage, peculiar to a hill country. Some of the hill tops are dry and arid, some are clothed with vegetation thinly, and some densely and, some are converted into grasslands formed mid the ridges and cliffs. The tree species otherwise in the rich jungle grow and vary according to the climatic conditions.

Rich in Mineral Resources: Apart from a few mineral resources that have been located, the vast mountain terrain has yet to be explored as scientifically as possible. The existence of coal as a precious mineral has been detected but at present it indicates a small seam located on the south near a place called *Chwangte* and on the north, coal in small quantities, has been located near a place named Bilkhawthlir.

The high peaks and mountains in the region have also shown the existence of salt wells and in a few pockets, the people have been acquainted to collect salt by boiling the salt water in certain urns and the solid lumps are extracted after the water has kept cold. They contain medical propensities which are helpful to cure the stomach pains, they may have contained some sodaic elements. These salt springs also exist in Mizoram. The qualitative yield so far has not been collected. It is maintained also that oil seepages may be found in the northwest and the possible existence of oil in southern Meghalaya and western Nagaland may be viewed simultaneously. Until the latest researches conducted by scholars, Mizoram appears not to be so rich in mineral wealth.

Besides the valuable timber species, there are several shrubs, palms and straw. It shares a kind of a semi-tropical vegetation in the lowlands, a temperate kind on the hills and perhaps, an alpine type yet, on the higher summits. The agricultural crops also vary largely according to the climate. The dearth of mineral resources excluding a few located ones can be attributed to a system of stratification of rocks which appear to have taken place more recently compared with the other cases of formation, which occurred in the more ancient period.

Occurrences of the high intensity earthquake tremors could have similarly caused a severe alteration in the crust. This accounts for the lack of fossiliferous elements. The sandstones and shales, however, have revealed the marine fossils of the tertiary age towards the south.

Important Peaks

Among the important peaks, Phawangpui anglicised Blue Mountain is the highest in the country. It measures a little more than 7,000 feet elevation resembling Shimla in altitude. Water heads as a rule are very few. The only known rivers are Tlawng which after draining the great length of the land is emptied in the Barak river in Assam. The other small rivers are Turial and Tuivawl on the north. The Tlawng is converged by one of the rivers named Dhairang before she debouches the hills for the plains.

The Tlawng is called Dhaleswari when she flows through the Hailakandi plain. The rivers flow for a considerable distance on the hills, on emerging out from the hills they touch a fringe of the plain and are emptied in the Barak in the Cachar plain. These rivers on receiving such streams flow northward. At places, it is known that these rivers flowing in the deep ravines underneath the mountain have made themselves inaccessible to the inhabitants occupying the upper spurs but at other places they are quite accessible to the villagers depending upon their location. Some of the central ridges form the great water partings so that the southern portion is washed by a major river called *Chhimtupui* having its name Her upper reach is in Burma, she winds west to Mizoram, bends like an arch and flows back to Burma.

She is known as Koladyne in the lower reaches. There is also Khawthlangluipal river known as Karnaphuli in the outer hills and she flows past the southern hills carrying a few small streams known as Tuipui, Tuichang and others. She flows southward to Chittagong until emptied in the Bay of Bengal.

Vegetation and Plants

The vegetation in the lower hills and narrow plain corridor of the state evidently is tropical or Semi-tropical. The central and eastern parts have accommodated large formidable jungle groves covered with the species of hill vegetation. And yet, there are places covered with thick bamboo groves. The viable planning of forest industries can now be undertaken; a few species have got also their medical propensities. Other constructional patterns may also be based. This can be done in the northeast only when a system of tree plantation can be undertaken as should be proportionate to the system of timber exploitation.

Evergreen Forest: Mizoram on the part of level land and lower hills, appears to have a kind of wet evergreen vegetation; part of it can also be classed as semi-tropical vegetation which confines itself to the outer hills. Bamboo, cane, palm and shrubby plants also intersperse the places on the lower altitudes. The bordering areas once formed "a tract of most intricate hill ranges and impenetrable cane-brakes lying between Manipur and

Cachar on the north, and the Arrakan Hill tracts on the south and the Chittagong Hill tracts and Hill Tipperal on the west. On the edges of this tract on all sides the hills are low, covered with dense forest and trackless jungle, the only paths being for the most part the bed of torrents. Further in the hills are much higher and more open, so that there would be less difficulty in exploring them". Timber felled here serves the multifarious purpose of building, cabinet and construction. We find towards the plain, large groves of trees forming the formidable conopies on their tops and affording great shades in the ground. Bamboo plantation if further extended can be helpful for the installation of paper, match sticks and other industries. Many timber factories can be planned. As regards bamboo and cane, some craftsmen think that the hill bamboo serves better for their purpose. Different bamboo species can be allotted for different purposes including bridges, platforms, house constructions and factorial uses. Hill vegetation dominates the higher altitudes. Straw is still used for thatching.

Forests serve to meet the multifarious needs. They shelter birds, fowls, animals and brute more so because the state forms a meeting ground of the Chin, Arrakan and Chittagong fauna. There is collection of rich orchids and even rare flora in the state. However, the variety of flora and fauna is not distributed uniformly. One kind is scarce somewhere and profuse elsewhere. It is known that forests are relied on because they supply firewood and provide resources for making posts, troughs, mortars, articles of furniture and other things of use. Bamboo and cane provide the necessary materials for basketry and other wicker works. Oak, chestnut, firs and other hill species had been close to the inhabitants both for constructional and cultural purpose.

Flora and Fauna

The lush green vegetations and forests infested with many type of animals signify the rich Mizoram Flora and Fauna. The excellent flora and fauna of Mizoram is a strong reason behind its popularity among the tourists.

The abundance of bamboo forests is one high point of Mizoram's flora. The hills of Mizoram have dense deciduous vegetations. The valleys and the mountain peaks are blessed with many known and unknown orchids. The ever admirable rhododendron is seen in abundance in these areas. The Blue Mountain is one such place where the Veitchiunum and Arboretum species of Rhododendron are found in plenty.

The presence of thick forests and good climate facilitated the fauna of Mizoram. The animal kingdom of Mizoram comprises of several rare and endangered species. Some of the animals found in the Mizoram forests, wildlife sanctuaries and national parks are:

- Bear.
- Tiger.
- Hoolock Gibbon.

- Leopard.
- Porcupine.
- Mongoose.
- Clawless Otter.
- Chinese Pangolin.

The forest areas and the lakes of Mizoram attract large number of migratory birds beside the local birds. Several species of Pheasants, Hawks, Eagles, Bulbuls, Herons and Egrets are sighted in Mizoram. Numerous species of butterflies, moths and many colourful insects are also found in these regions.

Agriculture and Irrigation

About 80 per cent of the people of Mizoram are engaged in agricultural pursuits. The main pattern of agriculture followed is Jhum or Shifting cultivation. Of the total 21 lakh ha of land estimated, 6.30 lakh hectares of land is available for cultivation of horticulture crops. The existing area under different horticulture crops account for about 4,127.6 hectares, which is only 6.55 per cent of the estimated potential area. This indicates the vast scope for horticulture crops to flourish in Mizoram. The main horticulture crops are fruit crops, viz. Mandarin Orange, Banana, Passion Fruit, Grapes, Hatkora, Pineapple, Papaya, etc., and flowers like Anthurium, Bird of Paradise, Orchid, Chrysanthemum, Rose and other subsidiary seasonal flowers. Spices like Ginger, Turmeric, Black Pepper and Bird's eye Chillies are also grown. People have also started extensive cultivation of oilpalm, medicinal and aromatic plants. The ultimate surface irrigation potential is estimated at 70,000 hectares of which 45,000 hectares is under flow and 25,000 hectares by construction and completing 70 pucca minor irrigation projects and six lift irrigation projects for raising double and triple crops in a year.

Animals

Mizoram appears to have a good collection of fauna. The indiscriminate felling of Trees and the progress of constructional works, however, have reduced the number of typical ones. The dense jungles and dry places have sheltered different kinds of wild animals. The tiger tribe once was more numerous. The important wild animals once included the monkey, ape and jackal tribes but now, are more diminished. Different deer families make their homes at the different altitudes. Snakes of different kinds are also seen at the different soils according to the hills' elevation.

The outer hills appear at one time to be the resort of elephant and leopard tribes which were taking themselves to the habit of migration at winter seasons, especially from Bengal side. The upper hills have sheltered recently some species of Himalayan fauna. Bisons and Rhinos are known to be the favourite objects of hunting among the tribes. They are valued not only for their meat but also they stand as the cultural symbols of the tribe. Squirrels, bats antlers, musk and bamboo rats and the other different varieties exist, wild pigs, wild bears, wild dogs and wild buffalos were more numerous in the past. Birds and fowls of several families which choose different jungles are known as well to be the favourite games to hunters.

Environment

Mizoram like the other neighbouring Hill States has the kind of a temperate climate. Summers generally are cool, invigorating and pleasant. The summer temperature varies from 11° to 21° centigrades while in winter it varies between 11° and 21° centigrades. Owing to the varying heights especially in the central and southern parts of the state, rainfall at places is heavy, the average amount of rain being 208 centimetres in Aizawl. But Aizawl is not so rainy, there being many other rainier places in Mizoram such as Sunglei which records 350 cm. Evidently the climate in the foothills bordering Cachar, Tripura and Bangladesh is hotter, the incidence of malarial diseases earlier being high at the lowlands. Cold places during the winter may have had little bit of frost accumulating at height time.

The incidence of the frequent cold waves in the winter times has affected the region and Mizoram as well so that, when such cold waves occur, the winters during their occurrences are severely cold. In fact, climatic alterations perceptibly and imperceptibly have become frequent all over the globe. In this regard, I have pin-pointed that "the topographical distortions presenting the climatic alterations upsetting other things in the phenomenon have become more and more prevalent".

The reasons are due as follows "Environmental pollution caused by the heavy industrial, civil aviation and nuclear installations and the road traffic congestions have been prevalent. The frequent conduct of nuclear tests, over ground and inside the ocean, the building of nuclear equippages along with the infallibility of man-made destructive weapons coupled with the heavy population explosion, have caused the fast changing weather conditions almost everywhere and heavy pollution is caused. Science has not made advances yet with regard to curtailing the intrusion caused from beneath the world. These explosions from the Subterranean world occurring on the earth's outer crust, have disturbed the system of relief causing the usually known disasters to the human establishments, the flora and fauna families alike". These influences have directly hit the heavy industrial zones and indirectly, the more isolated places as well.

5

Society

The total population of the State under the census of 2001 is 8,91,058 persons. Compared with the earlier censuses, the population had considerably increased. The population in 1951 consisted of 196,000 persons. But the earliest census of 1901 disclosed a population of 82, 434 persons scattered in 239 villages.

The District in 1900 comprised Aijal subdivision (containing an area of 4,701 sq mi) and 2,526 sq mi for Lungleh Subdivision, the population distributed subdivision wise being 59,936 in Aijal against 20,498 in Lungleh subdivision; incidentally the proportion of literate persons was 2,058 against the total population of 82,434 while yet, education was started only 1894. 87 per cent of the population used the Duhlian dialect as their *lingua franca*. Up-till 1900, only 26 per cent were Christians. 93 per cent of the people lived by agriculture.

The proportion of the population in 1901 was Lushai (36,400), Poi (15,000) Hmar (10,400) and the Ralte (13,800) The minor subgroups were Lakher Thado and Paite. The proportion of the Hindus was 4 per cent. The difficulty to working out the first census due the cumbrous spade work then being done against the lack of facilities can also be understood. The number of Christians was then insignificant but it was only in 1897 that the Welsh Mission undertook to carry on the work which had been begun by the two pioneer Missionaries'. The census of 1971 shows a fantastic increase of the population to 3,32,390 persons in all.

The tribes are Lushai, Ralte, Hmar, Paite, Pawi, Lakher and the smaller groups of tribes are Khiangte, Chawngthu, Fanai, Ngente, Pang, Pautu, who all are called Mizos. The other tribes are Riang and Chakma; as regards Riang, they are one of the Tribes who inhabit Tripura and a group of whose who have settled in Mizoram: as regards Chakma, they live in the hills and plains in Chittagong bordering on Mizoram and several groups from Bangladesh have also settled in Mizoram.

All the tribes excepting Chakma and Riang speak Lushai, a Lushai dialect called Duhlian being a *lingua franca* and medium of instruction among most of the tribes. It appears, only a few groups are bilingual using their own dialect and Duhlian. The Chakmas use a broken Bengali dialect and Riang speak their own language. Lushai being once predominant, this probably had prompted the British Government to carve a District called a century ago the Lushai Hills District.

Social Structure

The patriarchal structure dominated the society. Chiefdom itself was based on a strong patrilineal system of organisation. The system of village organisation based on the concept of patrilineal lineage groups and the closest kinship ties developing as such has continued. But the present transformation has also caused some reverses to the system. The transformation with its emphasis on education, administration, new trades and occupations, has affected the system of a joint household organisation and has caused diversions to other family interests in the country as the whole and the tribal areas as well. The increase of female literary, spread of education and occupational diversions must have caused considerable alterations in the old household organisation.

Among the other trends, the universal suffrage has its effect in ensuring the liberties of women and their sharing of social responsibilities with men.

Democratic and occupational trends have caused alternations in the household and community organisation. Growth of the nuclear and subsidiary families has been accounted to a System of change.

Another parallel with regard to the working of the village Councils can be enunciated briefly in the following:

> With the elimination of the rights and privileges hitherto given to the old chieftains, the people now have shared power in running their village Councils in a new set up. The Councils are constituted through their representatives; we see that both the systems, old and contemporary, have their mixed results. In the light of the social and political transformation we see also that new townships have sprung.

The rehabitation of families in the system of village re-grouping that had taken place since the sixties has provided a new perspective. In this way, safeguarding of tribal laws and customs had been adhered to in a Constitutional provision. The retention of tribal characteristics in all the Hill States has become indispensable. The situation now has been that the past and the present have become mingled more and more.

Marriages by negotiations were in vogue. Even if they were love marriages cases of these later on, were finalised by negotiations acceptable to the families. The system of paying bride price was inherent among many of the tribes now occupying the States and Territories on the northeast. It was essential in the case of many Kuki and non-Kuki tribes as well. Bride price among the tribes other than Mizo, has its connotation to a system of transfer of several movable items of property and which were considered as part of wealth among the tribes from the bride to the bridegroom.

Among the Hmars, the bride price was shared among the nearest relatives of the bride herself such as her maternal uncle, her aunt, nephews and nieces, elder sisters, her own bride's-maid and more so her parents. The bride price among the other Mizos, is shared among the bride's mother's father or brother, the bride's father's sister, the bride's elder sister, the bride's maid and her elder unmarried sister.

The stability and corporate character can be reiterated in assessing the historical conditions as discerned from the modern. The village corporate organisation was strong due perhaps to the important community roles which existed under the patrilineal organisation. This had caused the independent character of the people. The corporate structuring was strengthened by the strong community or team enterprises under the direction of the veterans; the system of training to enliven the community or corporate undertakings for the village welfare and ensuring a practical system of relief, rehabilitation and other kinds of assistance to the disabled or even displaced persons among most of the tribes has already been mentioned by many writers. The system of training was propagated by the chief but the more vital institution of training was the Zawl bilk, a Murung which every night, made the training compulsory to boys and male young persons.

The stringent rules for enforcing discipline in the circumstances stated were unavoidable. There were social constraints with regard to the use of undue liberties; consequently, there were constraints to the growth of the individual character. Most of the marriage and household usages were prescribed consistently to suit with the village discipline. Bride price in term of the material offering was transacted in the shape of a mithun, pet animals or their meat, a baby carrying girdle and others during the premarital visits, the bethrotal and the actual marriage ceremony. The bride retained some personal possessions like baskets, garments and ceremonial wears and ornaments. The marriages were made relaxable according to the mode of divorce by mutual consent among the wife and husband, or by the acceptance of demand moved from either side. Marriage feasts were either restricted to or opened at the community level.

Rural Activity

As regards disposal of the dead, burial was generally, accepted. The corpse generally was retained for a night. An extract from the Gazetteer on these slowly dying mortuary customs reads: "After death, the corpse is dressed in its best clothes and fastened to a bamboo frame in a sitting posture. A big feast is then given to the friends and neighbours and food and drink are offered to the corpse. On the evening following the death, the body is entered just opposite the house, the grave consisting of a shaft about 4 or 5 feet deep, from which a tunnel branches off in which the corpse is placed. People who belong to wealthy families are not buried at all. They are placed in a hollow tree-trunk, the lid of which is carefully plastered with mud, and put in the centre of the house. A hollow bamboo connects the coffin with the earth..."

Most of the old religious practices have become extinct. Consequently many of the social traditions and institutions have considerably been transformed. The ancient system of priestdom and practice of sorcery is no longer tenable. The affiliation to Christianity has considerably changed the face of Mizoram. Consequently as in the other neighbouring Hill States, the Church ministers, pastors and clergy have played more important roles in the conduct of death, marriage and other ceremonies. Education has opened the society to the present system of transformation.

Education has been greatly assisted by the other factors caused by trade and new occupational trends. These trends have vitally affected the system of social integration which transcends the racial barriers. The material changes in the system of house buildings and constructions, dress, food habits and the other models in a social scene have thus become more and more noticeable. The ethnological and sociological patterns have been reviewed in context of a change. The concepts have largely been concretised on the theme of topical relevance which concerns the home, the society and the state.

Influence of Christianity

Christianity evidently gave, during the early years, an impetus for elevating the spiritual life according to the teaching of Christianity. It had given the believers the new insights and values; it had given the Christians some experience in Church organisation, administration and participation in the other affairs.

So strong was its appeal that the Zawlbuk, a village dormitory organisation which gave training to young males in community life was used as a venue for the propagation of Christianity. It was admitted that 'the large gathering of the Zawlbuk' afforded opportunities for the Missionories to make known 'to the youths of Lushai the message of a gospel and it is here that some of their most successful meetings are held. Traditionally the Zawlbuk functioned for emphasising and intensifying training to the youths in martial arts and the other arts well known.

A great drift was caused. Evidently the Zawlbuk later on greatly assisted to shape the development of education. No wonder that the young persons took the lead to become Christians-Khuma and Khera, were the first young men who were baptised on the 25th June, 1899 at Aizawl".

A reminiscene can also be gathered in the following excerpt quoted from The Voice Of The Northeastern Hill Tribes on matters relating to the Mizos:

> "The Chief distributes the land for cultivation and decides cases. His house is a place where the poor and needy find shelter and food free of cost. He has his Ministers called 'Upa'.

They build their houses on the top or slope of the hill and they are well fenced with bamboo spikes. All the houses surround the palace and the young people's hall is in the middle of the village. Every house has a bamboo gate in front. There are beds on both sides of the fire place and a passage which leads to the back of the house. The posts are of wood, but the wall, floor and roof are of bamboo, and they cover the roof with cane leaves and bind with bamboo bindings.

Their dress is a coat for male and female as well and a shawl for covering their shoulders and body. The women wear another petticoat and ivory earrings on their ears. Their weapons of war are a sword and a spear of medium size. Both males and females dress their hair long.

Their constant are not very different from other hill tribes. Their trace of inheritance is from the male side. When the eldest son marriage, he gets some houses and becomes a chief. The youngest son remains at home with his father and when his father dies he gets all the wealth and property of the father and becomes a chief…

'The chief occupation is cultivation. They cultivate rice and millet by jhumming. The agricultural implements are a dao, a hoe and an axe. There is also some cotton cultivation. They also make earthern pots, daos and cloth'.

The administration and education played simultaneously their roles in causing the important sweeping transformation. Education played its notable role in disseminating ideas to the moral, material and scientific development of the race in context of the current situation. A uniform system of law and administration would have been feasible to developing a sense of social integration. The adoption of more less a common medium of instruction became necessary. The lack of social cohesion in other respects can be attributed to other factors. The life-styles and traditions had become affected; house, dress and food habits had also become slowly altered. The pattern of change worked on the same lines among all the tribes in the northeast.

The teaching of Christianity with regard to the concept of Trinity, the redemption of the soul, the resurrection of the dead, the winning of other souls, the efficacy of Christian faith among the Christianised Societies, attempts in those and other doctrines had been sought to be intensified for developing a qualitative outlook and pattern of life among the devout and dedicated Churches.

In course of time, belief in Pathian, a supreme Being and more especially the dominant spirits named Ram Huai and Khuavang became discarded; these spirits had been appeased or propitiated for ages. The place of the Puithian or priest was taken over by a Pastor. The concept of the eternal paradise worked among the Christians and with the progress that Christian conversions made, many of the ancient belief, fertility and sacrificial rites became less and less restrained. Many have become forgotten.

Otherwise in the erstwhile situation, "every circumstance — birth, death, burial, marriage, sowing, weeding, reaping, is made an occasion for drinking and feasting". Now these have become reduced. Entertainments have now taken their social form. Christian festivals have now become extant. It is learnt in this context that the Christian Revival which occurred in 1905 originating from the Presbyterian Church in the Khasi Hills, had its effect in causing a great and sweeping transformation in modern Mizoram. Consequently churches rose by leaps and bounds. It had affected southern Lushai also. In the Welsh record, there were already one church, 5 preaching stations, 32 communicants, total in church 57, adherants 200 that too as early as 1904. Therefore, most of the social characteristics in the process of change have already altered. It is learnt that villages once were largely populated each village accommodating 400 to 800 houses. Most of them for ensuring security were encircled by two or three levels of stockades. The physical changes in all the tribal societies with regard to house construction, dress, food habits have been noted. Birth, naming, marriage and death ceremonies similarly have been radically altered; this was due to the great sequences caused in the history of Christianity.

A change in music had become indispensable as at present the category of western or neo-western music, Church music, traditional music and folk music has existed and music in its variegated roles, under this division, has catered to the social needs. Urbanisation indeed was one of the decisive factors considered essential to a system of social transformation. Also a network of communications devised for the state could have their far-reaching consequences for working out a rapid process for change. As such, some of the traditional bases which afford a concept of a tribal identity need their utmost care which would have been deemed feasible, to provide the symbols in a system of cultural orientation. Among other recent denomination, mention may be made of Salvation Army; it provides a scene of one of the formal church systems and abides through a wall formulated discipline. The Seventh day Adventist as well has its importance as a Church organisation. The Roman Catholics have also established their own congregation and set up few schools. According to a report, "two Roman Catholic Missionaries have already established themselves in Aijal in 1947-48." There is also the Isua Krista Kohran, a small denomination. It is known that nowadays some *ad hoc* organisations known generally as Fellowship Societies exist in the Hill States.

Tribes in State

As regards the distribution of tribes, the Pawi and Lakher are settled in the south and east, the Hmar are distributed on the east and north and the Ralte, Lushai, Hmar, Paite and others stay mostly on the north and the Central portion in the State. The use of Mizo evidently connotes a process of transformation tantamount to a concept of tribal identity representing the tribes or sub-tribes of a uniform or cognate background among them. This process of identity most probably must have occurred for some time before it was finally adopted. The regularisation of place names has occurred recently. For instance Aizawl now is used in place of its old name Aijal and Lunglei in place of Lungleh. The use of the new nomenclatures evidently is in response to the new needs which have become indispensible in the system of social and political reorganisation.

This race of tribe beyond doubt is held by the intrinsic ties of kinship through the ages. During the contacts made with the British Administration, Lushai inhabiting the more accessible areas was recognised by Government and the formation of North Lushai hills was followed by the opening of the South Lushai Hills district or subdivisions whose jurisdictions would cover also the far flung tribes. It is also known that Mizo is a generic name which includes Lushai, Hmar, Ralte and the allied subgroups. The Lakher and Pawi also fall within it. As regards the ethnic composition, the homogeneity of customs, traditions and institutions or otherwise is so essential to our consideration, as no complete system of homogeneity among the different races of people, can be possible everywhere. Most of the tribes are the cognate of Kuki.

Riangs: The Riang autochthonous to the Riang tribe of Tripura are distributed in some Mizo villages. The Chakmas who had moved to and were recently rehabitated in Mizoram are now fairly distributed. We have noticed that during the earlier decades, frequent expatriations of Chakmas were caused into the neighbouring States and the heavy swarms had taken place in Mizoram as well. This made the further addition to the existing population. The bifurcation of Mizo hills from Assam and the Constitution of Mizoram into a Union Territory and then into the state had, provided further rooms for promoting the concept of social integration for making adjustments among the tribes mutually, in pivoting the affairs of the state.

As regards language, it is noted that most of the tribes, excepting Riang and Chakma, speak and understand the same language among themselves. During one Church meeting at Halflong, I noticed that the Ralte, Hmar and Lushai persons speaking the same language. It has been admitted that all the cognate tribes have used the same language. It appears, Chakmas on the other hand use the Bengali medium for instructional purposes. The linguistic barriers have not been so formidable compared with the states having a multi-linguistic background.

Mizos: As regards Religion, the Mizos are all Christians. Approximately about 90 per cent of the population have embraced Christianity. As regards the process of Christianisation of the tribe, in respect of Christian conversation, an analysis into the matter would have been as much necessary and interesting. The Chakmas are grouped with the Bodo race of people who lived in the hills and valleys of Chittagong and those groups have been sheltered any rehabitated in parts of Mizoram are Buddhists.

Most of the Riangs have become Christian; yet a large portion of Riangs in Tripura still practise their ancient religious usages and rites. It is in this regard that our knowledge of the old Mizo religion based on the Kuki, Lushai and Lakher customs, beliefs and rites has become necessary. The account of Christian conversation among the Mizos who form the bulk of population is essential; a same time, a review into their ancient religion has its foremost importance.

Lushais: The old Lushais believed in a Supreme Being called *Panthian*. He is according to a tradition, considered a God, Overlord, Creator and Dispenser of human destiny. The old Kukis and Lushais in spite of their largely unsettled state, the migratory habits essentially followed in their struggle and a series of warfare conducted among themselves and with their neighbours, have cherished a strong conception of religion. The world is reckoned as a scramble between the good and the evil. This strikes the tribal religion at its root.

The existence of the benevolent and malevolent spirits is subscribed to. The religion reveals the manifestation of the powers of those spirits who reside in sky, the earth and the underworld. The natural phenomenon exercises tremendous influences in causing the religious beliefs, some of their beliefs relatings to the manifestation of these spirits and their power over mankind resemble those of other Kachin and Sino-Tibetan speaking races. The religion although primitive also provides sufficiently strong moral causes to espouse the cause of a man rising before the deities for obtaining their blessings.

Social Traits of Tribes

Some social traits of the indigenous tribes, the Pawi and the Lakher may be briefly assessed for a comparative evaluation. The formative event with regard to the last entry of the uncontrolled area in the British administration was recorded in 1924 only when 'the hitherto independent Zuahnang and Sebeu villages lying between Assam and Burma were first brought under control. In that year was affected also the final demarcation of the boundary between the Lushai Hills, the Chin Mills and the Arakan Hill tracts, when meeting between the Superintendent, Lushai Hills and the two Deputy Commissioners of the Districts was held in 1922 and the boundary adjustment was finally worked out'.

Since then therefore, 'all the Lakhers have been under the British rule'. The Shendoos or Lakhers had given the enormous troubles to the frontier administration due o their raids caused for plundering the neighbouring areas, which had caused a great deal of insecurity to the British subjects. The raids dated to 1847 when hey raided the subjects of Kalindi Rani and of the Phru'. Since then, raids with he heavy consequential havocal consequences were caused almost uninterruptedly till the establishment of the British administration.

Most of the Lakhers are confined in Chhimtuipui district. The best known groups are Tlongsai, Hawthai, Zeuhnang, Lialai and Heima. The parallel tribe is Poi or Pawi and midway between the Pawi and Lakher there are sub-tribes who practise both Pawi and the Lakher customs. The Pawi, Lakher, Lhakma and other minor tribes under he present arrangement are mostly confined in that District. The Maras are supposed to be the branch of the Lai tribe and speak a language which resembles Lai. The Pawis also call themselves Lai, the name of the tribe that is known so well as Chin; the Pawi although speaking Lai, yet they have accepted Lushei or Duhlian as their medium of instruction and for other uses as well. Shendoo earlier was used to denote both the Pawi and Lakher.

Lakher dress in minor points is typically Mizo. It has preserved the essential common features of dress with the other tribes. A formal dress suiting itself with the decorum of festivals, has, therefore, a greater essence. Most of the original dress patterns have become now extinct.

Turbans once featured as the composite dress items. Men's turban is seen in that two rims of the sheet wound were clumped upward leaving a small compression above the forehead or that the hair of person wearing it was twisted from all directions and rolled into a bun leaving it bare or covered as the matter would have been preferred. Such a clump was seen tied in the tarban of a person wearing it above his forehead.' Otherwise one end of a turban from behind was decked upward 'and then thrown down behind looking like a loop.

The woman's pagri vas seen kept flat on the surface of the dead or sometimes as in the case of men, the ends were amalgamated upward the head and tied into a knot. The upper body garment was a sheet of cloth suspended from one side of the shoulder and thrown down around the body or both its ends were clumped round the shoulder leaving its lower sheet to cover the body. It was worn also like an apron with its two ends tied on one shoulder and the whole lot was thrown down, to reach the legs. Evidently the mode of wearing a mantle for the full or partial covering depended upon the climatic conditions.

Along with these, a typical loongi was worn on the upper portion tied on the position of the waist and the whole sheet thrown down to the legs. The warrior's dress was more bare; the turban was wound round the head; on its back a long dark tassel rose upward on top of the turban and fell down behind like a long tail. The upper garments of a warrior consisted of two crossed sashes, each one suspended from the shoulder and thrown down to the reverse.

The used waist-dresses also with some outer flaps when they were armed with swords, spears, guns and shields. They used also a Kilt for other purposes. For ordinary occasions, they used plain white clothes. Sisai a hnang, a sheet of dark blue cloth carrying some stripes was worn as the most valued skirt; it was confined only to the royal houses carrying on its border, patches of ornamental cowries and beads. They used belts-brass and metals for their purpose. Many clothes had black bands in rows, single or more.

Cheulopang is a cloth with a dark blue background, two columns of white stripes running down the middle portion heavily embroidered with many figures like the eyes of birds and animals. The viapang is dark blue background embroidered with red.

They used a profusion of ornaments to which we find mention of:

> Brass belts, women's brass pins, women's conch shells, lacquer combs, earring, men's brass hairpins, women's white metal belt, and bamboo lacquered hairpins. They were called by various names such as Chongchi, Hrokei, Hra-khaw, kihlong, sakia, chaiphiapha, sathichapawa and others.

To the above we can add the bracelets (viahchipang), earrings (takaraheu), syphont joint (pakong), necklace (naba), wooden earrings (thanghareu), necklace (dopachhi), necklace (sisai), brass bracelet (rohungpachhi), comb (sathichanongpa), comb (sathichapawpa), hairpin (sawkahrong).

About music, it is remarked that 'gongs are of all sizes, and vary greatly in sweetness and depth of tone .... The Lakhers also use of pairs of small metal gongs known as dawchheu and pairs of small gongs known as ladaw. At a dance, there is a regular band beating on gongs and drums and blowing on bugles and managing to evolve, if not a very definite tune, at any rate a very strongly marked rhythm. Gongs, bugles and cymbals are imported from Burma; the drums are made in the village.

The bugles are called *Chiami* and the cymbals photla. Other drums are made usually of deer skin. The gong looks like a dish and emphatically, a round bell beaten with a striker. The violin is suspended by a gourd across the middle position carrying a peg and a string (a sort of a fibre of a palm), the bow is a thin split of bamboo. They use the jew's harp and many flutes and pipes.

Faith and Religion

Ancient Religion

Belief in Rebirth: They believe strongly in the state of rebirth in the world hereafter. They believe in the state of eternal reward and punishment to men and women according to deeds done during one's life time. They have the conception in the state of paradise and the supreme bliss especially to those who have attained moral or chivalrous conquests at their earthly existence. Therefore, Pial Ral is a Mizo heaven and Mitthi Khua is a hell where those who have failed to accomplish according to their religious beliefs, are retributed and tormented eternally.

Religious Morals

Like other tribal religious, the Mizo religion lays emphasis on the efficacy of a good moral and one's triumph in his or her struggle with the evil forces. It upholds a belief in the system of appeasement, invocation and beseeching good and evil spirits alike, the former to assist them and the latter to be removed from causing ailing or suffering to mankind. They believe in the obstruction of bad spirits rendered to the soul in its journey to the eternal abode.

However, they believe that the successful hunters and givers of village feasts would have their first preference to attain paradise. Thunder and lightning are the manifestation of the power of spirits and the rains are the manifestation of the deity's blessing. They believe also in the spirits which are attributed with learning. They believe in the existence of bad spirits known as Rambuai who reside in the jungles, hills and dales whom they therefore seek to appease. They offer sacrificial offerings with the kinds of animals named by them and the entrails are appropriated respectively as the mark of their offerings.

They make clay altars for the purpose to symbolise their communion with the infinite power of the spirits. The Tihuai are some of the water spirits which they seek to appease. Hunting is one of the great feats and a successful hunter by their community's usage is extolled. Therefore, Lasi a spirit of hunting, is propitiated. In the same way, a successful head-hunter in the past was exalted in society. The religion beyond doubt aims at enhancing the concept of martialism. The system is minutely connected with priestdom and the essence of conducting frequent sacrifices.

Sacrificial Activity

They believe in a series of purgatory and sacrificial rites which they perform for attainting spiritual strength. The propitiations mainly relate to the concept of agricultural fertility, cure of sicknesses, attaining of health and prosperity and other purposes. They also propitiate thanks givings, to protectors of family with a view to avert bad spirits from frequenting the human abodes.

During death and burial, the tribe was in practice of displaying grave goods and even building an effigy to represent the dead. This resembles the practice of some other tribes in the northeast.

As almost the whole of the population have embraced Christianity, most of the old age customs, beliefs and other sacrificial rites have nowadays become obsolete. This necessitates us to review the stages marking the spread of Christianity. The beginning of Christianity is traced to 1893 when the process of administrative consolidation had progressed on and was nearing its completion. The importance of social traditions, institutions, laws and customs can also be viewed in this perspective.

Christian Religion

Christianity was born in 1893, the date which marked the arrival of two missionaries named J. H. Lorrain and F. W. Savidge; they belonged to the London. Baptist Mission which took steps to' cover the far-flung areas not yet covered by any Mission. The missionaries despite the insurmountable difficulties took up residence at Aizawl; a school subsequently was opened. The Missionaries sought to reduce Lusha to writing in Duhlian dialect. Their efforts had borne fruits in view of the tremendous progress that education has now made in Mizoram apart from the growth of Mizo literature.

At the outset they faced considerable hindrances. They were considered as strangers. Their efforts an education were not immediately paying. There were frequently school drops out. In that situation, education would be very helpful as the converts would acquainted to read the Bible, sing the hymns and help the Church. Despite these hazards confronted, they persisted in their struggle to strengthen their work. In course of time they befriended the local persons and the situation became better.

In this connection, a report of Mr. A. Porteous, ICS political officer, in 1894-97 makes reference to "the labours of Messrs Savidge and Lorrain who had been in these Hills since the spring of 1893 and had been wonderfully successful in introducing education".

Consequently the situation improved when a Welsh missionary, D. E. Jones joined the branch of the Baptists in a Mission Station. That happened in 1897. The Welsh Presbyterian missionaries had earlier worked among the Khasis for about 50 years, opened a few stations in the Cachar and Sylhet districts and built their first tiny Church congregations at the Centres where they were opened. D. E. Jones proved to be the useful asset in the first stage of Christian propagation, Jones joined the English Baptists in 1897.

The two Baptist missionaries later on took a short leave. It was known that they availed the leave to explore the Abor (now Adi) country now Arunachal, they stayed among the people, learnt their language and had even produced the first gospel or primer in that language. Jones meanwhile was coping with his services to Christianise the Lushais. Therefore, Jones on their absence was coping with the Mission work.

As the present century opened, Lorrain and Savidge came back to Lushai Hills. A decision among the Missions was reached with regard to their spheres of jurisdiction in which the Baptist Mission agreed to confine themselves to South Lushai Hills leaving the north to the Welsh Mission. A close liaisoning in other respects would be maintained among them. These relations are now kept among the Mizo Baptists and Presbyterians.

The Missionary who joined Jones later on was Edwins Rowlands. He made immense efforts to establish education; he sought to produce the necessary literature as would be suitable to education. The missionaries started the bulk of Bible translations. Christian conversion evidently started to gain ground from the dawn of a century.

Schools had shown a steady increase in number. This had helped the growth of the Middle School education commencing roughly when the present century opened. The Missionaries at this stage were authorised to handle the monopoly of education in respect both to its numerical increase and administrative management. By then the essence of Christian conversions which had their penetrating effects were recognised by the Lushai,

Hniar, Ralte, Lakher and other tribes, near and far. This would provide them ample means for the spread of education and for transaction of affairs in a modern way. Subsequently, many of the chiefs gave way and became Christian to adjust themselves with the new spiritual urges and concepts propagated by Christianity after a few village churches sprang in their land. The increase of Christianity may be dealt with subsequently.

Report of the Foreign Mission, 1947 of the Welsh Calvinistic Methodists Presbyterian Church of Wales, 1948, Liverpool, gives us an important base of knowledge regarding the Mission enterprises in the Lushai Hills. We serialise the events below:

> David Evan Jones the first ever Welsh Missionary reached India a few months "after the 'great earthquake of 1897" which according to the report, caused the destruction of several stations and buildings, together with a heavy loss of life. The field into which he entered also was a field whose inhabitants were notorious for their cruelty and their murderous raids upon the adjacent plains. About him, 'his faith and courage, however, never wavered and were richly rewarded'. He had baptised the first converts among the Lushais, and travelled extensively through scattered villages: had a large share in translating the scriptures into Lushai; published a Sunday School magazine; contributed greatly to a magazine published by Government.

"At the time he entered the field not a single Christian could be found among the Lushais; at the time of his retirement through ill health in 1928, the converts numbered 37,000 and by the end of last year had increased to as many as 88,926. Jones saw much fruits to his labour, truly, "a nation born in a day".

The converts fostered by him and others, had realised their own responsibility and "there is found today on the Lushai Hills a strong Church which is practically self supporting and self propagating. The memory of his ....indefagitable labours will long remain a precious heritage on the distant hills of Lushai". The impetus to the rapid conversions is also attributed to the forceful sway of two Church revivals which brought so great and sweeping additions of Christians year by year. Dr. Rev. Jones passed away in Wales on 10th August, 1947.

Facts about the Mission enterprises 'in other respects: Dr. John Williams served so competently as a medical Missionary; had attained his supreme desire "of becoming a Missionary, and a Medical Missionary in Lushai" he was credited 'by his tireless efforts' in effective planning and expeditious building of Durtlang Hospital; served this hospital from 1928 to 1936 and left it on his retirement to Dr. Gwyneth Roberts. He threw himself with wonderful energy into his work, travelling continually over the high hills from village to village, healing the sick and preaching the gospel.

Lewis Evans first worked under the auspices of the Mission, Wales and a Missionary society formed by the lurches belonging to the connections with the Mission, Wales at the earlier Welsh Mission field in Shaista Gonj, Sylhet; then served from 1928 in Sylhet and Cachar plains as Superintendent, fission Buildings; moved to Lushai Hills in 1931 in the same capacity and raised the Mission buildings; left Lushai Hills in 1936, died May 4, 1947. The Mission further set up a printing press to cater with printing both the school and religious books. Samued Davies a Missionary while during a furlough, appealed for funds from his country men towards purchasing a press the printing office, Aijal. The total £ 551 was collected. The first printing press appears, to have been stalled during the first decade of this century by Mr. Fraser.

The progress in the field of education was tremendous. One of the greatest achievements was the Mission management of a High school in 1946-47 which had grown from the previous years. Consequently the school roll strength, had increased. Two classes were added and two more teachers were taken. The school was accommodated in a Mission building, all the available mission halls including bungalows were converted into a school and hostel.

The new school site with the existing old buildings was converted into temporary classrooms and hostel. Mr. Meirion Llyod wrote: "The school is not a Mission school, but, as I mentioned above, it has been housed in mission buildings, and several of our Mission staff have helped considerably in the teaching, while I have acted as Headmaster. It may for want of a better term be called a 'Public School; Early in 1947 it had its own committee formed and both the public and the chiefs have representatives in it. There is a likelihood that it will later on become a Government school". The Girls' school under Miss. Gwen Rees Robert was progressing on, from kindergarten to Class VI, there were 300 students all girls, except for small boys reading kindergarten. More details follow in the subsequent chapters.

Until the end of 1947, there were in all 323 Presbyterian Churches, 344 preaching stations, 38 Ministers, 42 preachers, 638 deacons, 39,034 communicants, 18,206 candidates, 33,312 children, 1,306 baptised adults, 2,050 baptised children. Collections: Church Collection — Rs. 35,423, Home Mission — Rs. 185, Rice Collection — Rs. 4,960, Other Collections: Rs. 13,498.

The Mission was actively engaged in the construction and maintenance of buildings involved in educational and literary work, organisation of churches and setting up the branches of the Medical Mission.

According to L. B. Thanga, Savidge and Lorrain on return from modern Arunachal, established themselves at Serkawn near Lungleh. Lorrain since 1893 evolved Lushai into a written language. His brother later on came and joined his Mission and this led to the opening of a station at Sherkor prompting them to work among the Lakher tribe. These were the germs of the Baptist Mission in the making.'

On this basis, we find that R. A. Lorrain came to Lushai Hills and took off the Mission from his brother in 1905-08 Besides a school, he set up a dispensary. The Missionaries did much to reduce Lakher to writing. The first Lakher to become Christian was only a small boy of about ten years old. But his conversion took place till 1910 and within a few years, the whole of the Lakher tribe embraced Christianity.

Housing Pattern

Most of the houses are mechang structures elevated from the ground. Timber and more universally bamboo is used for stilting, fencing and flooring. The roof is thatched with either came leaves or straw. The former seems to serve better and is more endurable. This necessitates overhauling or repair in parts of roofs or fences followed on particular seasons. There is a small portico at the entrance to the main house used also for keeping certain implements and bamboo crafts.

Fences are made up of timber and bamboo usually plaits or otherwise. The inside of the house is partitioned into apartments with varied sizes used as kitchen, bedrooms and stores. More than one side portico may be provided to keep it exposed to air and sun light. Mizo like other tribes must have used kitchen racks for the purpose of drying things and keeping some foodstuffs and accessories. Stilting houses in regular level land can be easier than stilting on higher steeps owing to the irregular heights on which the lever of the mechang can be maintained.

Social form and organisation counts considerably in our scope of dissertation, which includes village structure, dress and ornamentation, arts and crafts, music and dance, arms and weapons, food and drinks; other social habits and behavioural patterns are essential to our consideration with regard to both the traditional and modern aspects. A brief assessment to these trends is of considerable importance.

House pattern is essentially tribal in character. The British explorers, found in their earliest contacts that villages were preferred to be built on tops of hills or hill spurs and parts thereof. The village road ran through the centre and houses in conglomeration face the road mostly in straighward alignment to it. Houses belonged to the category of chieftains, nobles and commoners as well and accommodated families fit for various undertakings.

The chiefs house was crowded with persons attached to and serving him in different capacities. His house occupied a predominant position and close to him, there were houses next of his kin or persons having the posts of trust and responsibilities. A system of polygamy is said to have been limited to powerful chiefs and rich persons who, in view of their Atifarious undertakings in administration and trade, kept more than one wife, the others served as concubines. They looked after their husband's interests over lands, cultivation, forests and trade.

The chief employed several craftmen, warriors, messengers and priests at his disposal. The house of chiefs was more spacious for this purse. Apart from cultivating the land, hunting formally organised on household or village level was an important enterprise followed at the particular seasons. Hunting was one of the vile rituals receiving considerable attachment from the village folk, were the chiefs powerful, they would be attached to with a number of slaves, and gifted ones could be the valuable assets to the society. Another noted feature was the existence of a bachelors' dormitory known as Zawlbulk.

According to Lt. Col. Thomas H. Lewin when embarking on journey from Chitttagong Hill tracts to an interior the hills into a village of one great chieftains name Rutton Poia believed have been implicated in raids before July 1866, wrote as follows:

> "The village is surrounded by a palisade of enormous logs, as thick as the leg of an elephant and ten feet high. The entrance lay through a stockaded passage, thickly studded with downward - pointing bamboo spikes, and defended by two heavy doors of rough hewn timber, so thick as to be practically fire and bullet proof".

H. Lewin was impressed about R. Poia's house which was like:

> "A large barn like structure, a hundred and fifty feet long by forty broad, raised on a low platform about three feet from the ground. It was thatched with wild palm leaves, and its entrance adorned with by lines of skulls, buffalo, pig, deer, over the door way". The house was led from the ground by a staircase, a long properly surfaced and cut in steps. The broad plaits of split bamboo are most of the formidable items in the traditional system of construction.

Style of Living

Dress

The people were more barely dressed. However, the chieftains' style of dress was more formal. Some of the dress items are known as Siap Suap, Hnaw Khal, Piian hlap, Kappui Zikzial and Dwlrerrz Kawr, the latter is graded as the more elaborate form of clothing. Garments and attires are home spun: the women gin and weave cloths out of cotton grown sufficiently in a few villages.

They prefer dark colour. They use mostly wrappers or large size baldrics of a few colours. Like other tribes; dyes are processed from tree barks, roots and tubers; the system of steaming the yarn of cloth with the dyeing materials is kept, the whole mixture is exposed to sunshine. In this way, they procure the coloured threads and yarns varying in size, then woven into apparels.

Their traditional system of dyeing is usually rendered into a deep dark blue background of a shawl, mantle, or loongi they usually wear or the original white; stripes either are velvet or yellow or blue. They keep their hairs long, twisted and inserted into a knot suspended down to the back side neck. Men wear earrings mostly oval in shape. At one time, they tucked the feathers of light colours on their heads by clasping them into bunches. They are items of the traditional fashion of men. They wear loin cloths on their waist and downward. Men keep necklets of beads also.

The women use kilts usually dark and deep blue and another sheet of cloth serves as an upper body apparel suspended from below the shoulder downward. The system of plaiting hairs among the ladies is practised. The traditional dress appears now to have been more elaborately oriented which suits with the modern times. Dress and ornaments at festivals have their own style, being devised to be more colourful conforming to the exultant notes of joy at the performances. Cotton weaving till Independence was confined only to domestic use; they turned out their dress materials in quantities sufficiently to clothe the members of the family; there was very little left for trade.

Long skirts used nowadays are sheets of white cloths usually striped in yellow, red and dark. I have seen men wearing long loongis mostly meant for indoor. The siap soap the aboriginal clothing used was woven from the fibres of tree bark or tuber plants or soft canes. The dresses as stated bear different names. Fragments of ivory and cornelian served mostly for the purpose of jewelleries. The other metals traditionally used are conspicuous by their absence. Most probably use of some metals by now must have been needed. The ornaments most known are Kawppui, Saingho bangbeh Zikzial in ivory and thrhna (stones).

According to the Gazetteer, small ivory earrings and amber necklaces and rough uncut cornelians were worn as the necklets inserted in a string. Necklets composed of silver or copper discs or coins and small, white balls and items of glass are also worn, Girls use many kinds of hair decorations.

"All the males wear their hair long, the prevailing fashion being to tie a knot in position with long, heavy pins of iron or brass. The women's distinguishing ornament is the large earring fixed firmly in the lobe of the ear. The ear is pierced in early childhood and a small disc of wood or clay inserted. The discs are continually increased in size until the lobe is at length sufficiently distended to hold a piece of ivory an inch and a half or two inches in diameter". Some of these very original patterns in hair style, dress and jewelleries must now have been rare.

Food

Food in Mizoram is one of the main attractions for the tourists who plan to visit this Indian state on a vacation. The Mizoram cuisine offers mainly non-vegetarian delicacies. The people who belong to this place do eat vegetables, but they prefer to add some non-vegetarian ingredients to each and every dish they prepare.

One of the main specialties of the food of Mizoram is that it is very different from the food available in other parts of the country of India other than the northeast. However, the food in Mizoram is quite similar to the food in the other Northeastern States of India. The cuisine of the Northeastern States of the country including Mizoram has an identity of its own.

The staple food of these people is primarily rice. One of the most popular non-vegetarian items of the people of the state is fish. The most commonly used medium of cooking is mustard oil. The Mizos do not like to eat oily food and they prefer to cook most of the dishes with little oil.

Some of the most demanded delicacies of Mizoram are made with ingredients like bamboo shoots and ducks. Some very well known Mizo dishes are Misa Mach Poora, Panch Phoron Taarkari, which is actually a grilled preparation of shrimps, Dal with Eggs, Poora Mach and Koat Pitha.

Performing Arts

Dance and Music

Few of the tribes in the northeast use gongs as the valuable items of heirloom the gong usually is round and has columns or sides or its head dominantly modelled in brass. There are also drums structured with the wood frame, surfaced on its two flat ends with the skin sheets and held by the coils of skin straps along its body. The use of drums has become prevalent in a few church choirs. Drums according to the Christians give good accentuations to singing of hymns.

Darbu is a big gong which looks like a drum set with some sided columns; it tooks like a round bell and is intended to match with the different presentations such as solo, trilet, lyrics, choruses and orchestra." The essence of an orchestra is indicated by the existence of Rawchhem, a type of the wind instrument which carries a traditional bag-pipe and, a gourd at its base, in fact suspends its structure. There are other small gongs and drums.

Some of them resemble those used by the other tribes. Gongs produce beats and even the tunes depending upon the hitting styles. Wind instruments in the shape of pipes or flutes are many. There are bamboo structures used as hand instruments. Sometimes a split or surfaced Bamboo carrying a thin structure on its side and a string a sort of a soft cane inserted in it when tossed and strummed, produces the mild tune. They also use an instrument which looks like a violin most probably swung 'or its tune by a bow and played with fingering on the strings. "Most of these are typical to some of the aboriginal tribes who live on the Himalayas.

As regards, dances, Cheraw or the bamboo dance is almost universal among the tribes. Although funerary an origin, Cheraw has become one of he popular dance forms. The dance is an introversion of feet in and out the bamboo squares which when the squares are opened, the feet of the dancers fall in them and when they are chohered (the bamboos in proportionate number being hitten by clappers on the ground), the feet are drawn out. This works out the alternate insertion and hopping off the squares.

It is a style of introversion of the anklets in and out the squares, the system of striking in and lifting up of feet as the bamboos open and recede over them. The bamboo clappers strike in and out the bamboos. The dancers mostly are maidens and clappers are men. But perhaps the original mode of participation by men or women was not that originally rigid and men probably can also dance.

Gongs and drums provide mostly the fundamentals of beats essential to the maintenance of accent and rhythm. Percussion has its different traditional styles; the beats are connotative to the style of presentation and performance. As regards off-key singings, octaving, or notations, hand instruments like typical the violin, flute and pipe, these have served all the time as their target of music.

Nowadays the western songs and music have their permeating effect in a tribal society. Singers and musicians pick up the western music mostly by ear and a few by the prescribed discipline. As regards church music, knowledge and practice of tonic solfa or staff notation is highly indispensible among the tribes. Therefore, the traditional, church and western music dominate the scene nowadays.

Folklores and Dances

The Mizos are rich in their folk and musical lores. They recall their ancient legends and folktales in the strain of music. Some of the compositions could have been equivalent to myriad tunes aptly fetched like the minuets, odes, lyrics, heroic songs and other kinds. They recollect their heroes and heroines, the acts of chivalry and feat, the story of migration and settlement; some of the songs no doubt are elegaic or monotonous especially when rendered in slow fetching notes. Exploits and adventures find considerable mention in their lore.

As elsewhere songs sung in background to dances or cultural operations are tumultous and some run in regular rhythms. Part of these strains are the asset to entertainment and recreation programme; part of them have their profound philosophic or ethnic significance having the poetic form significantly brought out by bards and skilled music conductors. Bulk of our treatment will focus on the traditional or folk music in which the use of the musical instruments has become indispensable.

Chheihlam a dance with songs and lyrics against the background of drums, where dancers dance in a circle in company of men and women who make the rhythmic motion and symbolising partaking of drinks in their jovial mood. The songs echo the glorious exploits of their forefathers and many important events are recalled. Solakialam originally in Lakher style, is like a small group dance for young boys and girls displaying rhythmic expressions in some rounds.

The other dances are Zawl Kkawsir Lam, Pangparlam and other romantic dances. The former is a dance in a circle or group where boys and girls participate some sort of stepping in and out, dancing on, singing their traditional songs and ending their stanza with a loud accent. The former is a slow dance performed against a melodious tune and girls holding in their arms bunches of flowers.

There are ritual dances for entertaining guests and visitors at post-funerary celebrations and there are heroic songs sung to the celebrate the hunters' victories and attaining the other trophies. Dances, songs and musical relays centering these performances were resumed, regularly and more actively till roughly the first decade of our century. Some of these dances are called *Khullam*. Sarlammai, and Chawnglai Zawm, they have been exhibited at the stage from time to time.

The Lushais, Pawis, Lakhers and other tribes have frequent celebrations at agricultural seasons coinciding with performances of fertility riles for ensuring the successful operations in agriculture and thereby reaping a good harvest of crops. Some priestly observances have their implications in these rites. Merry making and feasting have their incidence at undertakings in jhumming, sowing, weeding, pre-harvesting and the actual harvest. The bulk of tribes have embraced Christianity; therefore, most of their ancient beliefs and customs have disappeared. Consequently the folk songs and dances, many of them, have been forgotten. Yet in search of the identity, some of the old dances and music have taken now their social connotation. Therefore, the colourful performances are held on the state and socially auspicious occasions nowadays.

Art and Crafts

Dress without ornaments is incomplete. They use different shapes of ornaments. Among a few tribes, ivory is essentially a major item. The other tribes use beads, cowries, shells and corals as part of their ornamentation. Their knowledge of using more precious jewels such as saphirres, sardonyx, emeralds is limited. It is interesting to note that a few tribes use helmets made of tusks which blend with their artistic dress. Others make use of plumes and horns for their helmets which also give an artistic insight. They use copper wires which are decked with their ornaments. Some use skins also. Hats and caps turned out from cane and bamboo make also their heritage to the tribe.

Because of their rich art treasure, tribal festivals therefore become quite colourful providing a spectrum of men and women clad in their charming dress and in their very originality.

Tribal dances are varied. From the war dance and war haunts we also see very typical groups and maidens dances so graceful in gesture, meaningful in movements, and full of other expressions. We see several fertility and thanks giving dances. The literary aspects can further be highlighted below.

Most of these dances are connected each with a story of their origin; some say this or that dance came into being in the midst of certain crises which befell the human beings. Some say such dances glowing in their folk attributes were meant to cement the ties of oneness between all sections of the people who have formed the entity with their Chieftain at the helm of affairs.

Some dances are held to the accompaniment of loud music played by an orchestra; even head-hunting was connected with fertility in the plain belief that the obtaining of human skulls was an appeasement to the spirits who bless in turn the human beings with a bountiful harvest. Maiden dance whether danced separately or with a group of men, becomes more graceful and at ease in the lifting of hand and feet and general balancing. In Mizoram and Kuki highlands, gongs appear to have more dominant role used at different festivals and in council sittings. Like the Garo and the Konyak tribes, they are quite demonstrative. Drumbeats or skits are so many which have multifarious significance.

Pipes and drums in the main characterise a good deal of tribal music. They are used during dancings and festivals. They are used by experts familiar to the meaning and the techniques. Most of the rhythms and drums have been forgotten especially in the areas where Christian hymns are dominant. A Jew's harp is vary common among almost all the tribes. It gives a light but penetrating accentuation.

In the more indigenous practices, we find that rhythmisation is the governing factor of composing poetry, music and dance and these faculties in the folk character are always integrated. Voice and vocal are varied. We hear different tribal chants. Soiree catch the incantations used in prayers. The tribes have many romantic features; their intimate connection with nature is reflected in their songs. They have songs expressed in joy at the harvest, and successful fish catching and hunting. They have traditional expressions on such themes. The tribes have different lamentations over certain mishaps which had occurred long time ago.

Oral literature in different forms and contacts has evolved. Thus poetry, wise sayings, moral lessons and other traits have come into being. Some of these along with naive folktales and fables have appeared in the books. Some tribes have developed a high sense of the poetic gift and have invented metrical rules for forming poetry. Some bards present the tales and wise sayings in music.

The paucity of textbooks among the tribes is also highlighted. Although the local language forms only one subject on the secondary and higher levels, the presentations of the cultural and secular needs, have to be aptly made. The great service of literary criticism and review of the Cultural inadequacies has to receive a larger emphasis so that the literary production would be worthwhile of being given the correct dissemination and use in the schools.

It is not possible in a condensed treatise like this cover all the essential aspects of a literature. We have, therefore, been impelled to highlight only the fundamental trends of the literary growth. Orientation of literature of course has become a great moving force among all the races of people. The matter to recreating it has been viewed from many angles to fit with the traditional and modern angle. Literature has its great impact in the number of its diverse themes.

Partly bulk of it among the tribes is to cater to the educational needs; partly it is to cater to the needs of the church. It is also to give adequate response to the other needs of the society and cater suitably to the cultural orientation. Journalism recently has made its impact in stimulating consciousness to the many needs in the society. The contributions of the poets, essayists, novelists, story writers, critics and journalists make their impacts in stimulating the growth of literature.

Significant Festivals

Therefore, some of their spring and autumn festivals have now been reinvigorated under the name of Chapchar Kut observed in March which winds up jhumming operation and a demonstrative dance is held in which dancers in jovial notes show mutual greetings and reciprocate each other and young persons accompany them in a row. The other dance is Minikut held in August or September. They celebrate the harvest of maize and beseech their ancestors' blessings. Pawl Kid is another jubilant post-harvest festival held in the winter.

There were other organised village activities which gave an impetus to a village corporate character. Feasts and festivals, rituals and observances took considerable time of the people in making arrangements for holding such programmes from time to time. Hunting and games are considered the very favourite and sometimes compulsory means for providing mean of social recreation. Some of them carry the ritualistic essence in their own way.

The shifting cultivation, on account of the unviability of permanent agriculture, entailed the shifting of the population from hill to hill and consequently the shifting further and further from the village every year. The village circle over plantations and farmings consequently by become more and more extended. It had become necessary to resort to hunting among the tribes for several reasons, for guarding the village and their plantations against the havocal intrusion of wild beasts and, therefore, on the scheduled seasons, the whole village or bulk of their men go hunting.

They embark on an organised expedition to set traps to the brute especially at the area where there would be traces of them, blocking the animals on their known routes or adodes, chasing them and fatally dealing with them, then rejoicing over the attaining of spoils.

The tribe was in possession of the muzzle-loading flint looks which facilitated them obtaining their spoils and nowadays, several of the habituated tribes men get licences for the supply of guns and ammunitions. It is considered among the tribes a disgrace for a hunting party to return home without bringing their spoils over the games. Hunting provides rooms for exercises and exertions on their part of explore the jungles which could be informative to them regarding their knowledge of wildlife. Wildlife sanctuaries and zoos here and elsewhere have been intended to serve the purpose of wildlife preservation. The successful hunters have their convicted status in society. Consequently a cruel or cunning beast is considered a menace to society. Hunting is considered the best means to strike off the offending beasts.

Hunting: Hunting also has its utilitarian role in that it can solve the problem of food scarcity and a successful hunting can bring home good quantities of meat, horns, skins, beaks, feathers which can have considerable importance for the purpose of decoration. Long feathers at one time had their importance because they served as items of head decoration. Squirrels, bats, pigeons and all kinds of birds large and small provide young persons means for light games.

Almost all the tribes relish them. They can provide delicious soups, curries, and meat smoked, baked and boiled. So also fisher caught from streams can provide similar delicacies. In spite of a network of communications built across the land and consequently the rapid increases of traffic and transport, hunting is still at large. In this regard, we note, that the shifting cultivation practised through the ages, had led to the disappearance of good jungles which shelter some rare species of fauna and flora.

A victorious hunting is highly acclaimed. Stories on the decisive hunts, considered as acts of feat on the part of their grandfathers, have been transmitted vocally and in songs from generation to generation. Sometimes the exploits in games are just similar to the exploits of head-hunters. These hobbies of course are common among other tribes.

Some stories attribute to hunting the stage of migration and settlement of a village which developed into an entity. This was due to the fact that it served best the purpose of winning games and also provided them a good opportunity for plouring the lands and other resources.

The erstwhile creations of circles in Lungleh and Aijal subdivisions gave the chieftains, jurisdictions, over the hunting and fishing grounds as, well as over the arable lands and forests. Forests are considered essential because they provide timber, firewood and other means for constructional purpose. Bamboo and cane as well have their multifarious uses in turning out various commercial crafts and items of furniture. It is known that the tribes came into conflicts with the British administration on several occasions. In fact some of the disputes centred on the question of jurisdictions as the Mizos then needed the outlying lands which would provide them ample means for fishing, hunting and making other exploits. It appear that they wanted also to control the routes in their close vicinity to protect their trade interests.

There were two kinds of festivals; they were the festivals of chiefs and those of the people. The former revealed their ethnic significance towards providing means for stabilising the village social organisation as should be feasible to the cultural and other institutions. The festivals highlighted the corporate structure and the social integration. The chiefs on the occasions of festival provided several resources for feasts, feastings and other performances sometimes on lavish scale in which herds of animals were slained and their meat cooked for food and great quantities of grains were provided for the feast. Beers in huge quantities were brewed.

The chiefs gave the feast to the whole village in token of some auspicious events and in elevating their social status as should meet with the social requirements. Feasts served in this way were considered prestigious to the society. These feasts according to the belief would give an added qualification to their rank and file; they would even assure them a better repose to their souls to the world here after. Music, dances and marks of jubilance interspersed through in a series of ceremonies and observances held. This custom persisted among them as among the Angami Nagas and their neighbours when a rich or resourceful chief, having provided such feasts, became highly exalted. These feasts of merit could even occur more than once during the chiefs, life time. They connoted their philosophic implication that chiefs were to perform manifold functions for ensuring their people's prosperity and happiness and were related also to promoting the ties of kinship and cooperation among the lineage groups who constituted the society. The other festivals had their similar impact in promoting amicable relations and forging the village unity. Songs, dances, merry-making provided a fitting system of recreation but the demonstrative moods, gestures and behavioural patterns also counted. The cultural importance beyond doubt was upheld.

As the Mizos have almost all become Christians, most of their ancient beliefs and practices, rituals and sacrifices have disappeared. Most of their ancient institutions in the wake of new upsurges, as it is with Christians, have become extinct. Some of their arts of dance and music as social traditions have now been renewed. New substitutes for Christian festivals have also been institute. For instance, the Christmas festival elongate to the New Year's week is now observed in the old community spirit but now singing Christian tunes either translated or indigenous compositions have been more dominant.

Prayers and services are also held. Other entertainment programmes are necessary for the observance on these joyous occasions. We have seen also the other cultural programmes and exhibitions being displayed occasionally. Community spirit and team undertakings appear to have their strong hold. The awakenings inscribed in the literature may have considerable impact in the field of orientation.

Sports

Sports of Mizoram are one arena where the state has carved out a niche of its own. In fact, Mizoram sports have left an indelible mark in the world of hockey, polo as well as wrestling. In fact, the unique culture of the Northeastern State is manifested through the traditional sports that range from wrestling, rod pulling as well as rope pulling to test the strength imbalance.

Inbuan is one of the most popular forms of sports in the state of Mizoram. The game attracts swarms of admiring crowds who cheer wildly as the wrestling match progresses. The sport started as a brainchild of the Fanai tribesmen, one of the subunits of the Mizos. A one-to-one game, Inbuan requires the individual participants to dexterously use all their physical strength and overthrow their opponents. It is imperative that the players are armed with consummate skill and expertise. This enables a player to overcome any physical disabilities and defeat a more powerful antagonist.

Another archetypal Mizoram sport is the Inkawibah. The game is centred around a piece of nut that is locally known as the 'kawi'. The game is a hit with the youngsters of Mizoram and it is hardly unusual to witness a gang of children enjoying themselves over a round of Inkawibah. The game states that the number of pieces of the nut must match the number of players. The nuts or the 'kawis' are placed in an erect position by one group of players while the other group desperately tries to displace it from its position.

Popular Sports

Most of their ancient games and sports were mostly gymnastics, wrestling, long jumps, shooting, javelin, stone weighing; they were indispensable as men's sports. In fact they characterised the ancient trial sports. Laying ambushes and pit-falls to animals characterised some of these games. Fishing and ankling also are very essential to the recreation programmes.

6

Education

The department of education is looked after by a council minister and the Education Directorate, who work under the Minister of Education. Initially, before this place was declared a union territory in the year 1987, the educational system of Mizoram was looked after by the missionaries of the state.

The Education Directorate was created in the year 1973. The important positions of this directorate are the education director, three deputy education directors and a joint education director. The system of education at Mizoram follows the 10+2 pattern. This state offers a number of schools, colleges and a major university, which cater to the different types of educational needs of the society of Mizoram.

The schools of the state form an important part of the educational system at Mizoram. There are quite a few schools in this state, which provide the basic school education to the children of the region. Some of the most well known schools of Mizoram are Mizoram Institute of Comprehensive Education, Jawahar Navodaya Vidyalaya of Thenzawal, Kendriya Vidyalaya and Jawahar Navodaya Vidyalaya of Thenzawl.

There are quite a few colleges in Mizoram, which offer a variety of courses on different subjects. The Mizoram colleges include Engineering colleges, Pharmacy colleges, Nursing colleges, Hotel Management colleges, Veterinary colleges, Computer institutes, Polytechnic colleges and Law colleges.

The Mizoram University, a significant part of Mizoram education, provides research facilities and regular courses in a variety of departments like natural sciences, humanities, physical sciences, forestry, social sciences and many others.

All the above educational institutes of Mizoram are quite popular throughout the entire northwestern region of India.

Traditional Education

The antecedents leading to the beginnings of education during the last century would be found interesting.

The Deputy Commissioner had a small cell concerned initially with the establishment of education. This was the event taking place shortly after the inception of the district administration. Education, however, was handed to the two Missionaries on the North and the South designated Honorary Inspectors of Schools. The situation lasted until after Independence when the Inspectorate of the Department was started and shaped from 1947 to 1952. Since then several branches of Directorates including community development were started in the District.

It is learnt that the first Welsh Missionary brought Rai Bhajur from Shillong who considerably assisted him in establishing education as well as propagating Christianity. He had earlier served as teacher and had attained educational experience. Another contractor from Shillong, Sahon Roy also assisted the Mission in doing a considerable spade work.' We reiterate the beginnings as follows — the field was first explored by the Indian Aborigines Mission. They wanted to enter Lushai Hills. In 1893, J. Herbert Lorrain and Frederick W. Savidge of this Mission came to Lushai Hills and took up residence at Aijal. This was followed by the arrival of D. E. Jones, accompanied by a Khasi Evangelist, Rai Bhajur and his wife. Bhajur was a teacher in a High School at Shillong and was earlier offered the post of Subinspector of Schools but however, 'he voluntarily relinquished to become an Evangelist'. During this time, a school already opened by Government for the chiefs existed.

Savidge and Lorrain also had opened a school but it discontinued and when it was reopened by Jones, it numbered thirty pupils. Bhajur stay however was very short and he returned soon to the Khasi Hills. It was Rev. Edwin Rowlands who came to Lushai Hills in December 1898 and was united with Mr. Jones.

U Shonroy, a Shillong contractor, had given at this time, the 'valuable and voluntary assistance' to the Welsh Mission. The Mission had received also so great the assistance from the British Baptists earlier before they left for modern Arunachal. In these circumstances, the General Assembly of the Mission held in 1902 at Liverpool had approved for the "transfer of the Southern portion of the Lushai field" to the care of the Baptists as the agents of the British Society were already labouring in the adjoining country of Chittagong and 'is as much also as the Directors of the Baptist Society were in a position to send workers immediately on the field, it was judged advantageously for the speedy evangelisation of the hills that the transfer should be effected'. The population was estimated at 30,000 in the south and 50,000 in the north.

As regards schools, a marked increase was noted as in 1904, there had been 12 schools and 300 pupils on the roll, 30 of whom were females. The work of the Mission was acknowledged so that the Commissioner of Assam when visiting Lushai Hills during those years, was pleased to affect an amalgamation of a Government School at Aijal with the Mission School, "the new institution being placed under the management of the Mission" whereas, Major Shakespear, Divisional SO, CIE made over a generous gift of Rs. 1,000 for the purpose of the building of schools.

The indefagitable labour of the Mission was noted that hardly within fifty years, schools under the Welsh Mission in all had totalled 165, the number of boys in the school enrolment being 16,686 and girls 11,897. This considerable increase happened in 1947-48.

Miss Gwen Rees Roberts brought out an ample report on this trend as follows.

"Up to May, 1946, my work was confined to the Girls' School and the High School. Then from January, 1947, I also began to teach in the Teachers' Training School, so that this year, together with the Girl Guides my work has been fivefold".

Firstly the Girls' School. In January I felt exactly like "the old woman who lived in a shoe", for I certainly had so many children I "didn't know what to do" with them".

"I wrote last year of the Cotton Project. I would like to tell you that each girl in Class 6 wove a cloth "puan" (shawl or mantle) for herself and Class 5 cooperated to weave a, table cloth for the school. The Class 6 girls worked on a Health Project and found out all kinds of valuable information about the Health Services that exist in Lushai. We are introducing an increasing amount of Physical training. I told you last year of the Domestic Science Class which we had started. This still flourishes and we hope to expand it to include simple cooking next year, so far we have been confined to cleaning, washing and ironing.

At the end of the year an Exhibition of knitting, weaving, sewing, drawing, etc., was held on Prize Giving Day. Although we seek to keep before us always a high standard of academic achievement and up to now have succeeded quite well, we feel that education which includes at least an introduction to the crafts which they will need to use later as wives and mothers, and to the music and drawing which help to bring harmony and colour into their rather restricted lives, is vitally important.

Closely connected with the Girls' School is the Girl Guide Movement. The School Companies and Bluebird Flocks gave a concert early in the year and so made enough money to buy a door in the new Girl Guide Headquarters of India. They were proud to be the first Guides in Assam to have done so".

"At the High School I have continued to teach Biology and Geography, but as the Girls' school continues to expand and there seems no hope of any other teacher coming out I shall gradually have to give up this teaching, much as I love it. I feel much happier about having to do this now than I did last year, for now we have Pi Sangpuii, B.A. (the only woman graduate in North Lushai) on the staff and I feel that she will continue to have the welfare of the girls at heart. There are about two boys to every girl in the High School.

In the Teachers' Training School I have taught them Geography, Map drawing, etc. In the Training School as the men were rather raw villagers it meant speaking in Lushai from beginning to end. It was a tremendous effort, but worth it — for my language as well as their Geography! At the end of the year they returned to their villages carrying a reasonable amount of apparatus for teaching, reading, arithmetic, geography and scripture especially. Thanks to the indefatigable Zalawra, Assistant General Secretary Lushai Sunday School Union, the Sunday School work has gone on at least in a skeleton fashion during Miss Hughes' absence. As I am so tied in the schools all the heavy office work has fallen to him".

The Mission had done a pioneering work in higher education. A proper infrastructure was laid down; the system of teachers' training and the dissemination of the healthy co-curricular activities had been indispensable for giving education its foundation. The field was provided for building the character and intellect of the students and helping them as well to use their skills. The report indicates that the Mission had prepared the field. The Mission's sway, however was short. The agreement later on was arrived at when, Government took over the school to become the first ever High School of the District.

At this stage so excellent were the responses given to education. The advice and assistance of the influential chiefs and churchmen is important to stress here. The people against the various setbacks donated generously to the Church funds and the bulk of the so-called rice collections fund raised annually was used for the maintenance of schools and support of teachers and students even.

Meanwhile the Teachers' Training School of the Mission was striving on to impart the requisite training and basic training true to its principle and purpose was sought to be adequately organised and managed.

Evidently the first High School was shaped as the first local venture of the prominent people and had attained considerable support. The people had raised it and entrusted its management to the Mission. The Mission, on their turn, had concentrated efforts to build an excellent system in which students were trained in school enterprises worth mentioning.

Basic and Secondary Education

There are a number of Mizoram schools, which provide the basic education to the children of the state. These schools are quite well known not only in the state but in the whole northeastern part of the state. The total number of primary schools in the state is 1,280 while the total middle schools in Mizoram are 770.

The Mizoram Institute of Comprehensive Education is one of the most well known schools at Mizoram. This school does not put immense pressure on the young minds and impart good-quality education.

One of the most popular schools of Mizoram is called the Kendriya Vidyalaya. This school is often preferred by the parents over the other schools of the state as it offers the basic school education in a very simple way.

The Jawahar Navodaya Vidyalaya of Thenzawl and the Jawahar Navodaya Vidyalaya of Chhimtuipui also offer all the basic amenities that the parents may expect in a good-quality school. The Jawahar Navodaya Vidyalaya of Hrangchalkhawn is well reputed in the educational field of the state. The teachers of the Jawahar Navodaya Vidyalaya of Thenzawal give personalised attention to the students and offer the basic school-level information.

All the above Mizoram schools provide almost all the facilities that are necessary to impart good-quality school education. The school infrastructure of this state is well equipped to train the young minds to strengthen the future of the state.

Different Kinds of Schools

Some of the schools in the state are affiliated to the state board while the rest are affiliated to other educational boards like CBSE or ICSE. The Mizoram Board of School Education is also entrusted with the duty of conducting examinations at the end of academic session of various classes as per the rules of the state.

Number of Schools

As per the data of 2001 Census Report, there are 2,427 (approx.) schools in Mizoram. This includes Primary schools, middle schools and high schools.

Medium of Teaching

Mizo is the language used for teaching students from class I to VI. English is used for teaching students of higher classes. The ICSE and CBSE schools generally use English as the medium of instruction.

Drop Outs in Schools

The rate of school drop out is quite high in Mizoram. The State Government is taking a lot of initiatives for overcoming this problem.

Famous Schools

Some of the most famous schools in Mizoram are Jawahar Navodaya Vidyalaya Chhimtuipui, Jawahar Navodaya Vidyalayas Thenzawal, Aizawl (serchip), Kendriya Vidyalaya, Aizawl, Jawahar Navodaya Vidyalayas Sedaikawn, Aizawl, Jawahar Navodaya Vidyalaya Thenzawl, Dt-Aizawl, Jawahar Navodaya Vidyalayas Mamit and Jawahar Navodaya Vidyalaya Hrangchalkhawn (minlokawn) Spo-Theiriat Lunglei.

Higher Education

There are quite a few Mizoram colleges, which form a very important part of the total education system of the state. The colleges of Mizoram offer educational courses in a number of different streams.

The various types of colleges that one can avail of in the state of Mizoram are Engineering colleges, Polytechnic colleges, Nursing colleges, Hotel Management colleges, Pharmacy colleges, Law colleges, Veterinary colleges and Computer institutes. There is one major Engineering college in Mizoram. It is called the Mizoram Engineering College. There are quite a few polytechnic colleges in Mizoram. The Regional Paramedical and Nursing Training Institute, the Government Polytechnic, the College of Veterinary Sciences and Animal Husbandry and the Women's Polytechnic are the main polytechnic institutes in Mizoram. The College of Nursing - Regional Paramedical and Nursing Institute is the leading nursing college of the state. There are two hotel management institutes in the region, namely, Lunglei Government Aizwal College and IGNOU Study Centre.

The main pharmacy college of Mizoram is Regional Institute of Para Medical and Nursing. The chief law college of Mizoram is Aizwal Law College. The College of Veterinary Sciences and Animal Husbandry, one of the popular colleges at Mizoram, offers quality education on the subject of veterinary.

There are three major computer institutes in the area. The names of these institutes are the DOEACC Centre, the Academy Of Computer and the Golden Republic Information Technology Centre. All the above Mizoram colleges impart high-quality education to the youth of the state and hence are quite popular among them as well as the students of the remaining parts of Northeastern India.

Colleges

Engineering Colleges

There is one major engineering college at Mizoram. The name of this college is Mizoram Engineering College. It offers a number of courses to the students of engineering in Mizoram.

An engineering degree from the Mizoram Engineering College has good value in the job market. The teachers of this college are well known for taking personalised care of the students. This institute has got the recognition of AICTE. The Mizoram Engineering College constitutes one of the most important segments of the department of education as it provides massive opportunities to the young people for building a strong career.

There are three major engineering courses that are on offer at this educational institute of the state. One of them is the course of Bachelor in Engineering in the department of Civil Engineering. This course spans for a time period of 4 years.

Another course is the Bachelor of Engineering in Computer Engineering. It takes 4 years for completing this course. The Bachelor of Engineering course in the department of Electronics and Communication Engineering is also offered by this college. This course also spans for 4 years. All the above courses are quite popular among the engineering students of the place. The minimum eligibility for all the above three courses is passing class 12 with the subjects of Chemistry, Physics and Mathematics or an equivalent subject.

This college of engineering at Mizoram imparts quality education to the young generation of the state. It is not only popular in the state of Mizoram but is well known throughout the entire Northeastern Region of India.

Nursing Colleges

The Mizoram nursing colleges form one of the most significant parts of the educational system of the state. There are two major nursing colleges in Mizoram. The names of these colleges are College of Nursing Regional Paramedical and Nursing Institute and Civil Hospital School of Nursing.

The College of Nursing Regional Paramedical and Nursing Institute is one of the most well known nursing colleges at Mizoram. It is also one of the leading colleges of India that provide education in the field of nursing.

This college is very popular among the students who want to pursue a course in the field of nursing. This is because it imparts all the latest information associated with nursing. The main nursing course offered by this educational institute is B.Sc. in nursing.

The Civil Hospital School of Nursing is one of the major nursing colleges of Mizoram. This college is also quite well known for imparting quality education in the field of nursing. The courses that are on offer at this college of Mizoram are quite in demand among the young women of the state as it has good market value.

Both the above Mizoram nursing colleges contribute greatly to the advancement of the young women of the state of Mizoram. Such colleges help the young girls to make a career and be financially independent. These colleges also play a big role in the medical sector of the region.

Polytechnic Colleges

Polytechnic Colleges impart valuable technical and vocational education to students of Mizoram. The polytechnic colleges in Mizoram cover a wide variety of subjects ranging from garment technology, computer science and engineering, medical lab technology, etc.

Some of the important polytechnic colleges at Mizoram are:

- Women's Polytechnic (AICTE Approved).
- Courses Offered — Modern Office Management Garment Technology Electronics and Telecom Engineering Culture and Cosmotology.

- Government Polytechnic (AICTE Approved).
- Courses Offered — Electrical Engineering Civil Engineering Computer Science and Engineering Mechanical Engineering.
- Regional Paramedical and Nursing Training Institute (AICTE Approved).
- Courses Offered — X Ray Technician ECG and Cardio Instru. Technician Medical Lab Technology Opthalmic Technician.

The women polytechnic colleges lay stress on a wide variety courses, including the women-oriented courses such as house decoration, culture and cosmetology. The women polytechnic colleges of Mizoram help the women to become independent and pursue their own independent careers.

Law Colleges

Liandig Puia Law College and Aizwal Law College are the law colleges in Mizoram that enable the students of Mizoram to opt for LLB degree. These law colleges of Mizoram are affiliated under the Mizoram University.

An estimate of the law colleges in Mizoram is given below:

- Liandig Puia Law College.
- Aizawl Law College.

It is noteworthy that both Liandig Puia Law College and Aizawl Law College are approved by the Bar Council of India (BCI), a statutory body that is constituted under the Advocate Act (1961) by the Government of India. The Education Committee of the Bar Council of India takes care of the law colleges situated in the different part of the countries. The law colleges at Mizoram, being a part of India, fall under the jurisdiction of the Education Committee of the BCI.

Computer Institutes

Computer institutes of Mizoram offer DOEACC 'O' Level courses to the students of Mizoram. The computer institutes in Mizoram help the students of Mizoram to opt for IT education and pursue a career in Information Technology.

Among the major computer institutes of Mizoram are:

- DOEACC Centre (Formerly known as CEDTI).
- Golden Republic Information Technology Centre.
- Academy of Computer Electronics Centre.

Each of the computer institutes provide specialised course in computer application. The eligibility for the DOEACC 'O' Level Course is 10+2 or ITI certificate followed by 'O' Level course. But, there are some parameters on which the eligibility of the candidates are judged. An estimate of the criteria that decides eligibility of the candidate is given below:

- 10+2 or ITI certificate from an accredited 'O' Level course (after class 10).

- Or completion of second year from a recognised polytechnic engineering course (after class 10) and simultaneously pursuing 'O' level diploma course in the third year of the diploma course.

- Or 10+2 or ITI certificate followed by a relevant experience (job experience in IT, including teaching as a faculty member in a recognised institution) of one year.

- A pass-out in NCVT-Data Preparation and Computer Software (conducted by DGE&T) is also eligible for the course.

The students opting for the DOEACC course can become Junior Programmer, Console Operator and Programmer Assistant. As the IT-sector is booming, the computer institutes in Mizoram is in great demand. The computer institutes provide an alternative for employment in this world of Information Technology.

University

Despite the fact that Mizoram is a small state in the Northeastern Region of India, it ranks first in India with a literacy rate of 89.9 per cent.

So far as the present educational scenario of higher education is concerned, the state of Mizoram has the presence of Mizoram University, a central university assisted by a number of vocational colleges spread across Mizoram.

The University of Mizoram is the bridge that connects the people of Mizoram to the outer rapidly changing and developing world and provides the fundamental understanding to the common people to recognise their duties to the nation.

So, it is easily comprehensible that Mizoram University helps the aspirants of the entire North Eastern region to culminate their strategies and plays the pioneering role in maintaining the unity in diversity.

Mizoram University

Mizoram University was founded on 2nd July, 2001, under the provision laid down by Mizoram University Act. Mizoram University aims at disseminating knowledge and providing research facilities in natural and physical sciences, humanities, social sciences and other allied disciplines. The permanent campus of the university is built on 978 acres of land, which is leased at Tanhril by the Government of Mizoram. Mizoram University gives affiliation to about 27 under-graduate colleges. Two professional institutions are also affiliated under the Mizoram University. At present, the total number of students enrolled in the university is around 8,279 students.

It is noteworthy that Mizoram University has received a grant of Rs. 43.50 crores (approximately) from UGC. As a result, the university has taken adequate steps for its development, so that it can work at par with the other universities in India.

Mizoram University offers a number of courses related to different streams. Some of the departments of Mizoram University are:

- Geography.
- History and Ethnography.
- Public Administration.
- Education.
- Botany.
- Physics.
- Economics.
- Commerce.
- Library and Information Science.
- Forest Ecology, Biodiversity and Environmental Sciences.
- Geology.
- Psychology.
- Political Science.
- Chemistry.
- Social Work.
- Mathematics and Computer Science.
- Zoology.
- Information Technology.
- Horticulture, Aromatic and Medicinal Plant.
- Electronic Engineering.
- Management.
- Extension Education and Rural Development.

Gradual Cultivation

The matter relating to updating and regularising Inspection works under the Inspectorates in the three new districts of the state after education was bifurcated from the Assam Government had become indispensable. The matter was pursued and implemented. Moreover the government had assumed control of primary education after the Union Territory was formed in 1972. The matter of updating university education occurred shortly after that event. As such different Departments with their defined spheres of jurisdiction and function came to exist.

The inherent problems of providing a highly utilitarian system and equipping the students under instruction with the necessary standards, have been pointed out. That the aims and purpose of education to provide the necessary critical, academic and even mechanical devices to shape the talents and mental faculties fully and consistently, this fact is ever accepted in the educational circles. The need to reinforcing these faculties is felt everywhere. It is not known how far the system of teachers' training has been feasible to all these issues.

In the absence of the facilities and resources compatible to these needs, teachers' training at present has been accepted as the most valuable asset to give teaching its requisite functioning. Therefore, education is the system of reinforcement of programmes suited to the diagnostic search of the inherent drawbacks and deficiencies and this issue is so necessary for our consideration in the present world situation. It provides certain devices and remedial measures to rectify them. Tapping the mental faculties with the reinforcement of critical acumen, critical tendencies, evaluationary tastes, analytical approaches and the power of deduction seems to be the most essential thing despite the inflationary and quantitative trends which education now has been subject to.

The advantages of utilising teachers training for giving impetus to education has been accepted by all the states in the region. More recently these institutions also updated in the Hill States within the confine of North Eastern Hill University. The services of State Councils for Educational Research and Training in these States are in demand for helping weak students in the subjects including science and mathematics. The task to updating teachers' training is looked to from many angles. More than that the need to giving a more prospective guidance to students with regard to prosecuting careers according to their aptitudes and participating in the regional, national and world affairs, has arisen from time to time.

On the infrastructure laid down, the amalgamation of basic training centre to the Undergraduate teachers' training in Mizoram was caused years ago. The task to coordinate teaching interests was held to suit best with the present situation in that State. Mizoram Institute of Education had already been set up which imparts teachers' training to the graduate level. It qualifies teachers and students for a Bachelor's degree in teaching. The Institute conducts the annual B.Ed. Examination in parity with the similar conditions in Meghalaya, and Nagaland where the Shillong Post-graduate Training College and Nagaland College of Education function their works under the university. The B.Ed. Colleges have been required to offer examination in written (exposition), sessional and practical (internal) and practice teaching.

These developments had shaped the growth of other institutions; one of the important measures was the establishment of a School Board of education which conducts the High School Leaving Certificate Examinations annually and which specifies some matters contained in the body of instructions. The rules for the conduct of Examinations now have become necessary for enabling the candidates to appear at examinations. These matters relate to conditions of eligibility, allotment of marks, selection of textbooks, the essence of the objective and essay type of examination and other particulars.

The university and other institutions of learning follow the rules framed and prescribed for the conduct of examinations. The matter regarding the present restructuring of education consequent upon the constitutional reorganisation have been reiterated.

New Institutions on Scene

Increase of the educational institutions in the campuses of North Eastern Hill University have also characterised themselves in a new set-up. The trends must have indicated an increase to almost 1 lakh pupils and students in almost every State. The number of Schools and colleges including the recognised and the other institutions (being upgraded) have constantly been on the increase. Literacy both within or outside the system of formal education must have also shown its significant increase.

The number of colleges in Mizoram is increasing. The colleges exist at new townships and centres. The setting up of a Campus of NEHU gave a definite increase of institutions in the constituent States within the university. The constitutional reorganisation and increases in the tempo of developmental and constructional activities must have led to the same conclusion. The rise in the number of colleges is due to the manifold increase of secondary institutions. The matter of providing post-graduate teaching in Mizoram was examined during the last decade. It is known in the above framework that a thousand of Primary, 450 Middle, 155 High Schools and many colleges exist in the state.

Panchhunga College was the first ever known college located at Aizawl started during the fifties of the last century; it was provincialised during the sixties of the last century. It had catered singly with college education during the first decade of its existence. The necessity for providing bases to college education at other places had arisen. The other colleges known to have existed during the early decade were Lunglei College (established in 1964) Champhai College (established in 1971), Sirchip College (established in 1973) and Aizawl College (established in 1975). From the statistics we find that a very few students took science during the final pre-university examination in 1978, as less than 250 students appeared for Pre-University Science against 1,515 male and 675 female students who sat for the P.U. Arts examination; over 460 boys and 154 girls appeared at the Arts Degree pass and over 180 male and 26 females appeared at Arts Degree Honours Course. Number of students who sat at B.Sc. pass and honours was negligible.

In these circumstances Lunglei College was afterwards upgraded to Government College; other colleges awaiting for recognition were on the list. Consequently, students were diverted to other courses traditional and new according to the pattern of syllabi adopted by the colleges. In 1979, the campus of NEHU concerned with teaching a few chosen post-graduate subjects was inaugurated. These also have substantiated the need to strengthening teachers' training as in parity of the procedure adopted in the advanced States.

Evidently there has been a considerable increase in course contents; use of new course contents and improved techniques has become indispensable. Few of the colleges have, therefore, offered interesting subjects such as commerce, geography, Home Science, sociology, besides the other science and art subject. In the matter of affiliation, most of the colleges in Mizoram, Nagaland and Meghalaya have been striving on to fulfil the terms and conditions laid down for upgradation and regular affiliation of colleges stage by stage. Inspection for evaluating the college prospectives already developed at the regular or temporary basis of affiliation would be most indispensable for the purpose. At the contemporary decade, among the colleges which have come to existence are Hnahthial, Kolasib, Hrangbana, Zintiri Women's and Saiha Colleges.

Further we note in 1987 that the introduction for +2 stage was sought for the following colleges: Kaichhunga, P.E. Thansela, Derlawn, Kawnpui, Saitual, North Eastern Khawdungsei and North Vanlaiphai Colleges. To the best of our belief, none of the colleges had ever been started under the Missionary sponsorship. They had started we believe as public initiative ventures which had involved a considerable organisational work and concentration of energy initially to fulfil the terms of the *ad hoc* or regular affiliation. We find on record that Pachhunga College was included in B.Sc. Examination of the university in 1979-80. Further the PUC Science examination had included Pachhunga and Lunglei Colleges. We find, in that year, B.A. Examination of NEHU included Pachhunga, Lunglei, Serchip and Aizawl Colleges. Further the above colleges, along with Saiha, Kolasib and Champai Colleges were included in the PU (Arts) Examination of the University.

The college included in B.Sc. (TDC) and 2-year Science course examination in 1984 was Pachhunga while PU (Sc.) examination was offered at Lunglei and Pachhunga colleges. At this stage, however, Hrangbana College offered PU (Com.) in that year. Colleges which had qualified themselves for B.A. (Hons.) were Pachhunga, Champai and Aizawl Colleges. Colleges listed in both B.A. : Ad course and TDC were Serchip, Lunglei Hrangbana and Saiha, they included also Lawngtlai, Saichal and Kolasib. Almost all the colleges along with Zintiri and Hnahthial offered PU Arts. Moreover, Hrangbana College had also offered B.Com. degree and PU (Com.) Examination in that year.

The Eleventh Report of Northeastern Hill University 1984-85 indicates the colleges as follows:

- Saiha College — Subjects: English, Alternative English, MIL (Mizo), Mizo Elective, History, Education, Political Science, Sociology and B.A. Honours in History and Political Sc.

- Lunglei College — Subjects: Honours - Economics, Political Science, History and Education; Pass - English, MIL, Political Science, History, Economics, Education, Mizo Elective, Chemistry, Physics, Mathematics, Biology.

- Serchip College — Subjects: English, Political Science, Economics, History, Mizo Elective, Foundation Course, Geography.

- Aizawl College — Subjects: Arts for PU & B.A. and Commerce for PU.

- Lawngtlai College — Subjects: English, Mizo (MIL) Political Science, Economics, Education, History, Mizo Elective.

- Zintiri: Women's College — B.A. English, Foundation Course, MIL, Food and Nutrition, Home Science, History, Education, Economics, Political Science, B.Sc. Home Science and subsidiary PU subjects.

- Champhai College — B.A. Hons. in History, Political Science, Geography, Education, B.A. & PU - English, History, Mizo, Economics Political Science, Geography and Education.

- Hrangbana College — Degree: English, M.I.L., Alternative English, Foundation Course, Accountancy, Auditing, Economics, Statistics, Business, Mathematics, Business Organisation and Commercial law.

The other colleges which figured in the University Tenth Annual Report were Kolasib College, Pachhunga College, Serchip College and Hanhthial College.

The infrastructure for developing university education was laid down. The Northeastern Hill University with headquarter at Shillong had initially been started in 1973 shortly after Mizoram was converted into the Union Territory. The university had started with the infrastructure of examination, affiliation, Boards of studies and the administrative set-up. A few post-graduate departments were initially started.

Meanwhile, the matter of updating university education in Nagaland and Mizoram was examined. The consensus of opinion was reached towards setting up campuses in the areas where NEHU extended their jurisdiction. The first step was the taking over of Pachhunga College for strengthening the teaching infrastructure to the selected subjects. Affiliation was given to the old and new colleges located in the three States under the university.

According to a Report, "the Mizoram Campus of the North Eastern Hill University came into being with the formal inauguration by the Vice Chancellor, Dr. A. K. Dhan on October 19, 1979". Three post-graduate Departments, viz. Education, English and

Economics were opened in the campus. This was a landmark to the development of education. Education till then had already made its notable expansion. The opening of Master Courses would help very much to build the different kinds of expertise in the different sciences.

In 1984-85, five batches of students completed their courses in M.Ed. programme. It was also proposed that M.A. Education would be offered as Master's programme instead of M.Ed. In the same year the Department of English and Economics were catering with running their normal functions. An important development was the starting of the Centre for Educational Technology which was expected "chiefly to promote the adoption of Educational Technology at different levels of education, both formal and non-formal sectors. The proposed activity spectrum includes development of a variety of software material, orientation training to different groups of functionaries, consultancy, research and extension".

The Campus Library meanwhile had considerably been strengthened.

As regards the Department of Psychology, this subject was taught at Pachhunga University College to the Degree level. Therefore, teachers were engaged to teach it. There was also the Department of Psychology at the Campus.

According to the Report 38th Meeting of the Academic Council, Northeastern Hill University, "this Department has been established with a view to organising regular programmes of post-graduate and Research Studies within this discipline. It will collaborate with the School of Education in the conduct of study and Research in the areas of Educational Psychology, Development Studies, Instructional Technology and Organisational behaviour. It will also undertake extension work in important areas like child development, delinquent crime, guidance and counselling in educational institutions and selection and placement work through a programme of test development".

The Mizo Accord had provided for the establishment of a full-fledged university in due course.

Immediately after the university was established in Shillong, the situation with regard to building the campus in Mizoram was considered. The matter of starting a Centre of study at Aizawl was taken up.

The increase of schools and colleges by leaps and bounds and consequently the explosion in the population of students, have reiterated the great needs for improving school management, discipline and the dissemination of instructions as would be proportionate with these quantitative yields.

The problem in the quantitative expansion of education in Mizoram as also in India as a whole has to be reviewed in the present situation so that the pattern of development would not deteriorate and that each and every student who has received education to that level and, who has taken advantage of counselling and guidance service, will have his or her proper role to play in the task of national reconstruction in the near future.

We have found in the previous years the population of pupils and students in all would have jumped up to a figure of a lakh.

Both the instructional and co-curricular activities make a great demand at present. The matter of updating instructional media is connected with promoting the healthy and constructive co-curricular activities. Physical training, excursions, sports and games, scouts and guides, library facilities, these and other activities are also formulated within the educational training.

The services of NSS and NCC have been rendered indispensable nowadays. In this connection we see that the camping intensification work of National Service Scheme of the university in the Territory in the year 1977-78 was organised due to the expected famine. "Over and above the money allocated for NSS special Camping programme, the Government of Mizoram gave an additional grant of Rs. 19,800 to help implement the programme.

Approximately a thousand of students were involved, at one time or other, in the rodent control programme"... "It was noticed that a number of campings were undertaken by the students that National Service Scheme, by going out to villages and helping the Agriculture Department in exterminating the rat population". The study of rat menace and the linkage between the rat menace, flowering of the bamboo and the Thingtam would have been constructively used.

Many of the schools and colleges provide sports and games, creation weeks, stage and concert entertainments, libraries and other facilities. There has been a proposal to provide a State library and a State museum as well as would be helpful to educate the public in many essential aspects of learning. The situation in journalism has considerably improved owing to the availability of printing presses in the state and the number of newspapers is now increasing.

7

Language and Literature

The languages of Mizoram reflect the cultural diversity of the North-East Indian state. Tribal communities belonging to the Mizo race are predominant in the state. The tribal people, however, give education its due importance and thus the state literacy rate is soaring at a phenomenal 89.9 per cent. The people of Mizoram speak a number of languages of which Mizo and English hold a special place.

The Mizo community is an amalgam of several indigenous tribes who had their own unique lifestyle and distinctive dialects. The Duhlian dialect, also known as the Lusei among the locals was the most popular language of Mizoram. Over the years, this local mode of speech and communication has evolved into the North-East Indian state's *lingua franca*. However, traditional Lusei language was interspersed with traces of other dialects like the Mara, Fanai and Changte and their collective medley led to the formation of the Mizo language.

Subsequently, the untiring efforts of the Christian missionaries led to the development of the Mizo script. This was a significant milestone that marked the development of a colloquial speech into a formal script. The writing pattern was a combination of the Roman script and Hunterian transliteration methodology with prominent traces of a phonetics-based spelling system. The development of the Mizo writing script has prompted the state to demand the official recognition of the language in the 8th schedule of the Constitution.

Another language that has gained wide acceptability in Mizoram is English, the universal language. English has paramount importance in the sphere of the state's education, all administrative units and government matters as well as all other formal ceremonies.

Mizo Languages

With regards to Kuki it is evidently one of the antiquated languages in the Asiatic mainland. The substram on which Kuki-Mizo rest must have been considerably old but it is not the oldest in the world. It must have been akin to the great oriental languages and must have branched off from the dominant languages spoken in China or in its close neighbourhood. It seems to have grown inflectionally or inversely from 'the well-known oriental languages which were largely monosyllabic in structure.

It has retained the components of simple fetching words which characterised themselves with some of the archaic languages lying most westward, once spoken in Middle East or eastern Europe. Kuki, therefore, was not an isolated language. It had developed some vital relations morphologically, orthographically or otherwise with some languages it came in contact while retaining its structure as adequately as simple and lucid. We also see that in the language formation, cases of mutual assimilation, absorption and adoption of certain glossories are not ruled out in respect of all the languages, great and small.

In its subsequent location, it attained its position in close proximity to Mon, the language of the once ruling race in Burma, Kachin, Karen, Tai, Bodo and Burmese. We have not come across any story of the Mizos connected in any form with the seashore but their forefathers must have at one time, been diffused elsewhere in the coastal region. We find too that although the language was influenced by Mikir or Singpho or Bodo and that it had alike influenced them, Mizo still retains its intrinsic character intensively. This is proved that the Konyak (semi-Bodic) and the Garo (Bodic; like the Kuki, use the gongs as the great treasure of their heir-looms and use them at their cultural demonstrations).

Characteristics of the Languages

In its written form, Mizo evinces considerably its power of flexibility, assimilation and adaptation and orthographically it can be adjusted quicker and in the easier way than other languages which carry with them the strong system of nasalisation and diphongtal character. It is conveyed much more legibly; as such, it is intelligibly brought out. The Mizo languages are not heavily structured with the compounds of words or metamorphics if we can use that term. This has rendered the work of Bible translation easier, compared with other languages in which the arrangement otherwise, is difficult.

The task of reducing the language to writing evidently was worked out from scratch. The need evidently was for adjusting and regularising the orthography and to experiment it for reading and writing. It entailed also the diagnotisation of the good, fetching letters and giving rectification thereto and usually took a longer time, to experiment and modify the alphabet. Sometimes besides the alphabet, the orthographers were compelled to a make use of a few asterics to facilitate pronunciation and legibility of words. Most of the first books published were subject to the subsequent revision to serve better for reading and improve the spelling as well. Evidently literature among the pre-literate tribes, start with the Bible translation. The need too had arisen for regularising the system of spelling in the books covered under the school instructions.

Literature

We find that we are confronted with the paucity of source materials in our efforts made to highlight the growth of literature. The service of literature in the propagation of Christianity and education especially at the first stage was considered essential. Evolving a qualitative pattern of society as equally responsive to the beginning of the Church, was also from the many angles emphasised. The era of Bible translation contained the seeds for the growth of literature.

The essence of the Christian writings was considered so much essential. And for the growth of education, the need of good books was also justified. In course of time this literature would also seek to cater itself to the cultural and secular aspirations as well. Mizo literature is already rich in oral ballads, dirges, heroic tales and their folklore provides the other distinct literary characteristics.

On the above grounds we find that Bible translation formed part and parcel of literature. We find too that the Bible translation entailed a longer time to put it to completion. There are several books, gospels, epistles and other manifestations contained in it. It can be found that bible translation took to about 50 (to be on safe side, say 60 years) to complete it. Usually the translation was the work of several translators, a single person usually would not be able to cope with. The task was done by a team of Missionaries. But the Missionaries alone without' the dedicated help of the' local Collaborators or Churchmen involved would not be able to do it. It would be beyond their means to perform it single-handed.

Actually when we compare Lushai or Lakher Bible translation with Khasi and Garo of Meghalaya, we find that in all cases of Bible translation took an average of 50 to 60 years to complete it. We find that the Serampore Baptist Mission, one of the oldest Missions, of William Carey, with the lightning speed they used, carried over the translations into several languages much more shorter.

Some of them in that case would not exceed even 10 years. But the Serampore Mission just relied on Pundits and Tutors without even in many cases, contacting the local society or working actually in the actual soil. But their works have served as the models for the future translations.

It was in Lakher and Lushai that the full Bible was translated and published in the previous decades. The progress of translation in the Riang language, however, was unsatisfactory during those years. As regards the Riang living on the border between Tripura and North Mizo, 'they have been evangelised and a volume containing Mark and the first epistle of John was issued in 1959'. This was the initial beginning of Riang Literature.' Many of them still follow their old religion.

Some of their sacrificial rites centering on the diagnotisation of the internal entrails for something auspicious and for reading some of the omens in their method of divination, provide some striking similarities to the similar practice of the old Khasis in Shillong. When serving the Union Christian College many years ago, I was in touch with a few Riang students in the Christian Mission at Agartala and was priviledged to be hosted probably by the last New Zealander Baptist Missionary. Now we examine the formative events of Bible translation in the erstwhile Lushai District.

When Lushai was reduced to writing and Mr. J. H. Lorrain having been acquainted with the task for translation, he stated 'we used Roman characters such as we use in English, and were able to follow more or less the system known in India as the Hunter System. Lorrain and Savidge evidently initiated Bible translation work in Aijal. This was in 1895. D. E. Jones later on joining them, considerably helped in the translation work; the success of the publication was due to the great help rendered by Mr. Suaka and Mr. Thangphungaphunga.

In these circumstances, the Gospels of John, Luke and the book of Acts, were published from London in 1899. Before 1911, ten editions of the portions translated from the New Testament came out to light; they were privately printed, they would have ranked eminently as the first conspicuous works in which credit was due to Jones, Rowlands and the Lushai collaborators. So great the progress was made that in 1924, under the supervision of Lorrain, the New Testament in one volume was printed in 1917, the work that was shared by many translators. Lorrain with the help of Rev.

Challiana and Rev. Chantera did considerable translation of the Old Testament; part translations of the scripture had also come to light. It was Mr. H. W. Carter and Rev Zathanga and Mr. J. M. Llyod who were involved in the bulk of translation and the translation of the Old Testament was completed in 1955. The printing of the whole Bible followed shortly thereafter. The Bible translation evidently was shared by the Welsh and the English Baptist Missionaries.

To evolve the language successfully with a view to put it properly to shape and also to provide information to the situation in the District, J. H. Lorrain did a considerable spade work in respect of orthography and vocabulary, he had compiled a Grammar and a Dictionary of the Lushai language. Savidge and Lorrain it is noted 'prepared also a Lushai Grammar and Dictionary, together with a small number of books for the schools.

Translation into Lakher started comparatively later. The first book ever published in the language was the Gospel of John, the translation being undertaken by Rev. R. A. Lorrain, the second man of the Mission. In 1928, the New Testament came out to light and the Old Testament was published in 1928. The help was given by Mr. A Bruce Lorrain

Foxall, (he seemed to be an English man) and own son-in-law of the Missionary, R.A. Lorrain' but the local collaborators who had exceedingly helped were Mr. Saro, Nyusa and Hratlu.

We are told that Mrs. Foxall born and brought up at Sherkor was so much loved and admired by the Lakhers who till her birth were for so long indifferent to the Missionary. She had attracted most of the visitors to their Mission since her infancy and even natives from the distant villages thronged to see her. She was called *Tlosai Zica*. No, a Lakher Princess and moved many of them to respond to the call of the new faith.

Evidently the Mission initiated the primary school books so designed to provide the basic knowledge in arithmetic, the local vernacular, geography and the subjects would include hand writing and drawing. On the upper primary stage, the pupils would start to learn English, history, hygiene and the already subjects prosecuted at the infrastructure.

There was great need to update the vernacular with better contents at the Middle and High school level. The bulk of the Biblical stories would have been included as they were intimately connected with the knowledge of Christianity.

This at the outset was unavoidable. Another thing, the Mission was given the authority over the school management and as such, a uniform system of instruction would have been applicable. It is understood at the incipient stage, few readers, arithmetic and geographical lessons were published from London. The increase of books subsequently had brought about the recognition of the language to the Matriculation level and that occurred most probably during the second world war.

Mizo as such was recognised to the secondary level by the Calcutta University only just before the end of the last world war. Textbooks introduced in the high schools which adopted the Lushai vernacular included mostly the portion from the scriptures; a translation of Pilgrim's Progress and a few religious treatises were also included in the course.

The Guwahati University recognised Mizo to the Pre-university level only from about the sixties. Later on, the university recognised it to the Bachelor's level. After the inception of NEHU, the matter to recognising it to the graduate level was considered on the criterion that due coverage would be given to the course contents in prose, poetry, fiction, plays and novels as Mizo Books would suit with the requirements. Already there has been some efforts made by the writers to highlight in their works some of the cultural landmarks.

It seems that the publications have been intended to suit with education; some of these are presented as Christian treatises; it is evident that literature which is responsive to the awakenings is in the making.

The literary orientation would have during the transitory epoch, been very essential. This is because the inexhaustible treasure of — folklore can be utilised for carving out the literary models. The oral characteristics of a literature have also been mentioned. There are many beautiful legends and folktales which are in circulation, transmitted from generation to generation through recitals, vocal and instrumental music and in the other media. There are rich philosophical concepts in the personification of streams, pools, caves, rocks and the natural motifs scattered about in the natural phenomenon and which have, ever inspired the feeling of awe, attachment and reverence. They have made their manifestations in the rich legends and folktales recited until today. Preservation of these things will serve as exceedingly a great purpose for maintaining their continuity and providing several connotative ideas on these themes. The folkloristic elements can be systematically reviewed for the purpose of literary assimilation.

It has been earlier remarked that culture' in context of our understanding is a level of learning attained; it also implies the level of dissemination of learning in the system of common knowledge and even a higher specialisation. Sometimes it means the refined tastes and behavioural pattern of a person or a society. It is, therefore, integrated with the different faculties of arts and sciences. Cultural orientation, in fact, implies the assumption of a culture inherited from the past as highlighted in the time-honoured traditions, institutions, folklore, arts and other cultural traits.

Further in the midst of tribal confines, there lie the picturesque and certain beauty spots. So the diverse natural objects have certain impact upon their life and this explains how these have tremendously shaped their imaginative and creative minds, besides developing certain inherent artistic attributes.

Mizo Literature

Mizo is the predominant language spoken by the inhabitants of Mizoram. The mountainous state of Mizoram or the erstwhile Lushai Hills District is the home of several tribal communities who are collectively known as the Mizos. The etymological connotation of the term Mizo implies highlander. In the local dialect 'Mi' is synonymous with people and 'Zo' means the inhabitant of an upland terrain. The Mizo language happens to be the *lingua franca* of the state. The language is an offshoot of the Kuki-Chin script that hails from the Tibeto-Burmese language. The several smaller tribal communities that include the Lushais, Kukis, Himars, Paithes, Pang, Raltes and Pawis agglomerate to form the Mizo tribe. Each of these tribes spoke a different dialect that was unique to its culture.

The Mizo language, an amalgam of several local dialects like the Mara, Fannai and the Chhangte reflect the gradual cultural enrichment intellectual appetite of the residents of Mizoram. In fact, Mizoram University has an exclusive department that caters to the study and research of this beautiful subject.

English Literature

English, the universal language, spoken in almost all countries also happens to be one of the most popular languages in the Northeastern State of Mizoram. The widespread proliferation of education throughout the state not only elevated the literacy rate to a phenomenal 89.9 per cent but also made a part and parcel of the people's everyday affairs.

In Mizoram, English is the official medium of communication in any formal occasion or ceremony. English language has also spread its wings to penetrate into the state's academic circuit as well as the administration. In fact, even the small children attending primary school in Mizoram are fairly adept in speaking the English language.

The simplicity and the flexibility of English have led to the acceptability and ever growing popularity of the language even in the remote reaches of the hilly terrains of Mizoram. Thus today the language is flourishing as one of the predominant languages of Mizoram. Ninety one years ago, not a single Mizo could read or write for the Mizo alphabet as we know it today, was only codified by the pioneer missionaries, Rev. F. J. Savidge and Rev J. H. Lorrain who landed in a small hamlet near Sairang by the banks of the River Tlawng in Mizoram in the chilly winter of 1894. If the true meaning of literature is to be taken literally, it may perhaps be a little presumptuous to claim the existence of any Mizo literature prior to that date.

Oral Literature

If we remember, however, that long before man wrote down his thoughts and emotions, he expresses them in songs. Untouched by learned influences from without, these songs are crystallised into the living language of the people – folk songs and folk stories were born out of such full and spontaneous expression which were then orally passed on from generation to generation. As we follow history of any literature through all its transformations, we are brought into direct and living contact with the motive forces of the inner life of each successive generation, and learn at first hand how it looked at life and how it thought about it, what were the things in which it was most willing to be amused, by what passions it was most deeply stirred, by what standard of conduct and of taste it was governed, and what types of characters it deemed worthy of its admiration.

Mizo Ltterature Begins with the History of the People

Mizo literature, we would therefore, claim did not begin with the day when the Duhlian dialect we now call the Mizo language was reduced into writing in the Roman script but in fact, started with the history of the Mizo people. Anything that, for good or evil, has entered into the making of Mizo society has also entered into the texture of Mizo literature – whether it was the travails of their migration, their fierce battles and ambuscades or the sweat and toils of raising their crops, their festivals and folk dances, all go to their general life, belief and aspirations which were profoundly imprinted in their literature. What we now call Mizo literature consists not only of the creation of literate writers or translations of the Bible and other Western literature but also of the collection of those folk songs and folk stories which go under the anonymous name of the people's creation.

Beginning of Written Literature

Thanks to the hard work of the pioneering missionaries, their earlier converts and to subsequent generations, no less, Mizo literature has now gained, within a span of less than a century, a status which is considered fit to be included in the curriculum right up to the university degree courses. The tales told by grandmas to the children, war chants and love songs provided the necessary ingredients to the literature. All these not only generate existence of Mizo literature but also inspire and promote its development.

Earlier Literature

The earliest Mizo songs are those which can be called nursery songs or cradle songs, most of which are apparently non-sensical repetitive mnemonic rhymes but on closer look they reveal the imprint of the simple milieu of yesteryears of Mizo society. Perhaps the earliest Mizo songs we know of are the following:

"Ur ur tak kai, ur ur tak kai

Hnung hnung tak kai, hnung hnung tak kai"

"Khawmhma pal a er an ti,

A duh duhin er rawh se"

Mothers carrying their babies on their backs would put their darlings to sleep with a lullaby like this:

"A khiah khian lungpui a lo lum dawn e,

Ka nauvi kha a del hang e, suan rawh u"

(High up from the hill is a rock rolling down

Remove my little darling, lest the rock will crush him)

"A khiah khian rammu an kal dial dial e,

Ka nauvi pa tel ve maw, ral that ve maw?"

(Yonder o'er there go the warriors does my darling's dad join there, did he too kill an enemy?).

Formulation of Mizo Script

Mizo language has no script of its own. Credit for reducing it into writing in the Roman script has been given to the pioneer missionaries. Their efforts were, however, preceded by commendable exercises of enterprising officers like Lt. Col. Thomas Herbert Lewin (affectionately called *Thangliana* by the Mizos – a corruption of Tom Lewin) who wrote Progressive Colloquial Exercise in the Lushai Dialect in 1874. Dr. Brojo Nath Saha, a civil medical officer of Chittagong, also published a book called Grammar of the Lushai

Language. Yet another British officer called C. A. Soppitt had compiled Rangkhol-Kuki-Lushai Grammar way back in 1885. All these efforts paved the way to the more systematic and organised efforts of the missionaries.

Original Works of Mizo Poets

Following publication of the Mizo Bible, a number of books on religious matters including translations of Christian hymns were published which were avidly learned by the new literates. Their thirst for more literature to read was nursed with the publication of the Mizo version of the Pilgrim's Progress (Kristiana Vanram Kawngzawh) translated by Rev Chuautera which remains one of the most readable books, apart from the Bible, in Mizo literature today. The contribution of the missionaries and the churches towards the development of Mizo literature cannot be overemphasised; they do not only provide the printed material but opened up their eyes to wider horizons to the world of literature and changed their outlook on life and life after death. Not being content with the translated hymns of the Western composers, many gifted Mizo poets came up with poems written in their own idioms and in tune with their own indigenous ethos and conception of Christianity. Such songs of worship are called *Lengkhawm Zai* and are sung in the traditional Mizo way with a drum. In style and profundity these songs are dearest to the hearts of the adult members of the society and are original contributions to the wealth of Mizo literature.

The codification of Mizo language and publication of Christian literature in that language not only paved the way for the development of Mizo literature but also resulted in the emergence of the Mizo language as the only language, the *lingua franca* as it were, for the entire Mizoram. Barring the Mara (Lakher) and the Chakmas, all the subtribes who used their own dialects switched over to the Mizo language. This has had a salutary effect on all aspects of development and the growth of literature.

Role of Journalism

Having been exposed to the world of literature, the need for publication of things mundane and secular was soon felt. The first Mizo journal of a sort called Mizo Chanchin Laishuih was published in 1898; it was a cyclostyled tabloid. This publication did not last long. A monthly journal published by the Superintendent of Lushai Hills and printed in Sylhet came out in 1902. This monthly journal called Mizo leh Vai Chanchin was in circulation for several years. Contributors to this journal were the first educated Mizos who were held in high esteem by the people.

Their writings on human interest did a yeoman's service to the people. Then came the Kristian Tlangau, a monthly mouthpiece of the Presbyterian Mission from Aizawl in 1911. The Baptist Mission of Lunglei also came up with a monthly magazine called *Tlawmngaihna* (1934). This magazine, though with an emphasis was more interested in highlighting whatever is good and worthwhile in Mizo tradition like Tlawngaihna and so on. Another monthly Kohhran Beng from the Baptist Church of Serkawn came out in 1947. This again is the mouthpiece of the church and is still in circulation. But the journal which took up the development of Mizo literature as its main object was the monthly mouthpiece of the Lushai Students' Association (LSA) which came out in 1935 till it ceased publication in 1980. The LSA was later changed to MZP – Mizo Zirlai Pawl. This magazine published, among other things, essays and other writings of purely literary nature. Many other newspapers and journals have since come up but the ones which have contributed most to the development of Mizo literature are those that have been enumerated. At the moment there is only one literary magazine called *Thu leh Hla*, a mouthpiece of the Mizo Academy of Letters.

Contemporary Literature

A study of contemporary Mizo literature reveals considerable maturity and depth from the 30s onwards with poets and writers producing works of lasting value on secular subjects. From Serkawn High School under the leadership of the headmaster Lalmama and Rev H. W. Carter a number of poems called *Sekawn Concert Hla* have been produced. These poems eulogise the legendary heroes of the Mizos and praise traditional values in Mizo society, the beauty of nature and other human interests. This type of poetry called *Hla Lenglawng* (Community songs) set a new chapter in Mizo literature. In the traditional Mizo style the creations of Awithangpa, Bualkunga and a host of others blossomed forth. In originality and content, the works of Kamlala stood out prominently. World War II and its aftermath saw the blossoming of many beautiful lovesongs from the pen of C. Lalzova, Vankhama, Lalzuia and others. The devastation caused by World War II and the political awakening which followed also brought about the spirit of nationalism and the need for moral development all over the world which also inspired writers like Rokunga and others to produce poems of inspiration and thought-provoking nature. The essays and writings of Biakliana, K. C. Lalvunga, C. Thuamluaia, J. Malsawma and others set the pace for literary prose writings.

No sufficient justice can be done to describe the spurt of literature coming up in recent years without a full-length study. Suffice it to say that the literary award given to Rev Liangkhaia by the Mizo Academy of Letters in 1978, and the Padma Shree award to James Dokhuma for literature in 1985 by the President of India, confirm that given the opportunity and necessary patronage, the door is open now for the massive development of Mizo literature.

8

Economy

- -

Mizoram during remote times was an isolated mountain tract. We have very little information with regard to the economic conditions during that time.

We find, therefore, that the economic necessities guide and pervade the human actions to meet the wants of man. Basically the wants of man were for food, clothing and shelter. Man initially used his physical strength to make exploits upon nature to provide him the basic needs. His wants at first were limited. Subsequently the economic necessities became broadly categorised into the bare necessities, the conventional and other supplementary necessities. The wants now are also confined to the very high cost of living which we call luxuries.

Economic Development

It seems that the political parties had not given sufficient time to look into this problem as they gave much time to the problem of party adjustment. Then again, a great deal of attention was given to the definition and adjustment of the powers between the two District Councils and the State Government. It would be difficult in the nick of time to revolutionise the entire economic system. By then it appears that Agriculture, Community Development, Public works, Transport and other Departments were not giving their dividends. The famine that broke out in 1957 and continued unabated till 1960 was a culmination of this event. The real infrastructure to economic development was neglected.

We find that the State Governments had borne the bulk of the expenditures of District Councils but these Councils had not laid down any infrastructure worth examining for development. Apart from the regular provision of budget laid on regular basis, and earmarked annually, the situation in 1958 demanded that the amount of Rs. 80,000 which was required for "payment of a grant-in-aid to the Mizo District Council to enable it to tide over its financial difficulties in running its day-to-day administration. This being an unforeseen expenditure, funds could not be provided in the current Year's budget. So necessary advance was obtained from the Contingencies Fund. Hence, the demand to regularise the same".

The economic infrastructure as would be suitable with the post-independence situation had emerged just as slightly on the feeble lines. Then came the period of insurrection based on the political grounds. The heavy system of village re-grouping which, brought about the near collapse of agriculture and the village industries, intervened. Good sense also prevailed from experience. Therefore, Road construction was actively undertaken.

These road projects had considerably involved themselves into the hazards of road alignment, survey, gravelling and black topping in so great an undulating terrain. The resources in adequate number, it was found, needed now the most scientific and objective analysis and tapping for building the industries. The task to provide industries then being reviewed for growth had also its effect into the system of analysis.

As regards the importance of village industries, the matter can be reiterated as follows:

"On the infrastructural base, it is known that the art of weaving and blacksmithy had existed as the most original among the village industries. But for a long time, they have not been practised on an active scale. Some of the arts are economically viable especially weaving and dyeing, ornamental arts and handicrafts. Weaving and dyeing in fact among the tribes of the throw different reflections. Most of the tribal woven clothes have shown a high standard of craftmanship and are renowned for both quality and endurability.

Some tribes use cotton yarn more while others, have errand and a few have been acquainted with silk. They use their traditional designs of spindles and weaving looms. With a handful of equipment, they produce different designs of shawls, scarves, kilt, waistcloths, girdles, stockings, and others; weaving is still a prolific village industry in Nagaland, Manipur, Tripura and Mizoram. They use different styles of colour combination.

They have traditional system of dyeing employing different plants, barks of wood and grass. Some use indigo either grown or collected from the jungle. They apply certain ornamental patterns, oval, horizontal, zigzag and many other figurines over their apparels which all reflect artistic skills of a high order.

The colour patterns are also different and quite varied in the reflection of shades and ornamental designs. The ceremonial dresses are even more artistic reflecting a greater degree of artistic skill and attainment. They have become highly valued among the foreign visitors and have found good markets. The tribes have now also been engaged in producing modern patterns such as neckties, bags, mufflers, bed covers, carpets and many other valuable designs". A lot is now done to study these traditional techniques into greater details.

McCall gave considerable boost to these undertakings in 1940 in which a craft-based centre was started at Aijal which introduced a system of wickerwork and basketry including mats, bags and many other articles. The centre was equipped with both the weaving and crafts sectors. However, reinstating weaving among the Mizos for a time being was rendered difficult. This was because the art of weaving in view of the growing popularity of Western dress models was almost forgotten. Now it is again planned to introduce the traditional and improved pattern of weaving.

Growth of Industry

Industrial growth at the grass-root level in the hills of the northeast can be based on the congenial ecological, climatic and geographical factors. The summers being cool and pleasant can be very helpful for larger undertakings but in the plains we see that with the availability of labour, in spite of the hot weather, the pace of production is considerably high. This marks the difference between the hills and plains with regard to industrial undertakings and production.

There is a great need now that more and more incentives be given to the tribal youths in the field of industrial organisations, undertakings — public, privately owned and aided and individual entrepreneurships. Creating the essential climate and temperament in the mentality and habits seems so much essential; training in trades, callings, practices and professions is indispensable to the present generation. The matter of imparting a suitable vocational or technical education and conservation of some selected training institutes to production centres require a review into these aspects.

It seems that the constituted authorities have envisaged the feasibility of introducing in Mizoram better vocational trades in spinning and weaving, cane hats and cane baskets, bamboo chairs, tables, teapots, racks, safes, etc., bamboo chicks and screen cages, umbrella handles and knitting and tailoring.

A few small scale industries which are now emerging on under incentives already laid, can have scope for further growth. The problems viewed on the light of Mizoram has have also been discussed as follows:

> The unavailability of yarn at the subsidised or cheaper cost has hindered the progress of weaving in the state. Cotton ginning and spinning by hand is a slow, laborious process. Traditional weaving can hardly compete with mill-made fabrics obtained at cheaper prices. The use of fly-shuttles can cater to a larger production under a good managerial supervision. In respect to oil extraction from the oilseeds and other crops, this technique requires the service of the oil extracting machines. The use of machines for crushing gur

in view of the availability of sugarcane under cultivation, will yield better results if cane crushing is introduced on a larger scale.

The new trends have slightly been increased in tailoring, bakery and printing. The number of workshops and carriages, watch repairing, knitting and embroidery units is increasing. The aluminium industry which require considerably welding of the old parts and modelling them, electrical services and leather work in shoe making have emerged. There is demand for dyes by weavers and saw-mills as well. The Industrial Training Institute so far has conducted training only for fitters, welders, motor mechanics and electricians. In the earlier years, a paper pulp industry was proposed to be installed and it appeared that the availability of bamboo in plenty for feeding the said mill would not be a problem to the constant functioning of the mill.

As regards animal husbandry and veterinary, 'The Government of Mizoram has commissioned three cattle-breeding farms for improved breed of cows. Government-run mill produces a sizeable quantity of mixed food for the dairy farmers. The central Hatchery cum poultry farm — also started functioning with 5,000 chicks imported from Bhubaneswar. Northeastern Council has also sponsored a Regional pig breedings farm to house 100 cows.

However, greater and more efforts and attentions must be paid in this direction". Upgradation of livestock, however, was started many decades ago and considerable attention to developing piggery and poultry through farming and improving the system of traditional care and upbringing was given both at the Departmental and village level.

Development of Community

Community development has its own etymology. It is one of the organs aimed at elevating the standard of living in towns and villages especially among the backward community. The works to evolve developmental progress is distributed through the blocks, each block following a hierachical order in staffing and having an allocation of villages with a total population brought under its jurisdiction. Uptil 1958 or so only two blocks were started in Mizoram, one of them was Kolasib NES Block and the other was Lungleh MPDC Block.

The sixties saw an increase in the number of Blocks which started to grow. The blocks have grown steadily and have been converted into Tribal Development Blocks. The blocks from the beginning and still more, during the regrouping of villages were confronted with difficulties of identifying and updating programmes especially, those relating to improving the living conditions of the people. During the insurrections most of them were closed. They were again reconstituted after the Government of Mizoram was formed.

The programmes followed, cover the different aspects of development with a view to improve the overall agricultural, educational, sanitary, health and road conditions and among others, to improve the craft and village industries and disseminate, among villagers, the mass communication services. In other States, some village access roads initially or temporarily were built by the Community Development Blocks. Some blocks elsewhere involved a considerable portion of the villagers in actual road constructions, road cutting, surfacing and gravelling on voluntary or non-voluntary basis. Some of the roads in the state appear to have been raised on self-help basis by the villagers.

The situation in Mizoram evidently has impelled the intensification of road construction to serve the delicately strategic purposes and evidently to maintain the feasible transport services. Communications and transport would assist quicker mobilisation. The better means of communication would also help to contain the insurrectionary and anti-state movements more conveniently.

The Public Works Department has catered to these needs. Road building indeed was confronted with many hazards in the steepish mountain. The longest roads maintained by the Department now are Aizawl-Thanazawla Lunglei road (171 km), Saiha-Saita Tapung road (120 km), Vanlaiphai Hnahthial road (90 km), Kolasib Zumuang-Kahnmun road (95 km), Khawsala-Lungdar road (71 km) and others. There are other shorter roads which have considerable importance in connecting other villages.

There are small approach and station roads. The assistance to road construction is considerably given by Border Road Task Force. Some of the major roads build under this system are Aizawl-Lunglei road (232 km), Aizawl-Silchar road (177 km), Lawngtlai-Ditlang-Chawngte road (203 km), Phaileng-Marpara Demagiri road (167 km), Aizawl-Selling-Tipaimukh road (139 km), S. Aizawl-Tuipuibari road (165 km), Lunglei-Tuipui road (156 km) and others. All the good roads having been completed were put to bus services. It appears that the success of agricultural and industrial improvement depends upon the coordination with the development measures such as the feasibility of transport services, health services, water supply, soil conservation and others.

The agricultural conditions, however, have not improved considerably. The event that occurred from 1966 onward produced some difficulties to conserving jhum more consistently and the execution of the planned proposals for improved fanning including the experimentation of certain suitable crops. The latest development seems to have been the restriction of agricultural improvement only to the opening of new agricultural farms are updating the necessary improvement techniques in them. Distribution of seeds and fertilizers and improvement of irrigation facilities and other measures have been taken on some scale.

At the other levels, power transmission and conservation of hydel projects are very essential for providing power to the industries. In fact, factories, workshops and laboratories function effectively and continuously with power facilities. Hydel projects can be successfully located in the hill terrain by damming rivers at the convenient sites. The installation of power transmissions already equipped at the headquarters and important stations would help to accelerate factory management and functioning to a greater extent. Ginger and fruit processing can adequately be met with the power driven apparatus. Also the workshops and other mills now particularly at Aizawl, are managing to provide sales and services with the help of power.

Moreover, industrial training and production for the various sectors have been sought to be successfully catered to by the Industries Corporation of the state as well as by the various Industrial estates already opened at a few centres. Assistance to entrepreneurs and unemployed educated youths has been extended under the usually prescribed Government and Banking schemes.

There has been now the concentrated efforts from many sides to reach some targeted goal of industrialisation. On the other hand, it has been found that small scale or medium industries suit very much for adoption in the hill areas of the northeast. As a result within a few years, rooms have been opened for more and more local participation in the industrial management and production. The parity of the village level development can also be examined in the present perspectives and in accordance with present progress made in the towns. The situation indeed has constantly helped to raise the standard of living among the elute.

Business and Trade

Evidently there were trade links connecting Mizoram with the rest of the region extending to Cachar, Chittagong, Tripura and the Arakans where a regular or seasonal trading must have persisted. Trade considerably suffered from the irregular communications which the country possessed. Most of the villages once were regarded as self sufficient in cereals. The volume of trade must have increased occasionally at the time of adversity than prosperity.

It is known that most of the villages provided their own clothings and dress materials. Most of the crafts, articles, implements and weapons were made by the village artisans, craftmen and blacksmiths. However, for a few metallic ingredients owing to the unavailability of the local iron pyrites, villages were made dependent for the supply of these metallic and iron components from outside where bulk of these materials were welded and moulded into the shape of their implements or weapons at their forges.

Bulk of the livestock in these circumstances could have been indigenous and at sacrifices and feastings, best of animals at their stock were sacrificed. However, the herd of cattle, goats and poultry were also brought from outside when, some times the country was running short of them. The community was no longer agrarian. They had diverted themselves to new trades and occupations. The Mizos were one of the trading communities. However, during the anterior times, barter dominated the economy. Trade was conducted among the Mizos friendly to each other and with the other communities outside the present State. Most of the chiefs were impelled patronise trade.

In course of time, trade was confined not only to the neighbouring hills and plains; trade in the passage of time had been extended to the further confines of Bengal. The tribes kept the practice to repair and renovate certain ancient roads when they were seized with the problem of soil erosion. Some of the roads served for the *ad hoc* purposes but they provided some means of intercourse with the outlying plain.

Trade was necessitated also with a view to solve the problem of food scarcity and ensuring arrival of supply from other places to those villages hard hit and which survived on the verge of a great famine. For these reasons, the opening of trade passages was resorted to. The system of production and distribution of goods was maintained with a view to further the trade pattern and this practice was kept among all the people of the globe.

With regard to the present times, we reiterate our view in the following:

> All the economic sectors — agriculture, forest, mining and mineral resources, industries and village enterprises in manufacturing and production have, decidedly their vital role in accelerating the economic progress. The system of coordination for effectual transport and transaction is indispensable to the factors of economy.

Referring to the trade pattern in the past, Lalrimawia in an article entitled Economy of Mizoram (1840 to 1947) states that:

> "Since the Anglo-Burmese war (182426), the Mizos got accustomed to the use of artillery; gun acid guts powder became a passion to the chiefs. They were in possession of flintlock guns mostly old tow muskets which were imported from Burma and Chittagong. Large hunting parties frequently made expeditions into the uninhabited parts in search of elephants, wild mithun or bison, bear, deer, tiger and other animals.
>
> In the economy of the Mizo people, hunting occupied an important position in the past. From time to time, hunting parties were arranged to procure meat. Elephant tusks were the medium of exchange; the bones and the skins were the valuable articles of commerce. Good markets were always available in the neighbouring plains".

During the first half of the last century, trading was also restrained by many factors. The situation improved when the more formidable contacts of the administration were made with the Lushai chiefs who agreed to promote trade and commerce. Trade stations consequently were opened which had considerably helped the mobilisation and exchanges of goods.

Trading in rubber conserved from the huge of reserve trees lying in the outlying hills and plains has also been referred to. Ivory used as a valuable ornament in the hills ranked next as the item of export. "In the Mizo economy ivory was the medium of exchange; the bones and hides of the elephant were valuable articles of commerce. The Mizos exported elephant hides to the Mughal traders of Bengal. Elephant hides were abundantly used in the Mughal armoury, and war shields made by the Sylhet artisans were in great demand in the Mughal army.

The Rajas of Manipur, Tripura and Cachar were also dependent on the Mizos for the supply of elephant hides, bones and tusks. It had a very good market in the neighbouring plains. The Mughal rulers of Delhi and the aristocracy of Bengal purchased ivory for the craftsmen of Sylhet who were dependent upon the Mizos for the raw materials. The Mizo chiefs supplied ivory to the traders of Sylhet, Cachar and Chittagong even during the British rule and used to pay the nazarana to the Sirkar in terms of elephant tusks. This kind of nazarana was given to Major Stewart, the Deputy of Cachar and Captain Verner, the Superintendent of Cachar by the Mizos.

The other intervening tribes appear to have performed considerable work in bartering or who actually supplied the hill produce to merchants in the plain; in fact roads were made more accessible to tribes who occupied the lower spurs of the hills. The bartering of goods had continued for ages. Actually the Mizos in Manipur, Cachar and Mizoram performed petty trades.

They came down to the weekly hats in the outlying hills and plains and bartered their crops (chillies, capsicum, ginger, cotton), hides (elephant, bison, buffalo), threads and other things which they exchanged with salt, dried fish, iron and metallic components and other things. There were considerable exchanges of bamboo, timber and certain fine tree species with the other necessities. They required some of these things for making arms, ammunitions and explosives. Some of the goods most probably must have been boarded on ships and canoes over the navigable rivers in the foothills.

The real media of currency for higher transactions were elephant tusks, horns, gongs and the mithuns. They used different baskets, trays, mugs and cups for measuring grains and vegetables especially when they were referred to as the loans in kind.

Barter provided means to procure their immediate necessities. Barter had some of its limitations also. It would entail longer time to affect an exchange in terms which would be reciprocally acceptable to parties engaged in a transaction. Therefore, it did not command a stability in the purchasing power like money. But the tribes were accustomed to practising it.

Scenario in British Period

The British administrators found that the greatest hazards with regard to promoting administration and trade was the want of good roads. On the whole till then, the wants of the people were few; not to speak of the lower hills, trade on the highlands had just started to develop rudimentally. Many persons on the hills persisted on the bare necessities. The lack of good communication was pointed out at that time and lack of good roads still persists today. Active road construction hence had started during the early British period.

The situation during the early British regime can better be reiterated below:

> The trade infrastructure had not then grown sufficiently; trade still maintained its feeble links. Therefore, the village economy with its system of self dependence still maintained itself. Slash and burn in particular in Lushai Hills did not help to promote a system of permanent cultivation which discouraged any effort at the accumulation of wealth. The concept of urbanisation had not properly developed. Some may think that cash has not made any considerable impact in the society. The view is tenable also for modification.

The value of money since the inception of administration had gained momentum. First and foremost, payment of wages to the local workmen on roads and buildings was in cash. The beginning of Lungleh and Aijal were the auspicious events. Activities were resumed in building and constructions when the residential and office quarters were raised. Supplies of goods and stationaries were made with the outside agencies. Circumstances necessitated the coming in of their instruments and equipment. There were other transactions of business made and payment against services was in cash. The essence of the district budgets and services of District Treasuries were maintained. The purchasing power of money, beyond doubt, was recognised. But perhaps, the trade structures, had not developed significantly.

The First World War caused the new transitional trends. Hundreds and hundreds of people were enlisted to services in the army, the labour corps and the other occupations. Several persons also served the army on a regular cadre. The new occupational trends had emerged. Many well-to-do parents could afford to provide higher education to their children and sent them to read in High schools and colleges.

The Mizos, out of their earnings and resources, donated generously to the Church funds. The Second World War boosted economic restructuring to a greater extent. These events helped considerably to improve the standard of living. Housings with better facilities had come to stay.

Yet a lot, the then administrators thought, was yet to be done to determine the new trade assets and liabilities. The deteriorating trade conditions had received the frequent attention of the district administration. Developmental planning, coordination and execution would have been most indispensable in context of a changing situation.

The advantages and disadvantages of money consciousness among the tribes can also be better appreciated and understood in the present context.

The movement of the other Mizos and their resettlement at Cachar Hills, Barak valley, Manipur directly and indirectly fostered a sense of economic adjustment during their recent move. But the question of restructuring trade among the tribes, seems also to depend on the suitable grounds which the concept of nationalism can provide some guidance for enlivening its cause.

It appears that the circulation of the cash when the administration was settled, killed the trade incentives of the people. Trade and supply were availed in the hills partly through the service of the other trading communities. Economic stagnation also resulted from the dwindling of many village industries. Consequently there was more stagnation and this situation applied to all the tribes inside and outside Mizoram.

Post-independence Scenario

Mr. McCall one of the last English Superintendents just on the eve of Independence, had sought to lay down a suitable policy statement which should take note of the principles and objectives enunciated vaguely below:

- Medical, Industrial, educational, agricultural and all development measures should be specifically designed and directed to ensure that the people would be able to absorb them as part and parcel of their own cultural system.

- All departmental budgets should be submitted through the District Officer as coordinating centre of all efforts.

- Educational curriculum should be so designed as to ensure that education reached the masses and would suit the genius of the people.

- Adequate public health measures should be taken.

The Independence of India hit hard upon the people. It had affected the prices adversely. The prices of the commodities which the Lushais obtained from the Chittagong side like sugar, molasses, salt, dry fish, coconut oil and kerosene hot up their prices to six or ten times whereas the prices of the commodities which they had for exporting cotton, oil seeds and oranges fell appreciably. This stable trade structuring was rapidly disintegrating itself.

On the review by the authorities, it was now generally accepted that the partition of India had caused several damages to trade and commerce. It had led to price fluctuations and had caused so great the inflation to the prices of commodities which the tribesmen used to draw from Chittagong and near about places in East Pakistan. All along the western and southern border.

On their part, the prices in respect of the hill exports were considerably squeezed out. The balance of payment was adversely affected. The situation now had necessitated the strengthening of transport and supply mobilisation to procure for the people living in the southern interior places, their vital necessities for them to live on. Most of the' proposals were worked out on paper; the matter to intensifying the agricultural produce was reviewed; the cooperatives which earlier were not successful in the hills were sought to be revitalised with a view to reach rapid relief to the hard-hit section of the community.

Other industries were proposed to be started; the upgradation of the livestock in the villages was recommended. However, their effectual implementation had to be successfully coped with by a properly constituted and dedicated machinery to give effect to all these schemes and projects. There had been other constraints also which taxed themselves to carrying the policies and programmes so stated.

The frequent outbreaks of the famines at the post-independence years had indeed highlighted the prior need to provide the rapid relief measures to the suffering people and, at the same time, to prepare the better schemes of economic reconstruction. The implementation again was constrained by the heavy inflationary trends in respect of the currency; there were other technical difficulties to working them out; the problem of frequently rehabilitating the worst-hit people had also featured itself.

Practical Difficulties

The problem of the District was reviewed from the other angles. Pu. Ch. Saprawnga, the first MLAs during his speech at the floor of the Assembly which had assembled in 1952 after the first general elections held under the Constitution of India addressed on the matter thus:

> "As I have said, the amount of money that has to go to Hill Districts appear to be quite a big sum. But on closer examination, one wonders if any real progress and achievement worth the name would ever be made in the coming year. The reasons are: In the first place, a very high percentage of money has to go to meet the expenses on the existing institutions which are to be reinforced with more staff here and there. This simply implies that the same old things are being repeated from year to year. Secondly, the proposed new schemes appeared to have missed the main key of development wide off the mark. The present suffering of the hill-men and the unsatisfactory state of affairs are mainly due to the absence of road communications. The Partition of India has placed some of these Hill areas in a position still worse than before".

He further stressed the need in his speech to concentrate efforts on road development as no real improvement including the opening of schools and dispensaries without the road communications could be possible. It was feared also that officials in the interior villages would not do justice to their work. Moreover, the Partition of India "has resulted in economic dislocation in some of these hill areas. Local produce have never been able to find favourable and ready market at the same time those articles brought from outside are very costly. The cost of these materials is rising higher and higher. So sooner or later the economic condition of the people will be going from bad to worse. So the only remedy is by opening roads".

There had been no considerable improvement in the succeeding years. The problem of food scarcity irrespective of some of the schemes which had been prepared, was acute in 1956-57. Such food shortages were never experienced earlier. Probably the warning to this calamity was not paid heed of in the previous year. On the problem of transport and supply, Mr. A. Thanglura, MLA spoke in the legislative Assembly on the 1st July 1957 as follows:

> "I have already stated that the people of Lushai Hills indeed depend entirely on the villages. When there is heavy rain in Lushai Hills, the communications become the most critical problem for the people. Not to speak of the absence of good inter-village communication, the condition of the so-called Aijal-Silchar road, which is the main line of communication for the people of Lushai Hills is not good enough. This has deteriorated the position of the Lushai people who are already hard hit. But, whereas if there is good communication, the condition of the people with regard to rice, etc., could be ameliorated, even when there is scarcity of rice. But for the people living in the Lushai Hills were the cardinal problem is evidently bad communication, their position is very bad."

His speech was related to the problem of food scarcity which Mizoram then faced. The supply situation had deteriorated owing to the bad means of communication. The state of agriculture also deteriorated as "the people in Lushai Hills depend entirely on jhum cultivation which is very unreliable method of cultivation. This system is .... detrimental to the land". He expressed that Aijal, the headquarters of the Mizo District, having a population of 8,000, entirely depend for the subsistence on the Villagers who are the main cultivators. "But strangely enough, though the Lushai Hills is the biggest District in Assam in area, there is not even a single fair price shop at Aijal which is the headquarters....".

"I am happy to know that the facilities have been extended to the people of South Lushai Hills by means of airdropping. Although quite a big amount of rice and other foodstuffs have been dropped there and the position of the people also to a great extent has been ameliorated yet there are people living in the border close to the Chin Hills who have been still confronted with the scarcity of salt and other necessary commodities, not to speak of rice ...... The Lushai Hills is sandwiched by Burma and Pakistan.

It appears that with regard to other problems, not only food scarcity but also the feasibility to improve the water supply, very little was done to alleviate their conditions. The progress of road construction evidently was slow. Initially very little planning was done to improve farming and industry. In this connection, difficulties to start forest-based industries were substantiated in the Assembly report quoted below:

"So far as the bamboo in the Mizo hills is concerned, it is available in large quantities, but at present it is being wasted. The difficulty in setting a paper pulp factory is due to the non-availability of coal in that area. We have not been able to locate coal in Cachar area and therefore it is necessary to convey coal from the Assam Valley which mean increased cost. Therefore, the Private Sector finds it difficult now to utilise Mizo Hills bamboo in Cachar area until the question of the bamboo in North Cachar Hills which is available in Lumding area is settled".

Agriculture

In 1900-01, 93 per cent of the population depended directly or indirectly on agriculture. The sweeping social transformation which has stayed and affected society during the last 100 years must have opened the society to many new trades, callings and professions. Besides there are other several developmental activities being undertake the District and State level. The state of agriculture has been tremendously affected and disturbed by the insurgencies which had taken place frequently. In spite of these trends, agriculture is still the main stay of the people where the largest proportion of population are engaged in it.

A cultivation by slash and burn is prevalent in all the Districts of the State as it is among the other Hill tribes of the region. This traditional system in spite of its disadvantage, still holds itself in the rugged mountain terrain the land. This is because the physical conditions in soil, climate and other topographical conditions are best suited it and an alternative has not yet been devised and introduced even at the cost of a scientific system of farming that has progressed on elsewhere. In all the high and the lower hills, jhumming is still the essential system of farming and the traditional system as such, subject to some modifications, will be unchangeable.

The plain tract of the state, however, provides room for a settled agriculture with its system of mixed cropping pattern in which paddy is the most important item. The low level lands although meagre and lying on the fringe of the state have a different pattern in which crops, fruits and vegetables continue to be cultivated and harvested in the same plot of land; the tradition that continues for ages. The agricultural experiments in horticulture and other farmings, however, have given their mixed results. The problem of agricultural pests, scarcity of water and diminishing returns of the soil recurs from time to time. There have been occasional reports of crop failures as well and the Department have constantly been devising important schemes to solve these difficulties. The occasional outbreaks of famines caused by rat infestions pose other difficulties.

Jhum Cultivation

Jhumming entails clearance of forests and exposure of felled trees along with the other plants. The debris resulting from the felling of trees remains to be sun-dried and exposed.

When they have dried out, they are burnt; the ashes being conserved as fertilizer to feed the soil with a compost manure of this type. The bamboo groves are supposed to yield better results than soils which retain the other types of vegetation. Grassy lands are not very much suitable in this process of cultivation.

The seeds count considerably and usually are admixed in the system of dibbling. The cultivators make light or heavy scratches on the surface of the soil, making small appertures for dibbling the seeds or seedlings. The rotation of jhum cycle works out from four to six years in case of bamboo groves but the wild land stays longer uncultivated, allowing a cycle to work which is prolonged form eight to ten years. After a couple of years' cultivation at the most, these arable lands are left fallow until the new shrubs or plants have grown and those lands, at the close of a cycle, are again put to cultivation. Terracing system of paddy cultivation as that existing in the Angami Naga Hills has now and then been tried but as regards their results, we do not know much.

The practice of shifting the villages in the process of cultivation is adhered to. At the first decade of our century it was marked: "According to the last census, the total number of villages in the country was 228 with 15,668 houses. The villages are frequently moved. Having cultivated the land in one neighbourhood for five or six years, the entire village removes to another locality".

Usually Jhum allows crops such as maize, millet, vegetables, cotton and paddy as the principal items among them. The cultivators adopting this system have developed the migratory habits since the earlier times. Yet it serves well for the purpose.

Jhumming where practices entail different stages of agricultural undertaking where felling of timber, as also sunning and burning of debris are the preliminary method involved in the arduous undertaking. Light scratching or digging occurs in the process of soil levelling or surface manuring. Weeding operations are later the necessary stages of undertaking. It is not known apart from the traditional crops what are the other crops which can stay and make good yields in jhurn soils in a cropping pattern in Mizoram and the rest of the Northeastern Region.

Cash Crops

The paucity of cash crops except a few has been pointed out. However, many villages without mentioning the occasional crop failure were till 50 years ago the self supporting units; the increase of population of course had considerably worked out to dwindle the rate of production; therefore, some village had to depend on the outside supplies with regard to the crops and even vegetables.

Ginger and chillies are the common cash crops grown till today.

Rubber Production

Among the other items, rubber exploited against its huge reserve of rubber trees was transacted on small scale even with the neighbouring plains tract, the Mizos taking it to the trade marts which sold well and which brought them a good income. During the great famines which swept Mizoram at the closing decade of the last century, several local inhabitants collected rubber and sold all the available rubber on their verge of starvation owing to the adverse results of crop failure recorded from about 1882. This led to the disappearance of the huge rubber trees and little has been done to introduce rubber plantation on a regular scale. The Mizos most of them are smokers of tobacco in which the pressed and dried leaves are utilised using their indigenous pipe having a copper clip on its edge. It is known that tobacco cultivation was practised in the last century and it is now one of the cash crops.

Cotton Production

As regards cotton, it is planted on home scale. Cotton plantation flourishes in some parts of the valleys and also jhum lands. It is known that cotton ginned, gently surfaced and polished after processing, fetches better prices than raw or just the plucked out cotton. Cotton is used for weaving clothes and guilts. There are two staples which may be considered as superior and inferior. Previously weavers catered to the domestic needs in respect of spinning and weaving their dress materials but now probably, the change in fashions, has led to the dwindling of this art at many places. Among the crops, cotton and rubber as a forest plantation have great scope to flourish. They may have scope to thrive under the silvicultural operation.

In 1976, at a Seminar held in Shillong under the auspicious of the Department of Economics and Centre for Continuing Education, NEHU, B. S. Kailiana opined that till then, "Out of 21 lakh hectares of land, so far only 67,000 hectares of land representing 32 per cent of the total area is under cultivation. It is estimated that more than 80 per cent of the land is under "jhum cultivation and only about 0.47 per cent of it is under permanent cultivation for more than 5,000 families".

The actual figures are essential to our understanding with regard to the proportion of lands then assigned to the temporary and permanent cultivation. Jhumming has its deleterious affect upon the soil, it replenishes the forest wealth immensely annually and poses the problem of frequent erosions. Till 1976 only about 2,500 hectares of land is covered under paddy but only 0.35 per cent of it is under the operation of fertilizer.

The outbreak of famines is anticipated once in 48 years and may be reduced to 18 years and the menace of rat infestation occurring has caused the problem of crop failure. The insurgencies which have occurred from time to time have brought about several adverse consequences upon the state of agriculture. It is known that the regrouping of villages during the previous decades has its adverse effect upon agriculture.

Paddy Cultivation

The paddy production has resulted in continual decreases. In 1976, the whole population stood in need of 6,78,800 quintals of rice but there was a shortfall to half of that quantity working to 3,72,510 quintals. Supplies from outside as such became inevitable. The administration, therefore, would have faced frequent problems in providing reliefs to the worst affected population, financially, physically or otherwise.

The continual decreases in production in the entire region caused difficulties to the problem of food shortages; the difficulties are also due to an increasing rate in the population structure. The difficulties have also been caused due to the institutionalisation of brewery based on rice and perhaps other minor crops, the habits which persist in Hill States such as Nagaland, Meghalaya and Mizoram. Moreover, drinks are considered a necessity at rituals and festivals.

The habits effectively curtailed would help to strengthen the cause of a staple than a supplementary one. Agriculture if it would not persist in multifarious and organised mixed cropping, would result in weakening the economy of the several States as well as Mizoram.

The opinion has been levelled that agriculture being one of the strongest backbones of economy especially in the backward and isolated places, an intensive planning and expeditious disposal for innovation in respect of horticulture, silviculture and sericulture farmings is so indispensible. Use of fertilizers and of natural, artificial, and power system of irrigation would be most indispensible.

Fruits and Vegetables

Among the items of agricultural produce, the cultivation of winged beans (posphocarpus petragenolobus) has persisted but is on small scale. In respect of ginger, it is known that Meghalaya and Mizoram take the lead in its production. A better marketing is feasible for fetching better incomes to the growers. We see too in some markets in the plain, the Mizos come there to sell chillies and ginger and other crops Betelvine plantations may also have scope to thrive in the outlying area in the state. Fruit cultivation including pineapple can be successfully tried in suitable soils and possibly temperate fruits on the hills. Limes and lemons also can be grown in the plain.

The yield per hectare depends on soil and climatic conditions. The strength of the economy, therefore depends mostly on the regulating factors for exporting the items from the state. These factors give us to understand that the system of food gathering of tubers, roots and plants as it is in the other hill areas may not have been viable as most of them have replenished due to the wanton destruction of the vast forest wealth.

Some of the indigenous vegetables grown on Jhums and homestead gardens are pumpkins, cucumber, melon, capsicum and perhaps arum and other eguminous plants. Modern vegetable plantation including cabbages, turnips, cauliflower, carrots and others are more limited., This may be due to the unsuitability of the soil. The other crops grown in rotation depending upon the altitude of hills are maize and millets and some indigenous beans.

Most of the areas in the plain belt of the region as a whole can be conserved for an improved method of farming. As most of the arable land has been squeezed out, it was recorded in 1987 till then that only a meagre section of the total area of the state was under cultivation. This included also the area covered under the cultivation of pulses, banana and other crops. Again against the total area under cultivation.

Only about 7 per cent of the total arable land was covered under the irrigation scheme.' It is known that the paucity of irrigation facilities counts a lot as a great drawback to agricultural prosperity. Therefore, conserving water storage at river drainages and installing reservoirs at the side of good streams can be feasible for the regular distribution of water on the locations nearest to the villages.

Intensive Agriculture

Agricultural improvement would have made considerably headway owing to the intensification of farming especially in turmeric, groundnuts, and cardamom. Wet-rice cultivation has shown increases already through schemes mainly of subsidised assistance. It is practised in the open valleys and places reserved specifically under the Departments and through encouragement in the private sectors as well. There have been more and more of functional uses of fertilizers, pesticides, implements and consequently the improved techniques have been more and more accepted.

Moreover under the soil conservation scheme, afforestation has received better care; soil conservation has been greatly utilised by introducing cash crop farming at the apportioned area. As a result irrigation facilities by flow irrigation and rive lift irrigation have further been extended. These measures to curtail agricultural wastages and making use of a utilitarian system are relevant to the present development. Some marketable surplus so far the Aizawl district is concerned, are oranges, banana, ginger and cotton. In other respects, the state is totally dependent on supplies from outside.

Under IRDP, Annual Plan, we find that in the primary sector, assistance is given to farming in ginger, sugarcane, banana, betel leaf, potato, chilli and few other crops. Wet rice cultivation and horticulture have also been encouraged.

Animal Wealth

As regards, livestock, mithuns were usually the items of domesticated animals, however, they were kept mostly in a semi-wild condition. They were highly valued. In course of time, they became fewer. Dogs are the great assets; they are trained for hunting or reconnoitring big games, they are trained also to averting other animals from injuring the crops in the field.

Earlier they provided means for sacrifices and propitiations to the spirits. Pigs rank next as the favourite animals, treated some times as pets. The goats reared are the long haired hill breed. Poultry are also domesticated. They are secured at night at baskets with improvise cushions suspended from the walls in the outer porch of the house.

The Mizos are good hunters. They use several means of a stratagem to waylay and trap the robust brute such as tiger, leopard, elephant, beer and smaller tribes such as wolf, ape, monkey and others. They lay ambushes also upon the roaring leopards and monstrous elephants by using devices, encircling and charging them singly or in a herd by hitting with spears or shooting at with their muskets. In the past they hunted snakes and serpents at random with other games. The system of spiking in laying traps has proved as much effective for catching the wild animals.

Young persons are fond of hunting all kinds of birds, pigeons, jungle fowls and minor games as well. They lay several fish traps and use their traditional devices of fish catching. Ankling is one of the favourite games among the many tribes. The hill streams provide fishermen with a variety of hill fish, crabs and fingerlings. In the lowlands, a variety of fish similar to those in the nearby plains are obtained. The trophies of hunting such as beaks, horns, skins, feathers are preserved and sometimes serve as items of house furniture. Skins, among many tribes, are used as items of bedding, flooring, matting and for making drums and other articles of use. The jungles and streams provide the hill men with ready food in meat and fish. Edible wild vegetables, tubers and roots are also some of the delicacies to them.

Till the close of the last century ivory was a very important item of merchandise. It was transacted in a large quantities to the neighbouring plains in exchange with other goads regarded as necessities. Mithuns during those times served as the medium of currency and one fully grown mithun could be equivalent to a sum of one hundred rupees.

In the Hill States in the northeast, the lower hills located near the centres of communication can afford good places for breeding. As such sanitary and veterinary methods can be successfully adopted for the purpose of breeding and upgrading of livestock. It is found at places that poultry sheddings and pigsties require a spacious accommodation and with a sufficient safeguard adopted, epidemics can also be successfully averted or that their frequencies can be sufficiently curtailed.

Animal Husbandry

Upgrading the Animal Husbandry and Veterinary services has now resulted in the opening of a Veterinary Hospital located at the state headquarter which has functioned during these years. It has resulted in the distribution also of veterinary dispensaries at different directions and the establishment of the rural animal health centres. Moreover the cattle breed, dairy and local cows, goats, piggeries and poultries have been fairly distributed through the Blocks and other agencies and the people have received incentives to carry on the trade for the increase of milk meat and eggs. There are other farms located at suitable places maintained by the Department. Several artificial and sub-artificial insemination centres have also been established.

There is now a broiler chick-cum-demonstration farm at Tanhril near Aizawl; subsidised assistance has been extended to the local keepers of dairy cows under the milk supply scheme at Aizawl. The bio-gas plants (with 535 units) are also being worked out for the rural development and upliftment of the rural economy. This has led to the opening of a central Medicine and Vaccine Depot and Disease Investigation Laboratory located at Aizawl.

Pisciculture

The development of fisheries has benefited the people and the care and upgradation of fish ponds, seeds and fingerlings can considerably be boosted. Some experimentation in this has yielded good results. By now the number of cultivators and pisciculturists must have increased who have made self efforts through Government assistance to develop pisciculture. Assistance at 50 per cent rate is given. Over 5,000 private fish ponds have sprung. This also works out the multiplication of fish seeds and the provision of facilities for improving the economy through these efforts.

We can also review the progress as briefly as possible. In fact the real work in organising the Department was undertaken only after Mizoram became the Union Territory. The greatest need to develop agriculture has been stressed also in the Census Handbooks and other departmental brochures. The policy enunciated in that direction is to achieve self-sufficiency in food production. First and foremost among the measures adopted was to introduce and intensify wet rice terracing in such the viably arable lands and convert all the available flat lands to a settled agriculture. The need has been emphasised also to educate the farmers to the use of the modern advanced techniques of cultivation and to adapt themselves to a productive method of cultivation.

Under this scheme, land reclamation is actively pursued in all the districts and many families wee benefited. The next step undertaken is to develop the minor irrigation facilities which have covered many thousands hectares of land. Moreover the agriculture link roads have been constructed in all the districts which provide connection with the important agriculture fields and stations. These measures would be helpful to extend the facilities and build the trade infrastructure. Under the scheme, many villages have also benefited.

Moreover, the department has adopted the scheme of garden colony connected with a time-bound programme on horticulture which like rice, will benefit a large number of families. At present, activities have been intensified to reduce more lands as would suit them with permanent cultivation. Efforts have also been intensified to introduce turmeric on a wide scale by distributing the improved seeds and the grinding machines to the cultivators at 50 per cent subsidy.

Similarly, some citrus seedlings nurtured at the Agriculture Farm, have also been distributed to the cultivators. At that Farm, many crops have been tried and experimented with successful results. Cardamom has also been introduced on experimental stage which, has also shown successful results. Various citrus fruits successfully introduced, have yielded good results.

Summing up we find that 'various schemes of agricultural development were being operated in the district such as irrigation, land reclamation, green manuring, subsidised supply of tools and implements, distribution of seeds, plant protection schemes'. The intensification of farming has made it necessary to diversity activities to other crops. Therefore, special attention is given to horticulture, cash crop plantation and afforestation. Cultivators are all the time 'encouraged to take up shifting cultivation' in favour of a more settled type of agriculture. 'They are also encouraged to take up plantation of cash crops like coffee, rubber, cardamom in selected areas'.

Transportation

Roads: Mizoram is connected through National Highway 54. NH-150 connects the state with Seling Mizoram to Imphal Manipur. NH-40A links Mizoram with Tripura. A road between Champhai and Tiddim in Burma will soon connect the two countries.

Air Service: Mizoram has only one airport, Lengpui Airport, near Aizawl and this Airport can be reached from Kolkata by Air within a short period of 40 minutes. Mizoram is also accessible from Kolkata via Silchar Airport, which is about 200 km from the state capital of Mizoram.

Railway: Mizoram can be easily reached by train at Bairabi rail station or via Silchar. Bairabi is about 110 km, where Silchar is about 180 km from the state capital.

Water Ways: Mizoram is in the process of developing water ways with the port of Akyab Sittwe in Burma along Chhimtuipui River. India is investing $103 million to develop the Sittwe port on Burma's northern coast, about 160 km from Mizoram. Military government of Burma committed $10 million for the venture, which is part of the Kaladan Multi-purpose Project.

Telecommunications

Major cellular service operators include cellular phone companies like Bharat Sanchar Nigam Limited (BSNL), Airtel, Reliance and Aircel.

9

Polity

With regard to political history we see that a new page of history opened with the formation of the Union Territory and then after the formation of State. The event was auspicious because it led to the conferring of State hood within a few years. Mizoram was governed as a Union Territory for about fifteen years.

A review into the inception of the District during the early years of its formation is worthy of notice. The sequences can be noted below.

The Superintendent was overall in charge of the District. He enforced his administration according to the prescribed rules and regulations. He was the pivot of the administration. He kept his relations very close to the chiefs, he, was, therefore, acquainted with tribal laws and customs.

Normally the chiefs were responsible for the village administration and welfare and his intervention was necessary on matters which affected law, order and security. Some of the earliest administrators had to tackle these problems on the spot. The chiefs were to report to him matters involving the civil and criminal justice and, therefore, held the prescribed powers for tackling the petty cases over which they were legally competent to settle.

It was summed up during the consolidation of the District that all criminal and civil cases which are not disposed of by the chiefs are heard by the Superintendent and his assistants. The Superintendent exercises powers of life and death, subject to the confirmation by the Lieutenant Governor, who is the chief appellate authority. The High Court at Calcutta has now jurisdiction in the hills, except in criminal cases against Europeans.

The powers of these courts as defined since 1874 had remained intact. One important provision was that the Superintendent retained his powers for adjudication of cases exceeding seven years' term of imprisonment which of course were held subject to the final confirmation of the Chief Commissioner who, otherwise would be eligible to accept or alter the sentence or annul it or order for retrial. The rules further provided that fine and imprisonment could be awarded in lieu of the terms prescribed above and the spirit of the Indian Penal code was to be adhered to in the matter of enforcing adjudication. The fine imposed should not in any case exceed the value of the property held by the offenders. The Assistant Commissioner under the Superintendent exercised the power of the Magistrate first class.

The village chiefs under the rules were competent to hold petty magisterial powers. They were entitled to try cases to the extent of Rs. 50, impose a fine to that amount and restitute, a compensation to the extent of injury sustained and enforce it by restraint of property of the offender. Appeal against their decision lay with the Superintendent.

As regards civil justice, the chiefs were authorised to try civil suits according to the rules. Appeals against the decision of the village court lay with the Superintendent who could either confirm or change the sentence or order for retrial. An appeal against his decision to the value of a suit fixed at Rs. 500 or above, lay with the Chief Commissioner.

By virtue of Government of India Act, 1935, the power of the Chief Commissioner was transferred to the Governor who was empowered to confirm sentences to death or otherwise, alter the substance of a sentence or order it for a retrial.

In 1948, the jurisdiction of the High Court was extended in the district.

The administration was organised for the first time against several difficulties caused by poor communications, as well as the want of codified laws and lack of trade infrastructural facilities. Most of the tours were done on foot. Yet, in spite of these hazards, most of the problems were solved. More and more acquaintances with the tribal Chieftains were made. Most of them came in and lent cooperation to Government.

Political Parties

There are two major political parties of Mizoram that dominate the political scenario of the state. They are the Mizo National Front and the Ephraim Union.

Mizo National Front, which is known as MNF in short, is a regional political party. MNF has come out of the Mizo Famine Front formed by Pu Laldenga. It was formed to protest against the inactivity of the Indian Government towards the famine-affected Mizo areas of Assam in the year 1959. In the same year the Mizo Hills were also destroyed by a devastating famine. The Mizo National Famine Front, originally formed to help the people suffering during the Mautam Famine, was afterwards converted into Mizo National Front on 22nd October in the year 1961. Pu Zoramthanga became the leader of MNF after the death of Laldenga. In the elections of 1998 and 2003, MNF won the state assembly elections, with Pu Zoramthanga as the Chief Minister.

The other main political party in the state of Mizoram is Ephraim Union. It is also a regional political party. It is known as EU and it belongs to the part of Mizoram that considers the Mizos to be the descendants of the tribes of Israel.

Sociopolitical Organisations

Mizo society is hierarchically organised on the basis of age, sex, standard of living, and knowledge. Those who work in high offices in urban and rural areas rank above those who work in the swidden. Those who are associated with the leading local church are held in high esteem.

Mizoram is a state in the Republic of India. Mizoram has three districts: Chhimtuipui, Lunglei, and Aizawl. In the latter two, Mizo sociopolitical activities dominate. Each village has a council headed by a president.

He, his secretary, and members of his council are elected through adult franchise on the basis of political party. This democratic system replaces the traditional system based on privilege and non-privilege. The village council manages the affairs of the village: matters concerning agricultural activities, allocation of agricultural plots, collection of taxes, distribution of water, control of the market, community activities, and welfare of the people. The religious activities are attended to by the different church denominations with the help of their members. The village crier and blacksmith are nominated by the village council. The State Government manages such matters as communication, education, social welfare, law and order, hospitals, transport, food supply, industry, the judiciary, forests, etc.

Mizo customary law is enforced through a village council that has judicial powers. The local church authority is another body that regulates the behaviour of the People. In this matter clergy play an important role in religious and village issues. If an individual family is not happy with conditions in the village, it may leave the village for another, with the permission of the president of the village council.

State Government

The Government of Mizoram also known as the State Government of Mizoram, or locally as State Government, is the supreme governing authority of the Indian state of Mizoram and its 8 districts. It consists of an executive, led by the Governor of Mizoram, a judiciary and a legislative branch.

Like other states in India, the head of state of Mizoram is the Governor, appointed by the President of India on the advice of the Central government. His or her post is largely ceremonial. The Chief Minister is the head of government and is vested with most of the executive powers. Aizawl is the capital of Mizoram, and houses the Vidhan Sabha (Legislative Assembly) and the secretariat. The Guwahati High Court, located in Guwahati,

Assam has an Aizawl Bench that exercises the jurisdiction and powers in respect of cases arising in the state of Mizoram.

The present Legislative Assembly of Mizoram is unicameral, consisting of 40 Member of the Legislative Assembly (MLA). Its term is 5 years, unless sooner dissolved.

Role of Governor

The Governor's assent to the Bill is essential to have its force of an Act. In certain cases he withholds his assent an sends it back to the Assembly for their consideration embodying some of his observations considered as rectification to it. The said Bill being reconsidered and passed with or without his recommendation at the second stage, the Governor can no longer withhold assent and the Bill automatically become an Act. As stated he can reserve the Bills also for the decision of the President.

The term of his office is five years. He is appointed by the President. He can also be removable, should the President desired, pending the ending of that term. This subject is stressed with regard to the allocation of power in the state.

The Governor summons, prorogue and dissolves the Legislative Assembly. He may send messages to the Assembly prescribing certain measures for legislation in the issue which has assumed importance. He is entitled to process the bill to the President for final action if he feels that it will endanger the position of the High Court or derogates the Court's power. He opens the important annual session of the House, broadly emphasising the government programme for the year. He lays before the Assembly the annual financial statement indicating the estimated receipts and expenditures of that year. No demand for a grant or money bill can be introduced. His personal opinion is very vital to deciding Centre-State relations.

The Governor reserves his judicial powers for appointing, transferring and promoting the District judges and other judicial officers. Under the provisions, he is empowered to grant pardons, reprieves and respite of punishment or suspend, remit or commute the sentence of any person who has been convicted for an offence against any law.

The Governor theoretically holds extensive powers but in most cases, abides with the advice of the Cabinet; this measure is essential to restrict frictions, for coordinating matters smoothly and for causing a unified approach. The proclamation of emergency makes him to act in response to the decision and mandate mostly of the President or the Central Government.

In this framework, the Governor reposes the Chief Minister's confidence and the Chief Minister commands the confidence of the House being essentially the leader of a dominant party. The Legislature is the arbiter of the final authority and the party in power thus obtains its mandate. The Chief Minister pivots the functioning of the administration of departments according to the allocation and functional role of the allocated Ministerial portfolios.

The Ministry is wholly responsible to the Assembly for each and every issue of the administration. The Chief Minister's functions are restricted to non-judicial subjects but holds the real executive and his Cabinet decides the priorities of legislation. The concerns of Government are diverted to law and order, normal functioning of departments and departmental restructuring, social legislation, redresses of public grievances and coping with the other public responsibilities. Practically the Chief Minister's opinion is vital for framing policies for the Governor's acceptance.

With regard to normal administration, the advice of Chief Minister is indispensable. With regard to the abnormal situation the view of the Cabinet or Chief Minister would be subject to rectification and in the situation that Government is incapable to settle, the Governor will be wholly responsible and act in concord with the Centre. Most of the Departmental initiation with regard to the suitability or otherwise of legislation is censored by the Ministry concerned and approved by the Cabinet. A situation has impelled that the Chief Minister directly or indirectly maintains his overall influence overall the Departments besides holding a few portfolios to himself.

The Assembly establishment or Secretariat performs the manifold duties to chalking out the agenda, coordinating the subject at issue, preparing the coordinated statements or reports and making arrangements at sessions. The Speaker holds the important post of trust and responsibility for the efficient functioning of the Assembly's establishment, conducting the sessions in proper decorum and administering the other issues.

Freedom of expression in the House is guaranteed in conformity with the rules of discipline laid down. The status of the Speaker is considerably elevated.

In a Parliamentary set-up, we note that the elections are very decisive in the formation and functioning of Government. The allocation of the Cabinet portfolios also has its basic importance in the working of the Government Departments. As regards the structure of Departments, the Chief Secretary has his overall role in the liaisoning and coordinating the affairs at the Secretariat level. Under this arrangement, all the Departments are headed by Secretaries to Government and Directorates function under the departments and the branches of the directorates function at the State and District level. A Deputy Commissioner keeps the important departmental liaison of the district. The administration of District Councils is conducted by their respective Executive Councils.

The Administrator

In the set up of Union Territory, the Commissioner or Lt. Governor designated Administrator was eligible to summon the Legislative Assembly at the given times; he could summon a special session; he could, subject to the advice of Chief Minister, prorogue the Legislative Assembly and was empowered alike, in a difficult situation even, to dissolve the Assembly. He held powers over the bills specified below

Except with his decision, no bill or Constitutional amendment to an existing Act could be presented in the Assembly if it affected "Judicial Commissioner(s) jurisdiction and powers of the court of the judicial Commissioner and with respect to any matter included in the List or the concurrent list".

Similarly no bill or amendment could be offered which affected the:

- the imposition, abolition, remission, alteration regulation of any tax;
- the amendment of any law with respect to any financial obligation undertaken by the Government of the Union territory;
- the appropriation of money out of the consolidated fund of the Union Territory;
- declaring any expenditure to be an expenditure charged on the consolidated fund of the Union Territory or increasing the amount of any such expenditure, the receipt of money on account of the consolidated fund of the Union Territory or the custody or issue of such money, or a bill which if enacted and brought into operation would involve expenditure from the consolidated fund of the Union Territory".

All the bills passed by the Legislative Assembly were to be presented to the administrator before passing it to the President. Addresses by the administrator in the Assembly was necessary to ensure its smooth functioning even if, the draft of the Address otherwise, was laid by the Council of Ministers.

Under the subsequent amendment, the administrator was allowed to keep his discretion to assent to the passing of the bill or to seek the President's advice or to send back the Bill not being the money bill for the Assembly's consideration under certain' rectifications that could be provided. Should the bill be passed by the Assembly with the rectification proposed thereto or without it, it was up to him to decide whether he gave in his consent or awaited the President's opinion.

He was entitled further to withhold assent or use his discretion with regard to such bills which affected or derogated the status, power and functions of the High Court as had been provided for in the Constitution or to any of the matters inserted in Act 31 (A) of the Constitution.

On behalf of the President, the administrator could reserve any particular bill passed by the assembly and which related to any area comprised in any Autonomous district under the sixth schedule. Any amendment proposed by the President with his message on being returned to the Assembly, it should within six months be considered and passed and should it be passed, with or without amendment, the President would retain his power to consider it.

The administrator was competent enough to exercise his power over their decisions taken by the Council of Ministers or a minister with regard to any area under the autonomous district. The security of the border was his special responsibility in which he was competent to decide and issue directions. In respect to other issues, the Council of Ministers was entitled to advise and assist him and the President's intervention would be necessary as and when some specific differences had arisen amongst them.

The administrator held special power to decide over matters affecting the security of the territory, matters affecting the interest of any minority community, the scheduled tribes and scheduled castes, matters affecting other States' relations with the territory, matters affecting the Secretariat of the administrator and all relating to its establishment and matters affecting new taxation; among others, the Constitution of Advisory Board under section 9 for the maintenance of Internal Security Act and matters related to the centre's role under the Union Territories' Act was very vital in this regard.

Matter relating to new taxation measures, resolutions of the Assembly, rule making under the Union Territory's Act, mercy petitions to criminals, revision of a judicial sentence, summoning, proroguing and dissolution of the Assembly, disqualification of voters, dates for holding elections and the planned proposals, all these issues have been covered also in this frame work.

The administrator in consultation with the Council of Ministers could seek measures to protect the property of the Union and decide the suitability of enforcing rules and regulations relating to the service conditions of persons employed in the service of the Union Territory vested in him. He was empowered to consult the Union Public Service Commission on the matters which affected the territory; lie performed his normal duties to lay before the Assembly the Audit report: he would report to the President any kind of Constitutional crisis and receive correspondences from the centre.

He was eligible under the recommendation of the Union Government to settle:

- "any contract for the purchase of property or goods or the sale of trees, timber or any forest produce whose value exceeds Rs. one lakh;
- any indent for stores of Rs. two lakhs;
- any contract for the purchase of property or goods whose value exceeds Rs. 15 lakhs;
- any contract for sale or lease for period which exceeds 20 years of any immovable property whose value exceeds Rs. one lakh;
- any agreement or contract for technical collaboration on consultation with any foreign firms or foreign Governments.

The administrator exercises these functions in his discretion". Evidently the power of the Assembly had been circumscribed. The administrator had taken the bulk of power pertaining to State Legislature.

Mizoram in its status of a State as in conformity with other States has a Government headed by the Governor but the Chief Minister actually pivots the administration. The powers of the Governor, the Assembly, the State Government and the Court have been defined. The Assembly has a total number of 40 MLAs returned from their respective constituencies. Normally the life of Assembly extends to five years but when the proclamation of emergency has occurred under the circumstances that might endanger the situation, one more year may be extended to the Assembly. The Assembly would choose a Speaker and a Deputy Speaker to chair and conduct the Assembly sessions. Rules have been prescribed for the conduct of members and for entitling with the rights and privileges due to them.

Administration of Superintendent

The administration initially depended upon the interpreters to convey rules and decisions. The Superintendent's Court became a great centre. In these circumstances, the Revenue Branch was started which was concerned with the collection of a house tax at Rs. 2 per house collected annually. A meagre police strength was provided; however, a contingent of military police strong enough, commanded by a European Officer was stationed. A small jail was attached.

Buildings and constructions were in the charge of District Engineer. The remarkable task was the opening of dispensaries for the sick patients; the dispensaries numbered initially seven in all and several cases were treated. A Civil Surgeon was stationed in charge of the District. Work was done also to start regular census operations. Water reserve Storages were installed at the headquarter. Three Government schools were started at Aijal, Khawnbawk and Lungleh which later on were transferred to the Missions. This was the infrastructure laid down.

Administration now had extended to the far-flung tracts. Hardly with forty or fifty years of the administration, the new rapid upsurges had also become formidable. Education subsequently made great progress and educated persons were taken to service in Government, the Church, the Arm and other agencies. A social transformation had become inevitable.

The administration made attempts on a limited scale to improve the system of farming; it yielded very little result. The administration on the occasion of draughts, famines and rat infestation, sought to provide relief to the worst stricken as the situation had become difficult for the chiefs alone to cope with the scheme of village rehabilitation which in that situation, became unavoidable. The administration was confronted almost frequently with the problem of restoring communications when roads were affected with landslides.

The Second World War had its far reaching consequences; it forged more unity and integration among the tribes; developing the fast means of communication was planned; the avenues of trade, supply and traffic became extended; quick movements in the hills, when the war was making its advent nearer, became inescapable; the functioning of the administration was strengthened. The opening of some new administrative branches was not ruled out. Finally the new trends of consciousness had emerged.

The responsibilities for an integrated approach was the periodical holding of durbars of village chiefs. The Superintendent convened them. The durbars or conferences opened the avenue for the exchange of view they provided scope also for a reciprocal understanding of problems and for the solution of some inter-village disputes or differences. The opportunity was grasped to appreciate the mutual problem and settle disputes. Durbars provided the good consultative machineries for working out certain programmes.

Towards the close of the British administration, the formal District Conferences which involved the principle of election of chiefs and other representatives were constituted but were soon superseded by the District Council. It appears that the British Government during the transfer of power had not conducted any far-reaching consultations with the Mizo chiefs and leaders with regard to their future set-up. The people themselves were to be the arbiters to their destiny. These events culminated in the inclusion of Lushai Hills in the sixth schedule of the Constitution.

Under a Constitution provision, the district was entitled to send three elected representations to the Assam Legislative Assembly. It occurred for the first time, the working out of a democratic principle for instituting a Constitutional Government. The Constitution enshrines the system of universal suffrage under which members of the Assembly and of the District Councils were to be returned by elections.

The system of delimitation of constituencies was worked out for holding the first General Assembly and District Council elections. This system had enabled most of the Hill districts to have their say in the Legislatures. The member of Legislative Assemblies in the Hill districts would coordinate their interest with the Assembly with regard to getting due protection to their constituencies and accelerate developmental progress. The District Council, it was hoped, would give the representatives a fair chance for experimenting themselves in the system of self Government in these matters which pertained to them. The Mizo Union consequently made its name during those elections.

The situation in 1969 necessitated the reorganisation of Mizoram into the Union Territory under which the administration was to be conducted by the President through a Chief Commissioner or any other authority to be appointed by him.

The President further could "make regulations for the peace and good government of any such territory and any regulations so made may repeal or amend any law made by Parliament or any existing law which is for the time being applicable to such territory and, when promulgated by the President, shall have the same force and effect as an Act of Parliament which applies to such authority".

The competent authority as such to govern vested in the Chief Commissioner or any other authority entitled with that power. A Legislative Assembly under the arrangement was provided which would maintain close liaison with the authority so constituted for the administration of the Territory.

The Government of the Union Territory, commenced to function in January, 1972. As a sequence to its elevation to the status of State, a nine member coalition MNF — Congress Ministry was installed in August 1986 as a caretaker Government. Then in February 1987, the first State General Assembly Elections were held. The inauguration of Mizoram took place only two and half years ago.

Legislative Assembly

The State Assembly legislates on matters of State; in the concurrent list and in the event of any misunderstanding with regard to their spheres of jurisdiction between the Centre and State, the Parliament can intervene and settle the issue. Evidently the Legislature is the ultimate authority. It is the authority which rectifies the old issues and takes up new ones. The Assembly exercises restraints on the executive and frames suitable policies to strengthen the departmental machineries.

The matters relating to the power of the Legislature and Governor are well known. Suffice to say that the Assembly has the power to approve or veto bills and the members can table the necessary adjournments, motions and even motions of no confidence against the Ministers; they can suggest alteration or modification in the contents of bills presented.

As regards its power over the finances, the allocation of sources and disbursement against Government expenditures, they are the responsibilities of Legislative Assembly to determine these priorities; but with regard to the consolidated fund, the Assembly members even when entitled to discuss are not competent to exercise their voting right on it. In case of a unicameral legislature, the final bills passed are presented to the Governor for his decisions. Rules have been framed for the formation of Assembly Committees with all the rights, obligations and privileges attached to them.

The Mizoram Assembly was to keep themselves in conformity with the terms and conditions laid down in the Memorandum of Settlement prior to the installation of Care Taker Government. Practically the Governor performs his status role. He plays decisive roles in all issues of legislation; lie plays the dominant role in the crystallisation of legislation. He is the final authority in the system of legislation making. He coordinates action with the President with regard to the enactment of the proposed bills depending on the nature of their contents, connotation and application. He is the repository and residual authority in law making.

Law making because of certain complex factors can be time taking with regard to the screening and scrutinisation of bills. In law making with regard to the state subjects, the

Governor, is responsible to the President. Bills of controversial or extraordinary character which are likely to be one sided or prejudicial have their system of transmittance from the Governor to the President and back to the Governor.

The Governor keeps the vital liaisoning with the Centre because he keeps informed the Centre on this issue and several other things. He has the power to issue ordinances in absentia of the Assembly which is deemed to extend themselves to two weeks even after re-assembly of the session has affected.

The Legislature can also advise for its repeal at or before the maturity of its application. Another important thing, the Governor can recommend for the President's rule in the event, certain circumstances have hampered the normal functioning of Government. The State of emergency in view of the conditions peculiar to themselves, can warrant the suspension of the Assembly and the assumption of power through his functionaries. In the event of the state of emergency, he can withdraw his concord from the Chief Minister.

District Councils

The District Council had during a short transition, conducted the primary education and looked after the affairs apportioned to them. In the previous and even present District Councils, there have been frequent shifts in instituting the regular chairmanship which have threatened to create rifts heading themselves towards some instability. In the frame work of statehood, the better results would have been anticipated. The wisdom of the electorate and political parties participating in the elections, could considerably help to improve the situation.

The District Councils have existed in Mizoram since 1952. The erstwhile District Council at Aizawl performed the legislative and function executive through the Executive Council and judicial functions through the Court. It elected its Chairman, the Chief Executive Member and Executive Members and constituted an Executive Council to run the administration within its prescribed power. Four District Council elections were held from 1952 to 1970. This Council was abolished when the Union Territory was set up in 1972.

The Pawi-Lakher Council also functioned since 1952. Elections were held from time to time which returned its members in 1953, 1958, 1964 and 1970. The tribes in the face of complication could not run smoothly the council. As such in the framework of Union Territory three Regional Councils were given to Mizoram.

The Departments grouped and regrouped according to the administrative convenience are Home, Finance, Law, Judicial, Revenue, Accounts and Treasury, Planning, Elections, Parliamentary Affairs, Public works, Power and Electricity, General Administration, Public Health, Excise and Taxation, Cooperatives, Tourism, Trade, Industries, Commerce, Agriculture, Soil Conservation, Public Health Engineering, Animal Husbandry, Forestry,

Education and Human Resource, Rural Development, Administrative Training Institute, Civil Aviation, Social Welfare, Rehabilitation, Labour and Employment, District Council Affairs and Public Health Engineering.

Few of Departmental Heads are designated Chief Conservator, Chief Commissioner, Registrar, etc., according to their functionaries.

The bulk of the Secretariat and Directorate establishments are concentrated at Aizawl, the state capital. Most of the Departments follow the hierarchy of officers designated Secretaries and Directors. Therefore, Public Health Engineering, Power and Electricity, Public Works Department are looked after by the respective Chief Engineers. The Chief Election Officer looks after the election affairs. A few officers under the other designations look after the other Departments. The Police follow their own way of hierarchy.

The units of these establishments under the officers with different designations — Agriculture, Power and Electricity, Health, PHE, PWD, Printing and Stationary, Forest, Soil Conservation, Animal Husbandry and Veterinary, Industries, Community Development, Public Relations, Excise, Social Welfare, Transport function at Lunglei, the new District Headquarter and the previous subdivisional headquarter in the state and few of them have been started at Saiha, the new district headquarter.

At the District level, the three Deputy Commissioners function under the Secretariat; by now the responsibilities of the district administration have increased. Many branches of the Directorates concerned with their functional roles have been gradually established in the three districts.

Party System

The reorganisation of Mizoram into a Union Territory during a crucial situation was responsible for the growth of a party system. The number of parties had recently increased. Some of them were *ad hoc* parties and were merged subsequently into the bigger parties. The parties known to have played their role were Mizo Union, United Mizo Freedom Organisation, People's Conference, Indian National Congress and the other minor parties are Mizoram Janata Party, Mizo Democratic Front, Mizo Convention and Socialist Party. The emergence of the District Council and later on the Union Territory has revealed the enormous growth of small parties which sought to cater with the needs of the smaller tribal groups; they have amply demonstrated their grievances and have sought redressal in this respect. With the complicated background the field as such, has been prepared for developing some important pattern of ethnic and social consciousness, among the larger and smaller tribes in the state.

At the outset the Mizo Union rallied considerable strength and in the election held in 1952, three MLAs were returned by the Party in the electorate of 38,000 voters in which they polled 29,100 votes in all. The major parties which contested at that election were

Mizo Union and United Mizo Freedom Organisation. The latter having been defeated, therefore, coordinated itself with Eastern Indian Tribal Union and in the election held in 1957, two of its candidates were returned as MLAs. Mizo Union, however, retained one seat. The Mizo Union and United Mizo Freedom Organisation had fielded candidates each of them for the Assembly seats in 1952 and 1957.

The Eastern India Tribal Union formed after their merger of Mizo Union and Mizo Freedom Organisation into the said Union owing, to the deplorable situation which followed since 1958 due to a famine could obtain only one seat in the election held in 1962. The two other seats were taken by Eastern Tribal Union. The involvement of the Front in providing relief to famine hit persons on their verge of starvation and death completely changed the situation that in the next bye-election to fill-up the two seats vacated by the two Mizo Union MLAs, the Mizo National Front was returned to the two seats and Eastern India Tribal Union now affiliated to APHLC was eclipsed from Mizoram.

Mizo National Front emerged as a strong party. It had mustered great strength. This was due to the breakdown caused by a famine. This was due to the fact also that the Mizos had opted for a constitutional pattern of their own. Moreover the Mizo Union had approved to coordinate itself with EITU, but it was only the right wing of the said Union that had developed such understanding. In spite of the party breakdown, the Mizo Union by then considerably had improved its strength.

It won by overwhelming majority over 21 seats against 30 seats in the first election to the Union Territory. In these circumstances as state, the Mizo Union entered into an alliance wit Indian National Congress in which Indian National Congress MLAs were abducted to the Council of Ministers. This was followed by their complete merger which was announced in January 1974.

The next important party was UMFO. It was able to hold itself with 2 MLA in the election which was held in 1957. Much of it was not heard after 1962-63.

Parties had played considerable role in acquainting themselves with affair and contesting at elections. These organisations have considerable experience in launching election campaigns, fielding candidates, adopting the election symbols and manipulating these and other affairs.

Evidently the displacement of EITU and the merger of Mizo Union with Congress had brought about a phenomenal change in party politics.

As regards the Congress, a branch of INC was opened in 1961; Mizoram District Congress beyond doubt was first affiliated to the Assam Pradesh Congress. This party definitely had rallied such strength and resources almost adequately disposed at their end by the state or National organisation. But at the election held in 1962 and the bye-election which still followed in 1963-64, their candidates were defeated by Mizo National Front.

In the general election held in 1967, the District appears to have opted to boycott the Assam Assembly except one seat and a member filled to it was declared elected unopposed. Congress men now tried to strengthen the organisation for which, a special meeting of District Congress Committee was held in 1968. There was again a break down of the party when a rift among leaders came out to surface. The Congress then sought to put maximum efforts and fielded candidates in the election held in 1972 but they won only 6 seats. Shortly after, the Pradesh Congress bifurcated themselves, from the Assam Congress. In the same year, the Mizo Labour and Mizo Socialist parties sank down their differences and got themselves merged with the Congress. This considerably strengthened the cause of the Congress.

The People's Conference, one of the best organisations, initially had grown out from the Human Rights' Committee, purely at first a non-political organisation which, had sought to provide relief to people badly affected after a regrouping of villages which occurred during the insurrections. It wanted also to give adequate protection to the citizens enshrined in the Constitution. Later on it became an important party with an elaborate system of organisation covering almost every area in the state.

It may be said that the Conference itself fished from the troubled waters to secure itself as a dominant organisation. So successful was its performance that 23 of its candidates were returned to the Assembly in the election recorded in 1978. It assumed office for five years with a break of a few months which led to the dissolution of the Assembly but when the elections were held in 1979, the Conference came back to power. A group of dissenters during a breakdown constituted themselves into the People's Conference (B).

Mizoram Janata Party the Janata Party was formed at the instance of descendent Congress and other party men who left their respective parties and flocked themselves under the banner of Janata in 1977. Janata in spite of their weak grass-root level fielded 20 candidates in the election held in 1978 and were able to return 2 of them as MLAs. However, in the election held in 1979, they won again 2 seats.

Mizo Convention: This was the party formed after the merger of People's Conference (B), Janata and Mizo Democratic Front which respectively were dissatisfied with their own party organisations; these parties and party groups had dissolved themselves and managed to win one seat in the election held in 1984. The Convention later merged themselves with Mizo National Front.

Evidently the system of party restructuring went very fast. The crucial situation and search of identity among the small groups considerably assisted in party restructuring from time to time. For instance the Mizo National Union constituted in 1986 was formed by merging the Mizo Union Christian Democratic Socialist party and Mizoram Congress for peace. It seems that it has taken recently the name of New Mizo Union. The other small parties had their basic importance with regard to shaping the Mizoram politics.

There was the United Pang People's Party composed of Pang, Tongougia and other groups. They wanted more autonomy and pressed this demand in 1975. Among others, Mizo Inzawmkhawn Pawl formed as early as 1971 advocated the integration of all the Mizo areas lying contagiously into a Mizo State. There was the Chin National Union formed by the Pawis in 1963 and for some years, it dominated the Pawi Lakher Regional Council. The Mara freedom party succeeded on their demand for a separate Lakher Regional Council; and even contested the first general election with one member returned. They were then merged with the Congress. There was Paite National Council formed in 1962 which wanted a Regional Council for the Saikal range. A minor organisation, Tribal union constituted as early as 1950 demanded as well the formation of a Regional Council for the Pawis and Lakhers. It was the first organisation which seriously took itself with the concept of Regional Councils.

The split was overwhelming and afterwards three new District Councils were started for the Union Territory which were Pawi, Lakher, Chakma as the Chakmas fought tooth and nail for their own Council. Among others, the Mizo Union Council was one of the earliest organisations, later on it merged itself with the Union Mizo Freedom organisation. The Mizo Union right wing in this regard was constituted by descendants from the Mizo Union and had played some considerable role in District Councils from 1954 to 1957. The Mizo Union left wing also played a similar role.

Mizo National Front originally grew from the National Famine Front which had taken considerable measures to extend relief to famine stricken people about 1960. Later on it declared its political affiliation and fielded candidates in the election held in 1962 and the bye-elections which followed. The dailies in the '80s tells us that the Front had worked out with the government in chalking out the Mizo Accord which resulted in conferring statehood to Mizoram. It won decidedly many seats in the 1987 election and formed the government in which their leader played the dominant role. It also formed a caretaker Government with INC shortly before the inauguration of a new State.

Two MPs were entitled to the Union Territory: One for Lok Sabha and the other for Rajya Sabha. At the first polls held in 1972, the Mizo Union candidate won. In 1972 Parliament election and in a midterm Parliament election held on 1980, the seat was filled up by the same candidate who had returned, having polled the biggest number of votes in the two polls held. In 1984, a Congress candidate was elected unopposed. Similarly for Rajya Sabha, the seat was filled in by 2 candidates in 1972 and 1978 elected unopposed. In 1984, a Congress candidate was elected to the Rajya Sabha after defeating his rival.

Beyond doubt, the Mizo Union, People's Conference and Mizo National Front have played their more decisive role. Their growth and emergence were timely and responsive to the crucial situations. They had left considerable impact in shaping and reshaping the Mizo State and Society.

Genesis of Mizo National Front

In 1959, there was a great famine all over Mizoram, due to the widespread acute shortage of food and other things, there were cases of starvation deaths. The government of Assam could not take up adequate measures to meet the situation. As a result of this misery, a non-political organisation called the Mizo Cultural Society was formed in the same year by John F. Manliana to help the starving people.

But this society did not last long as it could not be an effective media to help the famine-stricken people. SOR Vanlawma, Dengthuama and Laldenga resolved to help the famine-stricken people through the formation of a welfare organisation. Subsequently, they formed Mizo National Famine Front for organising relief work for the distressed people. R. Dengthuama and Laldenga were elected Chairman and Secretary of the Front.

This social service organisation took all credit for fighting the famine and helping the suffering people. It, thus, became too much popular. At the same time, the Mizo Union leaders, staunch supporters of the Congress government in the beginning, who were running the administration of the District Councils were unhappy either. They realised that government of Assam neither paid much attention to famine relief measures nor attached so much importance to the District Council as expected. As consequence, the relationship between the Chaliha government of Assam and the Mizo Union led District Council reached at bitter stage.

So Mizo Union drifted away from the Congress and became more and more critical in their public utterances mainly because of sharp differences on the famine relief and the state official language issues in 1960. In the same year the rift between the Congress and All Patty Hill Leaders Conference on the Assamese Language issue also appeared. Laldenga exploited this situation fully as well as took the advantage of relief works done for the distressed people.

At the same time he received special patronage of the Chaliha government. So Laldenga and other leaders of the MNF decided unanimously to convert this social service organisation into political party. Consequently, the Mizo National Front was formed on 22 October, 1961 with the objectives of attaining independence for greater Mizoram, reuniting all the Mizo people living in the contiguous areas, improving the social, economic and political conditions of the Mizos, safeguarding/promoting Christianity, planning a long-term strategy for violent movement to achieve its aims and acquiring dependable source of support of some foreign countries. The tail end of the party's aim yelled out "Mizoram for the Mizos."

Armed Revolt, Counter-Measures and Pacification: The MNF carried on hostile activities, yet the Government of Assam did not realise the gravity of the situation. The law and order was fast deteriorating. The situation was ripe for a conflict. The MNF insurgency broke out on the midnight of 28 February, 1966. The party resorted to acts of lawlessness, violence, attacks and killings at many important places in the district. The MNF declared independence on 1 March, 1966.

The declaration of independence appeared to be similar in style and content that of the American Declaration of Independence. Laldenga appealed for external help. The government of India adopted military measures to counter the menace of the grave anti-national activity. The Army troops were despatched to the territory in aid of the civil power. On 2 March, 1966 the whole district was declared as a disturbed area under the Assam Disturbed Areas Act, 1955 by the Government of Assam. This Act of 1955 along with the Armed Forces (Assam and Manipur) Special Power Act, 1958 was also in force in the area.

Not only but the Government of India on 6 March, 1966 declared the MNF as an unlawful organisation and also banned it under the Defence of India Rules. Though, there was no declaration of martial law at all, the government entrusted the responsibility of law and order in the district to the army and issued strict instructions that the army was not to fight with an enemy power. Despite the MNF leaders remained adamant.

They did not resile from the demands of independence. They also persisted in subversive and violent activities and continued all sorts of atrocities in Mizoram. The MNF parallel government also continued functioning. The Mizo Hills District was elevated to the status of Union Territory on 21 January, 1972 and popular government was formed. The MNF was later split into two groups moderate/intellectuals and extremists which confused the rank and file of the MNF. The most intellectuals surrendered. Both the split in the MNF and the creation/provision of social welfare services by the counter-insurgency forces caused mass surrenders occasionally.

The continued political consciousness and a realisation about the MNF movement's futility among the MIZO's were also at work in discouraging the anti-nationalist forces of the MNF's rebels and thereby 'contributed to the MNF's frustration at its waning influence in Mizoram. Thus the surrenders gave crippling blows to the MNF, kept them in complete disarray and shattered their morale. Simultaneously, the concentrated efforts on development activities and social welfare measures were going to create in the minds of the Mizo people a stake in peaceful conditions.

There has been a considerable progress in political, economic, social and cultural aspects of the Mizo people since 1972 in spite of the territory being disturbed by the Mizo National Front insurgency. Both the first and the second ministries led by the Congress and the People's Conference tried to bring the Central Government and the MNF leaders to peace dialogue in order to settle the vexed political problem of Mizoram. So there had been frequent peace talks/meetings between the Govt. of India and the MNF leaders.

But the talks could not yield any tangible results. The MNF insurgency and the security operations continued. Later the Home Secretary, Government of India and the

MNF Chief Laldenga signed the `Peace Accord' on 1st July, 1976 closing the bitter chapters of hardship and sufferings caused by the MNF hostilities since March 1966. Unfortunately, the July peace accord could not be translated into practice in spite of the best efforts of both the sides.

The Janata Party came to power in the centre in the polls of 1977. Talks regarding implementation of the July agreement were resumed on 18th May between the representatives of Central Government and the MNF Chief Laldenga. But it was not materialised probably due to rift, internal squabbles and contradictions within the MNF organisation. As a result, the talks were called off in March 1978. After the MNF stepped up their hostile activities all over the territory, the attacks were mostly on the security forces, civil officials and non-Mizos. The Central Government viewed fresh spurt of violence and killings seriously. So the MNF and its allied organisation were declared unlawful. Laldenga was taken into police custody on 8th July, 1979.

With the return of the Congress (I) party to power in the 1980 polls at the Centre, the Mizo Pradesh Congress (I) Leaders requested the Prime Minister Indira Gandhi to resume the peace talk with the MNF. The talks were resumed.

The central government withdrew all the pending cases and charges against Laldenga on 30th July, 1980. But the talks between the government and Laldenga failed because of sharp differences on some of the demands, such as constitution of a state with safeguards on Jammu and Kashmir type and constitution of greater Mizoram including Mizo-inhabited areas as submitted by him. The central government, however, agreed to elevate the Union Territory hood to the Statehood of Mizoram with certain constitutional safeguards.

The Central government also made clear to the MNF that issues, which were possible without their repercussion on the other groups, would be met in the course of discussion. Still the peace talks broke off. The MNF and its armed wing Mizo National Army were banned on 20th January, 1982. The central government, thus, honoured the commitment of 'safe conduct' given to him when he came to India from West Germany on 24th January, 1976 for settling the political problem through peaceful talks. But peace and progress for which the Mizo people had been longing for a long times became casualty in the atmosphere of revived violence, killings and indiscriminate harassment.

The Congress party came to power with an overwhelming majority in the fourth election to the Mizoram Legislative Assembly in 1984. The government was headed by Lalthanhawla. The Congress (I) government committed to bring peace and harmony to the disturbed Mizoram besides other development goals.

The MNF leaders also wanted to mediate through the Mizoram Pradesh Congress leaders. Laldenga from London was called back to Delhi on 29th October, 1984. The peace talks were resumed between the Central Government and the MNF Chief Laldenga on 17th December, 1984. Operations by the MNF insurgents and the security forces in order to facilitate settlement remained suspended.

Laldenga had a series of discussions on various issues with the central officials, leaders and finally the Prime Minister Rajiv Gandhi. As a consequence, the historic memorandum of settlement was signed by the Home Secretary, R. D. Pradhan, Govt. of India, and Laldenga on behalf of the Mizo National Front and the Chief Secretary Lalkhama, Government of Mizoram on 30th June, 1986 to ensure permanent peace and harmony in Mizoram.

The peace accord was clinched both at the official (Govt. level) and the non-official and political (Party level). The memorandum of settlement incorporates some of the important issues. The MNF party agreed to end all underground activities, bring out all underground MNF personnel with their arms to civil life and abjure violence within the stipulated timeframe. The MNF further agreed to delete objectives of "Independence and secession of Mizoram from the Union of India" from its constitution to ensure its working within the constitutional framework of India.

The Government of India, on the other hand, resettled and rehabilitated the Mizos. The government also agreed to confer statehood on the Union territory of Mizoram with certain safeguards to satisfy the desires and aspirations of the Mizo people. After the memorandum of settlement was signed, the Government of India and the MNF took steps to implement the historic peace accord peacefully.

The underground MNF and MNA personnel surrendered with arms and ammunition. The MNF party amended its constitution by deleting the party's main objective for a struggle of 'Independent Mizoram' and other objectionable provisions to conform to the laws of land. The Government of India, thereafter, lifted the ban on the MNF party. The Central Government with a view to elevating the Union territoryhood to the statehood of Mizoram introduced the Mizoram Statehood Bill, 1986 with special safeguards and provision of forty elective seats in the Legislative Assembly and the 53rd Constitution (Amendment) Bill, 1986 in the Parliament and got the bill passed by an absolute majority of votes.

The President also assented to the Mizoram statehood Bill, 1986 on 14th August, 1986. The state bill became an act but was not brought in force with immediate effect. Because it was politically agreed upon between the Central Government and the MNF Chief Laldenga to form the Interim Congress (1) and MNF coalition government, comprising nine ministers of Cabinet rank (5-Congress, 4-MNF) led by Laldenga as the Chief Minister and Lalthanhawla as the Deputy Chief Minister. The MNF party on its part completed laying down of arms and ammunition within July 1986.

The Congress Legislature party in its meeting resolved to accept Laldenga as the leader of the Congress (I)-MNF coalition in the Legislative Assembly. So the Chief Minister Lalthanhawla resigned his Chief Ministership to facilitate the formation of the Congress(I)-MNF coalition government to ensure permanent peace and harmony in Mizoram. The Congress-MNF coalition government headed by Laldenga as the Chief Minister and Lalthanhawla as the Deputy Chief Minister was sworn in on 21st August, 1986.

After the formation of Congress-MNF coalition government, the Chief Minister Laldenga described the vacation of seats of Chief Minister and ministers by Lalthanhawla and his colleagues as significant contribution towards the implementation of Mizoram Peace Accord. However, the coalition could not function well. There was hardly any Cabinet meeting. The assembly election was held on 16 February, 1987, where Congress (I) and MNF fought against each other.

Organisational Structure of MNF

After twenty years of insurgency, the MNF leaders have taken the constitutional path by accepting statehood for Mizoram as a component unit of the Indian federation. The party in its constitution pledges to achieve its objectives through democracy, secularism and non-violence. It further aims at promoting and safeguarding Mizo culture and language.

The constitution also talks of uniting all Mizos and integrating the contiguous areas predominantly inhabited by the Mizos into a homogeneous political unit. But the party in its constitution does not make any reference to the socio-economic condition of the Mizos nor to any religion. The party, thus, does not follow any political philosophy but it represents the local grievances of its areas. This is local in character and centres around influential personalities. Most functions performed by it are *ad hoc* and act on especially politically-oriented compulsions which are determined by the structural and geographical elements of the society.

The MNF has a pyramidical structure starting at bottom with the village units up to the apex called the headquarters in the state of capital of Mizoram and at the districts/divisions and blocks. As regards Block Headquarters, each constituency of the Mizoram Legislative Assembly has block headquarters. A general headquarters of the state comprises general Assembly/Special Assembly, National Council, National Executive Committee, office bearers, National Woman Front and National Senior Front.

The headquarters has many office bearers — President, Vice-President, Treasurer, General Secretary, seven secretaries appointed by the President for three years. The divisional headquarters, has elected/appointed office bearers — President, Treasurer, Divisional Secretary and five joint Secretaries appointed by the Divisional President for two years. President, Vice-President, Treasure, one Secretary and Financial Secretary and two Joint Secretaries appointed by the Block President are the office-bearers of the Block Headquarters. They remain in office for two years. The group committee also has office bearers—President, Vice-President, Treasurer, one Secretary, one Finance Secretary and one Assistant Secretary appointed by the group President. The unit committee has also the President, Vice-President, Treasurer, one Secretary, one Finance Secretary and two Assistant Secretaries appointed by the Unit President.

The office bearers of the group and unit committee remain in their offices for one year. The President, Vice-Presidents and Treasurers of the state Headquarters, Divisional Headquarters, Block Headquarters and group/unit committee are elected by the general assembly and conferences as provided in the election rules for the office-bearers. The state headquarters/divisional headquarters may create group committee comprising more than one unit. All headquarters, in order to execute the party's aims, objectives/policies — have their executive committee such as National Executive Committee, Divisional Executive Committee, Block Executive Committee, Group Executive Committee and unit executive organ of the party exercise a large measure of influence and power in deciding party's policies and programmes.

It has to carry out the policies adopted by the General assembly. This body also supervises and coordinates the activities of the divisional/block headquarters/ committees. The party within a short period has made a significant dent in the urban and rural segments and established its units in all urban areas and villages. The party, owing to its hierarchical structure, has been to carry out the programmes of the party to the lowest level. The MNF was also a partner in the Congress (I) coalition ministry of August, 1986, so the party has become a very important force in the Mizo politics.

As regards the membership of the party, it is open to all citizens. One who believes in the party's aims/objectives, can become a member of the party without paying membership fee. As the dominant party, it has made steady progress in enrolling a large number of people of various walks of life. The MNF in the beginning consisted of mostly non-propertied persons.

After memorandum of settlement, the party has brought the urban rich, the urban proletariat, the educated petty bourgeoisie, the upstart contractor and businessmen to its fold, who may have their specific needs and demands. The party has enrolled many people belonging to urban-rural middle class.

As regards the social and geographical support base of the party; it has tried strenuously to broaden its base in the state except the inhabited tribes such as Lakhers and Chakmas. But the party has certainly extended its support base to the areas of the Pawi district council inhabited by the Pawi tribes. As the fact remains true, mostly the party derives its support from the mizo clans found scattered only in the Aizawl and Lunglei districts.

The Leadership

Laldenga is the founder President of the Mizo National Front (October, 1962). He turned the party into an effective organisation and carried its message of independence of Mizoram into every corner of Mizoram. As a powerful speaker, he could be able to win the hearts of a large section of the Mizos. He, in fact, enjoyed wide appeal. But the Mizo National Front encouraged a trend towards personality cult, and helped in furthering centralisation of power structure and also prevented the practice of intra-party democracy or democratic functioning of the party organisation at all level. Besides, there were also other elements which encouraged the tendency towards autocratic leadership. There were two elements, the system of intra-party communication and the instrument of indoctrination (education of the party members) which ran vertically from top to the bottom of the party. As a consequence, leadership always remained with the extremist and had not emerged from the moderate or intellectual groups of the new cadres who joined much later. There were almost the same persons from extremist groups at the higher level, representing more or less the extremist ideas till memorandum of settlement was signed.

It may be also mentioned that the party in its basic structure was rather ultra-conservative whereas its leadership elite was modern in outlook, realistic in belief and meticulous in actions. But the MNF Chief could not skilfully bridge the gap between antagonistic currents within the MNF. The MNF Chief simply kept together the different wings, groups and factions by his unchallenged leadership/authority. This is true no doubt but the party had a devoted band of workers and was guided by leaders. After memorandum of settlement, the MNF no doubt, had amended its constitution and also deleted some objectionable provisions. It also built up a mass base. It had further acquired political maturity insofar as it accepted the discipline of a parliamentary party and the values of democratic government. The MNF has emerged as a secular, democratic and constitutional party. The party leadership has also claimed to be legitimate being based on elections.

It is interesting to note that the MNF has not yet prevented its trend towards personality cult or strengthened the democratic functioning of the party organisation at all levels. There is a reason behind it that the leadership of the party before and after memorandum of settlement has remained unchanged.

The MNF Chief and some of his devoted and trusted colleagues had been still guiding the party and also playing a very dominant role in its organisational set-up and policy formulation. When the MNF party led by Laldenga split into two MNF and MNF (Democratic), a spokesman for the new party said about leadership, "We expected a new era and Mizoram under Laldenga where corruption would be rooted out and moral value upheld. However, he suppressed democracy and introduced a totalitarian type of functioning in the party and the government." Mr. Lalherliana said: "instead of collective leadership, Mr. Laldenga turned himself into a supremo." He said, the dissidents had made several attempts to persuade Mr. Laldenga to change his style of functioning. Instead, he became worse and practised nepotism openly." As Maurice Durverger rightly observes, leadership of political parties presents dual characteristics: it is democratic in appearance and oligarchic in character.

Party and Election Politics

This was the first general election to the Legislative Assembly held on 16th Feb., 1987 after Mizoram was accorded statehood. For the purpose of election, Mizoram was divided into 40 single member constituencies. Of them, 28 were in Aizawl district, 7 in Lunglei district and 5 in Chhimtuipui district. Of 40 constituencies, 38 were reserved for scheduled tribes and 2 for (Lunglei south in Lunglei district and Lokicherra in Aizawl district) unreserved. Briefly, Mizoram is entirely a tribal area.

Even the candidates who contested from the two unreserved constituencies, were also from scheduled tribes. The National Regional political parties which contested the Assembly election were: the Indian National Congress (I), the People's Conference (reorganised), the Mizo National Front and the Mizo National Union (unrecognised). The Congress set up 40 candidates for 40 seats. The Mizo National Front had 37 candidates. The People's Conference fielded 36 candidates.

The Mizo National Union nominated 21 candidates, but 11 Independents were also in the election fray. But there was no electoral adjustment among the parties because each of the party wanted to have a majority of its own in the Assembly. Undoubtedly the contest in almost all the constituencies was very keen and tough, though all the parties fought the election battle on their own. While four parties and independents were in the election fray, the actual contest was between the Congress and the MNF.

The MNF for the first time entered the Assembly polls of 1987 after Mizoram became state. The overall percentage of poll in 1987 was 72.63 per cent. The Mizo National Front secured an overwhelming majority with 24 seats out of 37 it contested. The party had 36.62 per cent of the total votes polled. The Chief Minister Laldenga and his former colleagues of the coalition ministry also got elected. Laldenga was elected from two constituencies.

The female candidate fielded by the MNF also won the seat. The Congress, a National Party, however, out of 40 contested seats managed to get only 13 seats, securing 32.98 per cent of the total votes polled. The Congress suffered despite being the ruling party in the territory since 1984. The People's Conference bagged only 3 seats out of 36 seats it contested and secured 23.70 per cent of the votes cast. This recognised regional party had a complete setback at the polls suffering a further loss of 5 seats. The Mizo National Union which came out with 21 candidates drew a blank obtaining only 3.33 per cent of the total votes polled.

The Mizo National Front fought the election mostly on the local issues. The party pledged to implement all terms and conditions and other stipulations contained in the memorandum of settlement, ensure peace/normalcy, bring about all-round progress making Mizoram a 'model state', bridge widening gap between the rich and the poor, eradicate corruption of all sorts, combat different social evils in the society and improve the deplorable conditions of the general masses caused by inequality in various spheres.

Besides the party had 15-point election manifesto concerning political, social, administrative, economic development problems of the territory. Lastly, the party came out with slogan 'Mizoram is for the Mizos.' It appears from the party's manifesto that the party did nothing to have reasonable or equitable distribution of the planned development among the average Mizo people. Party's manifesto lacked land reforms measures. The party in its constitution/manifesto vaguely talked a great deal about integration of the contiguous areas inhabited by the Mizos with Mizoram. But this promise is nothing but an emotional appeal. Laldenga's electoral promise of a self-reliant economy was a farce.

The Mizo National Front's best performance in this election among all the parties of the state must be due to the charismatic towering leadership of the founder leader, Laldenga besides other factors. The MNF Chief made extensive election tours throughout the territory, projected his personal stature/skill, promised a reform and regeneration in Mizo society, upliftment of the status of women folk. The overwhelming majority of youth were among the voters. Briefly Laldenga's charismatic leadership, capability and widespread appeal contributed to the victory of his party in the election.

It seems that the Mizo electors also prefer change of government at certain intervals and vote an untried party to power. Thus, the MNF faired best in Aizawl and Lunglei districts and made almost a clean sweep in Aizawl town. 20 of its 24 MLAs were returned from Aizawl district which has a total of 28 seats. In Aizawl town, the MNF bagged 7 out of 8 seats. But the party in Chhimtuipui district drew a total blank. It clearly shows the distrust of the ethnic minority tribes — Pawi, Lakher and Chakma for the MNF.

Party and Government

After massive victory of the Mizo National Front in the Assembly poll of 1987, Laldenga, a leader of the house was sworn in as the first Chief Minister of the state on February 20, 1987. He installed a two-tier ministry of Cabinet rank and state rank. The Chief Minister offered offices to the more recent converts for which he was accused of treading on the path of political expediency. The Laldenga Cabinet hardly functioned for two years.

The 19-month old Mizo National Front Government headed by Laldenga was reduced to a minority on August 29, 1988 following the sudden withdrawal of support by 9 of the 25 MNF legislators in the 40-member Assembly. The nine legislators led by the MNF Vice-President Chawngzuala formed a new party, Mizo National Front (Democratic) and conveyed their decision to the speaker of the Assembly. They also requested the speaker to recognise them as a separate group or MNF (Democratic) party which has been formed as a result of the split in the original MNF party led by Laldenga.

The dissident legislators took decision to protest against the suspension of two MLAs, Vanlalruaia and Siamliana from the primary membership of the party by Laldenga without the consent of the party as well as to ensure democratic functioning in the party. The dissident legislators and the Congress (I) MLAs, as pointed out in the speech by the Governor, formed United Legislature Party (ULP) under the leadership of Lalthanhawla MIX and President MPOC (I). Lalthanhawla, the unanimous leader of the United Legislature party met the Governor and staked his claim for forming a ministry. But the Governor asked Lalthanhawla to wait for the Speakers' crucial verdict on the face of 8 MNF Legislators who had left the party. J. Thanghuama, the Speaker of the Assembly issued a show-cause notice to the 8 MLAs asking them why they should not be disqualified from their membership under the Anti-Defection Law within 7 days.

By the same show-cause notice the Speaker suspended these 8 MLAs from their membership during the pendency of the disqualification proceedings though there is no provision either in the tenth schedule of the constitution or under the Mizoram Legislative Assembly (Disqualification on grounds of Defection) Rules, 1987 for suspension of a member during the pendency of the proceedings. This was pointed out to the Speaker by the Governor.

The Speaker, however, pointed out that he was empowered to suspend them under the constitution and Rule 9 of the said Mizoram Rules. The Deputy Speaker K. Thanfianga, who was in Boston, USA for Medical treatment, also sent his decision through message to the Speaker to join the MNF (D), though his name was included in the list of 9 MLAs submitted to the Governor on 29 August, 1988, he of course did not sign. But he agreed to be on the side of the dissident legislators forming a separate breakaway MNF (Democratic) group.

All these factors led the Governor to arrive at the conclusion that the Speaker was determined to disqualify 8 MLAs, though he earlier claimed that for a split, 9 MLAs are required. Thus the simmering political crisis caused a deadlock. The open rift and confrontation between the two powerful groups in the legislature party-one led by Laldenga and the other by Chawnzualak, Vice-President of the original MNF party became so manifest that uneasy situation prevailed in Mizo politics, leading to intra-party squabbles, conflict and internal dissensions among the ranks of the MNF. In spite of this unstable stand of Mizo politics, Laldenga, however, did not resign from office.

So the Governor, in order to end the political instability advised the President of India to issue a proclamation of emergency under Article 356 of the Constitution of India. Accordingly the President of India placed Mizoram under President's Rule on 7 September, 1988 for a period of six months and also dissolved the Assembly. There was much relief in the state on the exit of ministers, end of horse trading among the legislators and the dissolution of the Assembly. Ultimately, this infight in the MNF had adverse impact on the rank and file of the MNF bringing about a complete split within the party termed as MNF. (Laldenga) and MNF (Democratic), the first led by Laldenga and second Chawngzuala, though the split in the party was not programme-based.

In fact, the split was a result of clash of personalities, personal rivalries, rank opportunism and race for ministerial berths in the two-tier ministry which was expanded twice during its 19-month tenure. The MNF leadership privately admitted that the main reason for the desertion of the party by the dissident legislators was not merely to accommodate them in the two-tier ministry in which there were 12 ministers out of 25 member legislature party. This was stated by Saingura Sailo, Minister of State of Law. As the fact remains true, since the inception of the MNF, the control of the party has passed into the hands of select group of elites which does not like the extremely unitary structure of leadership which has later proved disastrous for the MNF organisation.

As regards the impact of the MNF on the Mizo people, the MNF insurgency for two decades has certainly affected the social, political and economic conditions of the people adversely. Insurgency has disrupted the normal administrative system and the counter-insurgency measures have again affected the system in the feedback process. Briefly, insurgency has posed a serious problem to the nation-building process and economic development in Mizoram.

Economic ways and means are provided in the development plans. Social development takes place by educational and welfare projects. The MNF emergency has caused a serious harm to the average Mizo people though the party has given a sense of political unity to the Mizo people and also introduced a concept of Mizo nationhood." It has raised secessionist and communal demands and thereby became a strong force in Mizo politics.

- The MNF is regional in character and more concerned with the interest of the Mizos. The party impact at the national level is also limited, though this party works in a very close link with the National Congress (I) Party. There is no doubt that the party is now secular and constitutional in character.

- It is not programme-oriented party. Most functions performed by the party are not political/ideologically-oriented but are determined by the structural elements of the society.

- In fact the party is the result of a personal following of its popular/front ranking leader, Laldenga.

- The ruling MNF which was manifesting the signs of an ultra radical party prior to a memorandum of settlement, is now turning into a static middle class association.

It may conclude with a short-hand comment on the limited but positive impact of regional parties that they are at the base of our polity. Their impact had been limited since, given their class character which was much the same as that of the Congress and other non-left parties, basic restructuring of existing socio-economic relations is not on their agenda. Ritual homage to social justice and holistic claims on behalf of their regions notwithstanding, regional parties have by and large a status quest social philosophy with some top widow dressing of welfarist tokenism and populist gimmickry.

Within the liberal democratic frame of reference however, regional parties have made politics more competitive, and popular participation in the political process more extensive at the grass roots. There is, finally, some activisation, slow but growing of a process of rethinking on the problem of nation-building in India. Regional parties have helped this rethinking by compelling attention to the need for coming to terms with "territorial identity" they articulate and defend. Regional parties may well claim some credit for winning a measure of legitimacy for the view that, given our plural social structure, nation-building has to be a process of aggregation, not assimilation.

An Analysis of Mizoram State Assembly Election of 1987 : Election in a parliamentary democracy is a political means through which the political opinion and awareness of the masses are moulded and promoted. Election involves people into politics or public affairs through participation and mobilisation, provides political linkages, resolves conflicts and also brings about peaceful and orderly change of authority to new leaders. Through the election the authority of a government is clothed with legitimacy. Not only that but the right to govern in the election is also obtained in competition with parties.

The political parties as per the rules of representative democracy have also to accept the election results. Hence, a good election system is regarded as the life belt of genuine representative government, serving an important function for the citizens and the political system as well. In India also, elections to legislative bodies are conducted on the basis of adult franchise, single-member constituency, one voter one vote, secret ballot, direct election and election by simple majority. Briefly elections in India, however, appear to be an increasingly integrative process.

In the Mizo politics during the fifth general elections to the Mizoram Legislative Assembly of 1987, participation of regional and national political parties, analysis of their election manifestoes/issues/promises, results, reasons for the success and setback of the participating parties and their overall performances/prospects in the context of the state politics. It also intends to throw some light on the mobilisation, apathy and political awareness of the voters, voting turn-out and role of ethnic forces.

The Government of India with a view to elevating the union territory to the statehood of Mizoram introduced the Mizoram Statehood Bill, 1986 with special safeguards and provisions of forty elective seats (38 reserved for scheduled tribes and 2 unreserved) in the Mizoram Legislative Assembly and the 53rd Constitution (Amendment) Bill, 1986 in the Parliament and got the bill passed by a absolute majority of votes.

The President of India also assented the Mizoram Statehood Bill, 1986 on August, 14, 1986. The state bill, thus, became an act but was not brought in force with immediate effect. On February 20, 1987, Mizoram was inaugurated as the 23rd state of the Indian Union. The Legislative Assembly polls were held on February, 16, 1987. After the results of elections, the Mizo National Front formed the first popular ministry on February 20, headed by Laldenga as the Chief Minister.

This was the first general election to the Legislative Assembly, after Mizoram attained the status of statehood. For the purpose of election, Mizoram was divided into 40 single-member constituencies. Of them, 28 were in Aizawl district, 7 in Lunglei district and 5 in Chhimtuipui district. Of 40 constituencies, 38 were reserved for the scheduled tribes and 2 (Lunglei South in Lunglei district and Lokicherra in Aizawl district) unreserved. Briefly Mizoram it entirely a tribal area. Even the candidates who contested from the two unreserved constituencies were also scheduled tribes.

Each constituency in Mizoram consisted of the number of electorates about 3,237 to 12,337. But all the constituencies are not equal to one another regarding the number of electors mainly owing to topography and terrain. However, such disparities should not exist in constituencies where the number of electors is small, because the value of each vote is greater than in constituencies with greater number of voters. The successful candidate will have to secure smaller number of voters. So all these factors should have been considered by the Delimitation Commission at the time of formation of constituencies.

The total population of Mizoram at the time of election in 1987 was 4,93,757. Of them, there were 3,21,557 registered voters. In 1984, the total number of voters was 2,56,530. Thus there was an increase in the number of electors. Of the registered voters in 1987, 1,63,043 were male and 1,58,514 were female voters. The sex ratio in the electorate thus, appears to be equal. There are 938 females to every 100 male voters.

It is an interesting fact to mention that the national average of the electorate to total population is always 45 per cent. But in Mizoram in 1987 it is 62.12 per cent. Evidently some below the voting age must have been registered as electors. There were 2,25,387, 51,596 and 44,574 voters in Aizawl. Lunglei and Chhimtuipui districts respectively. There were 550 polling stations of them, 355 were in the Aizawl district, 95 in the Lunglei district and 100 in the Chhimtuipui district.

The number of polling stations increased in 1987 was 147 compared to 1984. Thus polling stations were located in such a way that the voters of almost all the villages could cast their votes conveniently. The last dates for filing nomination papers and the withdrawal of candidatures were fixed 23, 24, 27, January, 1987. The date for poll was fixed on February, 16, 1987 which took place between 7.30 A.M. to 3.30 P.M.

There were four national and regional political parties, namely, the Indian National Congress, the People's Conference (recognised), the Mizo National Front, the Mizo National Union (unrecognised) and some independents in the election fray. There were 145 candidates including independents in the field. Of the 145 candidates, the Congress fielded 40 candidates for 40 seats including one woman.

The Mizo National Front had 37 candidates including one woman. One of them (Laldenga) filed his nomination in two constituencies. The Mizo National Union nominated 21 candidates including one woman. Rochhunga Ralte, who left the Congress and joined the MNU, filed his nomination in two constituencies. Besides them, 11 independents also filed their nominations. 214 nominations for 40 seats were filed but 69 of them withdrew their candidatures.

The unique feature of this election was that the Congress fielded all the sitting members including Speaker, Deputy speaker, Chief Minister/Ministers except three. Similarly, the People's Conference nominated all its sitting members (MLAs). The MNF also fielded all its members of the coalition Cabinet. Thus 28 of the sitting MLAs of the dissolved Assembly were in the contest. There was a straight contest in the two constituencies (Tuipang and Saiha). In all other constituencies, there were 3 to 5 candidates.

Thus there were multiple contests in the remaining 37 seats. 13, 19 and 5 constituencies had triangular, four-cornered and five-cornered contests respectively. But there was no electoral adjustment among the parties because each of the parties wanted to have a majority of its own in the Assembly. Undoubtedly, the contest in almost all the constituencies was very keen and tough, though all the parties (recognised/unrecognised) fought the election battle on their own. While four parties and independents were involved in the elections, the actual contest was between the Congress and the MNF. The MNF for the first time entered the Assembly polls of 1987, when Mizoram became a state.

Election Results

The percentage of poll in Mizoram has always been good. But the overall percentage of poll in 1987 was 72.63. The total number of votes polled was 2,30,865 for 40 seats. The poll results, thus, signify that the Mizo National Front secured an overwhelming majority with 24 seats out of 37, it contested. The total number of votes polled by the party was 84,549. The party had 36.62 per cent of the total votes polled, the Chief Minister Laldenga and his former colleagues of the coalition ministry also got elected.

Laldenga was elected from two constituencies. The female candidate fielded by the MNF also won the seat. The Congress, a lone National Party, however, out of 40 contested seats, managed to get only 1 out of 3 seats, securing 71,526, votes or 32.98 of the total votes polled. It is a surprising to note that none of the stalwarts especially Speaker, Deputy Speaker, and the Ministers of Cabinet rank except the Chief Minister, Lalthanhawla could return to the Assembly.

The party suffered despite the Congress being the ruling party in the territory since 1984. The People's Conference bagged only 3 seats out of 36 seats, it contested and secured 54,717 votes or 23.70 per cent of the votes cast. Thus a recognised regional party had a complete setback at the polls, suffering a further loss of 5 seats. The founding president of the party and its many stalwarts could not also return to the Assembly. The party could not maintain its strength of seats that it had in the dissolved Assembly. Thus the party has been experiencing a steady decline in its influence and voting strength, since it split in 1978.

The Mizo National Union which came out with 21 candidates, drew a blank obtaining only 7,688 votes or 3.33 per cent of the total votes polled. The party suffered a complete setback perhaps due to its weak organisational base in the territory. It fought as an unorganised party in Mizoram. None of the Independents found place in the Assembly, though they polled 7,759 votes or 3.36 per cent of the total votes polled. Out of 28 seats in Aizawl district, MNF bagged 20, Congress, 6 and Peoples Conference, 2 seats. In Lunglei district MNF won 4 seats, while Congress got 3. In Chhimtuipui district, MNF drew blank Congress won 4 seats while Peoples Conference one. Later the party joined the MNF.

There was no uncontested return to the Assembly during the period 1972 to 1984. But an interesting thing about the election of 1987 is that Nirupam Chakma of the Congress party from the Chawngte constituency was elected uncontested, the first of its kind in the electoral politics of Mizoram.

Another feature of the election is that most of the candidates won without the majority support of the electorate. Since there were multiple contests in the 37 seats, it resulted in two evil consequences, viz. election of a substantial number of members by a minority vote and forfeiture of security deposit by the vanquished. For an instance, in 1987, 34 of the 40 elected members to the Assembly were elected by a minority vote. 21 of the 24 seats won by the Mizo National Front were elected by minority vote, Laldenga was one of them. Of the 13 elected Congress members, 10 were elected by a minority vote. All the three of the People's Conference were elected by a minority vote.

The Election of members by a minority vote is inevitable, so long as the present system of election, by single-member constituency and simple majority exist. But it should be admitted that this honour of being elected by a minority vote is shared by all the political parties and independent candidates. It must also be said that sometimes a candidate may be elected by an absolute majority, even though the contest is a multiple one. But in Mizoram it seems to be rare.

The general rule appears to be election of members in multiple contests by a minority vote. The second evil consequence of multiple contests is the forfeiture of the security deposits. There may be forfeiture of security deposits in straight contest, though it happens very rarely. A candidate forfeits his security deposit if he does not poll one-sixth of the total number of valid votes polled in his constituency. In 1987, 27 of the 145 candidates, who contested elections lost their security deposits.

The party-wise break-up of the candidates who forfeited their deposits was MNF-I, Independents, 7-MNU-19 of the 21 candidates and People's Conference-4 of the 36 candidates. None of the candidates set up by the Congress forfeited security deposit. Although the Congress party received a setback, its voting percentage went up in comparison to the 1984 elections. Briefly the Congress party improved its image in the electorate.

Table shows the seats contested by each party, seats won, valid votes polled in the elections to the Mizoram Legislative Assembly, 1987

Name of Party	Seats Contested Polled	Seats Won	Valid Votes	Percentage
Indian National Congress	40	13	76,549	32.98
Mizo National Front	37	24	84,549	36.62
People's Conference	36	3	54,717	23.70
Mizo National Union	21	Nil	7,688	3.33
Independents/Others	11	Nil	7,759	3.36

Source: Report on general election to Mizoram State Legislative Assembly, 1987, published by the chief electoral officer to the Government of Mizoram, Aizawl

Election Manifestos

The political parties which were in the contests, issued their election manifestos declaring important issues and divergent approaches to manifold problems. The parties had appeals to the electorate different from each other. However, the study of the manifestos of the parties provides a clue to the understanding of the election situation and the strategy and tactics of the parties.

The Congress

The Congress in its election pledges talked of achieving the programmes and policies of democracy, socialism, secularism and non-alignment. This apart, the election manifesto included the integration of the Mizos living in the contiguous areas under a single administrative unit as provided in the Constitution. The party also pledged to promote and safeguard the culture, customs and traditions of the Mizos, check the illegal entry of the foreigners to Mizoram and deport all foreigners living in the territory to their respective countries.

The steps to rehabilitate/settle the prevailing disturbances, MNF returnees and disabled persons would be taken. The party further included the provision for better service conditions to all government servants; reservation of more jobs for the local people, and safeguard and concession to the Mizos as a scheduled tribe in trade, commerce and contract, enhancement of the amount of housing loan to enable the most needy (urban/ rural) people to have benefits of such scheme.

The party apart from the above promises, was concerned with the socio-economic development of the Mizos especially economic self-sufficiency, abandonment of Jhuming cultivation and adoption of permanent occupation of different types by the people, supply of high-yielding seeds to the farmers for better production, construction of rural godown and cold storage and extension of all possible help to the cultivators for better marketing facilities within Mizoram or elsewhere in the country, establishment of industries to utilise the territory forest and natural resources, encouragement of handloom and handicrafts, abundant supply of drinking water to the rural and urban masses, better communications such as connecting all villages and places of agricultural importance to motorable roads, construction of railway line and airport to link Mizoram with the rest of the country, establishment of more hospitals/dispensaries, extension of healthy cooperation between the police and the village leaders to promote healthy social life. Finally, the Congress came out with bold stand to eradicate corruption of all types. The manifesto was in Mizo language.

Mizo National Front

The Mizo National Front fought the election mostly on the local issues. The party laid emphasis on the sole responsibility of the Mizos to uplift Mizoram. The party having faith in God and the people pledged to implement all terms, conditions and other stipulations contained in the memorandum of settlement (Mizoram Peace Accord), ensure lasting peace, normalcy and freedom, bring about all round progress making Mizoram a 'Model State', bridge widening gap/cleavage between the rich and the poor, eradicate corruption of all sorts, combat different social evils in the society and improve the deplorable condition of the general masses caused by inequality in various spheres.

Besides the party had 15-point election manifestos mainly concerning political, social, administrative and economic development problems of the territory. It being specially concerned with the welfare of the Mizo people proclaimed to make efforts:

- To defend the religious faith of the Mizo people and also to safeguard them from religious extremity.

- To preserve and promote the mizo culture, traditions/customs and to protect the people from cultural orthodoxy.

- To create consciousness and awareness in the people about the all-round progress of the territory could be only made/achieved by their collective efforts.

- To help removing 'beggars-mentality' and also malpractice terming it as 'sale of conscience' from political spheres.

- To review and codify if so necessary the existing Mizo customary-Laws and Social Practices. To improve the status of women and also to safeguard the rights and liberty of individuals.

- Prohibit all narcotic drugs and other intoxicants.
- To encourage cultivation of cash crops and create suitable marketing facilities and also to explore/utilise indigenous resources for industrial growth.
- To separate judiciary from executive for efficient judicial administration. To take efforts to have a separate High Court in Mizoram and also to bring efficiency in the administrative functioning of the state.
- To expand and develop the police department.
- To augment electricity and also to accelerate the steps taken in this regard.
- To develop and expand telecommunication to link the remotest part of the state.
- To develop roads and other road communications connecting all towns and villages.
- To supply drinking water to rural and urban masses abundantly.
- To extend possible help to families for permanent occupation.

Lastly, the party came out with slogan, 'Mizoram is for the Mizos'. The manifesto was in Mizo language.

People's Conference

The party promised the voters to eradicate party favouritism, nepotism, corruption of all sorts, strive for justice in the expenditure of public money and also consult the church leaders and voluntary organisations as regards social reforms.

The party, besides, had 19-point election manifestos relating to political, social, administration and economic planning.

Political

- To stop illegal entry of Bangladesh Nationals to Mizoram.
- To work to integrate the contiguous Mizo inhabited areas if possible.
- To clearly demarcate the boundaries of Mizoram with neighbouring states.
- To formulate a scheme for reasonable compensation to the victims of political and government high handedness.

Social

- To preserve and promote the mizo traditions/customs/culture/heritage.
- To improve the educational system and programmes.
- To improve public health services and social welfare works.
- To create employment opportunities for the unemployed.

- To enforce effectively the section 27 of the Mizoram Excise Act, 1973 and also sections 211, 218 of Rules, 1983.

- To plan to provide a fair compensation for the MNF returnees.

- To develop youth welfare activities especially sports/games.

Administration

- To form a clean, efficient, effective, impartial administration to promote and meet the needs of the people and the region as a whole.

- To preserve Mizo customary laws and introduce separation of judiciary from executive so that quick and impartial justice may be available to the people.

- To look into and settle the cases/problems of the government servants.

Economic Planning

- To accelerate urban and rural electrification and water supply.

- To develop means of communications especially Air, Railways and waterways and other road communications connecting all villages.

- To create better conditions to have self-sufficiency in agricultural products within 10 years.

- To give priority to the cultivation of cash crops and create suitable marketing facilities for the farmers.

- To develop industries on priority with maximum utilisation of indigenous resources. The party manifesto was in mizo language.

Mizo National Union

The Mizo National Union, an unrecognised splinter party with its weak organisational base in the territory, entered the elections with lofty ideas of sloganeering that the MNU ministry will be people's ministry instead of party ministry, safeguard the Mizo society and protect the poor Mizos from exploitation and unsecured conditions.

The party further promised to strive for economic justice and improve the socio-economic conditions of the weaker Mizos by abolishing the wide gap between the rich and poor, advocate fairness instead of nepotism, impartiality instead of partiality, production instead of corruption, eradicate social evils caused by poverty, establish unity in social life and improve church activities, talk of every household to be self-sufficient and also of eradication of corruption, protection of the services of both the government servants and the labourers.

The party proposed to allot land to homeless/shelterless for their houses, make land ceiling for those having a vast stretch of land, arrange/food for work enabling the poor to earn their daily bread and provide employment for the qualified members of those poor families having none in the government services. It, apart from the above promises, assured the electorate to prohibit all intoxicating drinks/drugs, and cancel liquor permits, construct/develop road communications, Railways, waterways and air fields in order to enable the farmers/cultivators to sell their agricultural products and give priority to the development of small-scale industries and hydel projects. The manifesto was in Mizo language.

It appears from the manifestos of the National and Regional parties that no election manifestos emphasised the progressive measures to bring about the socio-economic transformation in the traditional society of the Mizos. Nothing to have the reasonable equitable distribution of the planned development among the average-Mizo people was pledged. Not only but the parties, manifestos completely lacked Land Reform Measures. The parties further vaguely talked a great deal about integration of the contiguous areas inhabited by the Mizo with Mizoram. But this promise is nothing but an emotional appeal. Because the areas inhabited by the Mizos are found in most states of the Northeastern India and also in foreign countries like Burma and Bangladesh. The Chief Ministers of the Northeastern States have categorically stated that no land of their territory would be transferred to Mizoram.

10

Tourism

The places of historical and social interest have their importance; they highlight the important events which have ever occurred in their own spheres and the important social and cultural trends which suit themselves with the folk attribute and character. Excepting Aizawl and to some extent Lunglei, urbanisation in the whole of the state is now working at a slow pace. However, some new administrative townships have sprung. The village settlements are still very important for our consideration.

Mizoram, also known as the land of Blue Mountains, is known for its picturesque beauty. Mizoram tourism implies a vivid tour across the romantic valleys, charismatic hills, quaint villages, deep gorges and the beautiful mountains of the territory.

Places of Interest

There are quite a number of places in Mizoram which may be described as 'must see' for tourist sports, anyone wishing to see a little more than the conventional tourist sports, anyone interests to know about the local culture and traditions is advised/expected to do/visit some of the Mizoram's historic memorials and fabled caves scattered all over the state. Travelling in Mizoram, not unlike in any other mountainous regions, is pain staking and little hazardous at times, but it has its own rewards.

Blue Mountain: The Highest peak in Mizoram, the Blue Mountain (Phawngpui) is situated in Chhimtuipui District overlooking the bend of the River Koldyne (Chhimtuipui) close on the state's border with Myanmar. The peak 2,157 metre in height and encircled by bamboo groves at the top where there is a level ground of about 200 hectares, offers a grand view of the height hills and the meandering undulated valleys. The woods around are home to various species of beautiful and rare flora and fauna.

Pukzing Cave: The largest cave in Mizoram, it is situated at Pukzing village near Marpara in the district of Aizawl District (Mamit). Legend has it that cave was carved out of the hills with the help of only a hair pin by a very strong man called *Mualzavata.*

Milu Puk: In the Mizo language, puk means a cave. Situated near Mamte village over 100 km, from Lunglei town, the Milu Puk, which is a large cave, was found many years ago to contain heaps of human skeleton.

Lamsial Puk: Situated near Farkawn village in Aizawl (Champhai) District, the cave is a silent testimony to a battle between two neighbouring villages in which many lost their lives. The bodies of the fighters from village Lamsial are said to have been kept in the cave.

Kungawrhi Puk: Another cave in Aizawl District, it is situated on a hill between Farkawn and Vaphai villages. According to the folktales, a beautiful young girl by the name of Kungawrhi was abducted and kept confined in the forlorn cave by some evil spirits when she was on her way to her husband's village. Kungawrhi, however, was later rescued by her husband from the prison of the spirits.

Sibuta Lung: Erected about three hundreds years ago by a tribal chief, this memorial stone is named after him. The memorial offers a story of jilted love and lust for revenge. Having been rejected by a girl he fell headlong in love with, Sibuta went mad for revenge and decided to raise a memorial to himself in a manner which displayed an insane mind. A huge rock awash with the blood of three people sacrificed by Sibuta was carried over a distance of 10 km from the Tlawng River. Darlalpuii, a beautiful young girl, was crushed alive in a pit dug to erect the mausoleum. The memorial was raised over Darlai who lost her life under weight of the stone.

Phulpui Grave: A tale of love and tragedy also hangs by this grave located at Phulpui village in Aizawl District. Tualvungi, a raging beauty in her time, was married to Zawlpala, the Phulpui chief. She was later forced by circumstances to marry Phuntia, chief of another village. But Tualvungi could not forget her first love. She came to Phulpui years after Zawlpala's death, hah, a pit dug by the side of his grave and persuaded an old woman to kill and bury there.

Chhingpuii Memorial: Raised to the memory of a young woman called Chhingpuii who was exceedingly beautiful, it is situated between Baktawng and Chhingchhip villages on the Aizawl-Lunglei Road. Chhingpuii, born to an aristocratic family, selected Kaptluanga as her husband from among her many suitors. But her happiness was short-lived, as a war broke out afterwards. Chhingpuii was abducted and killed. A grief-stricken Kaptluanga took his own life. The stone memorial reminds one of the legendary love story of Chhingpuii and Kaptluanga.

Mangkhai Lung: A large memorial stone, it was erected about three-hundred years ago at Champhai to the memory of a well-known Ralte chief, Mangkhaia.

Buddha's Image: An engraved image of Lord Buddha, with those of dancing girls on either side, was found at a site near Mualcheng village about 50 km from Lunglei town. The site also has another stone slab on which some human footmarks and a few implements like spearhead and Dao are engraved. The area is close to the Chittagong Hill Tracts which was under which the Buddhist influence a few centuries ago. It is assumed that some visiting Buddhists from the Hill Tracts were responsible for the Buddha engraving.

Suangpuilawn Inscriptions: A stone slab lie by a stream at Suangpuilawn village in Aizawl District with strange words inscribed on it. The inscription remain to be deciphered till date. However, it is believed that the inscriptions were done by some people who inhabited the area in ancient times.

Thangliana Lung: Captain T. H. Lewin was one of the first Englishmen to come to Mizoram. The District Commissioner of the Chittagong Hills Tracts, who entered Mizoram by way of Demagiri (Tlabung) in 1865, became so popular with the local tribesmen that as a mark of respect, he was called Thangliana which meant 'greatly famous'. He lived with the Mizos for nine years and authored the first Lushai book. His memorial stone at Demagiri remains as evidence of the extent of his popularity with the Mizos.

Natural Beauty

Mizoram offers a rich scenery. It is still one of the states which possesses the good forest and natural resources, rich in bamboo and timber species of various kinds. Till 1986-87, 35 per cent of land is covered by forests. At one time her forests sheltered host of animals and winged tribes according to the altitudes and soils and species of fauna suiting with them. They were really the natural wild sanctuaries. Jhumming has already altered the soil conditions and the agricultural output has gone on dwindling. The wanton destruction of the valuable timber species, owing to the expansion of work in construction, road building and other undertakings, has considerably reduced the number of wild animals. The same picture obtains in the other Hill States. Soil conservation and afforestation, therefore, have their immense importance towards maintaining the ecology in the present State.

Village Regrouping

There are approximately between 300 and 400 villages. The regrouping of villages in the earlier years had even reduced their number. The villages when, they were removed from their old sites to the new paces, retained their old names. The ancient villages, many of which are forgotten, had cradled the virile system of chiefdom; they had left their marks on their ancient institutions. The villages provided the scene of activities which enhanced the concept of the folk attributes. There are many villages now not yet made accessible to the present roads.

The inaccessibility to the remote villages in the past had shaped the village subsistence of economy which was self reliant at least in the essential necessities. The inaccessibility to the communication had kept few of them in complete isolation. They had created difficulties to trading and commerce. Water supply at some places was rendered difficult. The traditional and indigenous character is still noticed especially in the far-off isolated places. The undulating character of the terrain along with the practice of shifting cultivation, have obliterated the position of the interior villages.

Administration and Christianity have played their roles consistently to forge the inter-village integration. Evidently the gospel was reached to the distant places in the most difficult circumstances. The acceptance of Christianity had led to an integrated system of the Church community. The integration of villages into Circles led to the forging of the administrative integration among the chieftains. These were the concepts of the spiritual and administrative bonds.

The regrouping of villages which occurred recently brought about a great transitional system which affected the position of the previous villages adversely. The regrouping worked out some concepts of village integration. The villages with the admixed social moods, characteristics, temperament all of sudden sprang. The system of regrouping introduced at places a mixed concept of culture and economy.

The regrouping, however, was considered from the point of security indispensable. It taxed enormously upon the energies and exertions of the village folk and also on the part of the authorities. The matter of rehabilitating a sizeable section of the people taxed considerably upon them. It was a transitional upsurge which inevitably had involved for a time being, the dislocation of trade, educational and agricultural pursuits and sometimes changed radically the village habits and concepts. The country was gradually emerging as a resettlement after this phase was past.

The Administrative Headquarters and Historical Places: The places where the historical events of far-reaching importance had occurred, have found their earlier references. Now, therefore, the contemporaneous importance of places as headquarters, educational and business centres will be dealt with from the modern angle. There can be places where the provision of public amenities can be more perceptible. Bulk of villages, therefore, screened away from roads, retain their traditional character. The importance of places can now be analysed.

Aizawl is the state capital. The two District Headquarters besides Aizawl are Lunglei and Saiha. The process of elevation of Aizawl to its present position worked out to more 100 years. Other important places are road stations, and centres of education and of community development.

Aizawl originated as a stockade built in 1890 by Daly and Col. G. J. Skinner when a great expedition from Cachar traversed across the country to permanently occupying it and reduce the Lushais to a settled civilization. It lies on the northern portion and had, prior to the birth of a State, served as the potential centre of administration. It was the capital of the Political Officer from 1890 who represented the Chief Commissioner of Assam. We find that the inception of the administration of South Lushai Hills took place from 1891 then tagged on to Chittagong Hills Tract.

In 1898, South Lushai was integrated into the Lushai Hills District and was since then united to the latter District over which a Political Officer now redesignated Superintendent was placed in charge, with his headquarter at Aijal. Aijal was emerging to limelight. It became the first administrative as well as the first Mission headquarter; it had kept itself as a strategic position and saw to the occurrences of many events which would have historically been interesting. Aizawl aptly responded to the happenings which culminated in the formation of the state and had kept the transactions with the erstwhile Subdivisions in administration, judiciary and other matters.

The first jeepable road connecting with Silchar was brought only during the first world war. Another road was built and completed in 1950 which connects Aizawl and Lunglei. Now, a network of communications has extended to the near and far-off places.

Aizawl houses now the State Legislative Assembly, the Raj Bhavan and the Secretariat functioning from the state headquarter. Many new educational institutions have been functioning in the town. The small industrial installations and training centres have also appeared. Its importance has been greatly enhanced as the seat of legislation, besides being a Government and business centre. It is the headquarter of most of the political parties. Most of the works of the Christian organisations are directed from here. It served earlier as the headquarter of the District Council uptil the birth of the Union Territory.

Places of Interest

Lunglei - it started as a fort built by F.V.W. Tregear and D. Lyall when an expedition was taken into the hills to subjugate the marauding tribes. It became the capital of South Lushai Hills when a Superintendent was stationed here in 1891. In 1898 when the South Lushai and the North Lushai Hills were amalgamated, the Assistant to the Superintendent was placed in charge who was later on known as the Subdivisional Officer. For long years it was the Subdivisional headquarter of the southern tract and since 1952, housed the District Council and became the new District Headquarter after Mizoram attained the status of Union Territory.

Some District branches of administration function from Lunglei which are School Inspection, agriculture, power and electricity, PHE, PWD, printing and stationary, forest, soil conservation, industries, community development block, information and public relations, social welfare, transport, excise and others. Lunglei occupies the mid-southern position. The town is treated as class IV category in 1981 census.

Saiha is another new born District Headquarter located in the far south. There is the office of the Deputy Commissioner. It is also the head quarter of Lakher District Council. There are now some important Departments started on a district scale.

We find in this connection that Lawngtlai is the headquarter of Pawi District Council and Chawngte, the headquarter of Chakma District Council.

Vairangte lying in the outlying hills and plain on the north with its immediate proximity to the Barak valley on the other side. It is one of the stations which has a nearest approach to Cachar District in Assam. Now sericultural and a few agro-based enterprises have sprang at this place.

Kolasib it is another station on the Vairangte Aizawl road. It has grown into an important centre where there are a few office establishments. Demagiri or Tablung it occupies a very strategic position and had served earlier as the important base for despatching the various expeditions into Lushai Hills. It provides one of the main accesses to Lunglei from the Chittagong Hills Tract. It attained a very important position when South Lushai Hills was administered from Bengal. It is now a Subdivisional headquarter lying close to Bangladesh boundary.

Satrang lying very close to Aizawl and has become important for some industrial activities.

Durtlang it is another Mission centre. There was here a Mission hospital also. It was in 1947 or 1948 that the first Batch of nurses sat at the Assam External Examination Nurses, Midwives and Health visitors Council in which one nurse appearing her midwifery examination came out with Honours; one nurse also topped in the whole of Assam. In January 1948, the Governor of Assam, Mr. Akbar Hydari and Lady Hydari saw the hospital and at the special function held where a service of dedicated nurses was included, Lady Hydari gave away the certificates to nurses. Now it is one of the Presbyterian Church centres perhaps next to Aizawl.

Serkawr — it was one of the first Missions; bulk of the translation work both in the Duhlian and in a Lakher dialect was done at Serkawr; the educational administration during the first decades was conducted from here. There was also a Mission dispensary which acquainted the people with health services.

Champhai — it is one of small subdivisional headquarters located close to the Burma boundary.

There are a few lakes. One of them named Tamdil lies in the mid of a picturesque scenery; it is approached from Saitual village. The lake shows a variety of crabs, fish and provides a rich breading to the prawns.

Another lake, Rungdil is located on the northeastern portion of the state. It is called a twin lake because they are two lakes lying contiguous to one another and are very alike.

Birds throng to the lake side to refresh themselves and a host of patridges make the lake their favourite resort. It is believed that an underground tunnel of water connects them.

Palak is another lake which lies in Chhimtuipui District near Tuipung; it has a maximum radius of 660 yards. A host of the 'rare aquatic birds' are the permanent dwellers on the lake.'

The Blue mountain on its crest known as Phawngphui provides a rich, soothing and exhilarating scenery all around it. It is the home of the multi-colour orchids, wild flowers and a diverse foliage. It is famous for the rhododendrons blooming in their seasons. It is said that its upper range affords a resort to the birds and small animals.

Vantawng is a famous waterfall with its considerable height and the sheer sheet of water enveloping it from top to the bottom of the ridge. It is said to measure about 750 feet. It is approached from Jhenza village where a road connects that village with Aizawl Lunglei national highway.

Owing to the vastness of the District, the Districts split into Subdivisions have been found helpful in the matter of affecting the smooth functioning of administration. There are a few hotels in Aizawl. Tourist lodges are located at Saitual, Kolasib, Chatlang (Aizawl); there is a Highway restaurant at Thingdawl also.

The State reviewed as a whole, we find that there are a few towns; the rural character with the naive traditional traits that abound, is, therefore, a dominant aspect of society. On the other hand, a tempo of development characterises itself in the different sectors. A desolate vast of forests and wild lands' tracts is still formidable outside mostly the inhabited or cultivated places.

It is in this context that the wildlife sanctuaries have their importance in the preservation of fauna. It is assumed at present that there are wildlife sanctuaries at Dampa with a total area of 691 sq km at the sanctuaries located at Nyengpui and Phawangpui; moreover the lower column in Phawangpui has been converted into a biosphere.

Ka Hri Tha is one of the dominant ranges in the South. There are in it Khaisia Tlang or Ka Hri peak measuring 6,292 feet, Tliatlu or Mizen Thang 6,368 feet and Pheupi or Phawngpui, the blue mountain about 7,160 feet from the sea level. There is also a Seichawl range in Mizoram. Besides Aizawl and Lunglei, the other places treated recently as census towns are; Saiha, Champhai, Kolasib, Serchhip.

Bibliography

Abhinav, Shankar: *Making of Mizoram: Role of Laldenga*, Kashik Publication, Mizoram, 1994.

Agarwal, A. K.: *Administrative Review: Special Issue on Judicial Administration in Mizoram*, The Indian Institute of Public Administration Mizoram Regional Branch, Mizoram, 2001.

Animesh, R.: *India-The Land and the People: Mizoram*, National Book Trust of India, New Delhi, 1993.

Balwally, Darshan: *Growth of Totalitarianism in Arunachal Pradesh, Mizoram and Nagaland*, Spectrum Publications, Guwahati, 2003.

Bareh, H.: *Our Cultural Heritage, North-East India*, Omas Pub., Tripura, 1999.

Bhagabati, K. Abani and Kar, K. Bimal: *Survey of Research in Geography on North-East India 1970-1990*, Regency Publication, New Delhi, 1999.

Bhasak, R.G.: *History of North-eastern Fronetier*, Param Pub., Calcutta, 1917.

Bhattacharjee, J.B.: *North East Indian Perspectives in History*, Vikas Publishing House, New Delhi, 1995.

Bhattacharyya, N.N.: *Religious Culture of North-Eastern India*, Manohar Publishers & Distributors, New Delhi, 1995.

Bhaumik, Subir: *Insurgent Cross Fire: North-East India*, Lancer Publishers, New Delhi, 1996.

Bhuyan, B. C.: *Political Development of the North East*, Omsons Publications, New Delhi, 1989.

Bordoloi, B. N.: *District Handbook: United Mikir and North Cachar Hills*, Tribal Research Institute, Shillong, 1972.

Brown, R.: *Statistical Account of the Native State of Manipur and the Hill Territory under its Rule*, Govt. Printing, Kolkata, 1873.

Chasie, Charles: *The Naga Imbroglio: A Personal Perspective*, Standard Printers & Publishers, Kohima, 1999.

Chatterjee, Suhas: *Making of Mizoram: Role of Laldenga,* M. D. Publications Pvt. Ltd., New Delhi, 1994.

Chaube, S. K.: *Hill Politics in Northeast India,* Orient Longman Limited, Patna, 1973.

Choudhury, P.C.: *The History of the Civilisation of the People of North-East to the Twelfth Century A.D.,* Concept Pub., Madras, 1959.

Chowdury, Prosenjit: *The Turbulent North East,* New Delhi, 1996.

Coloney, L. Sailo, L. R. Zaihmingthanga, and Sailo, Lalthangfala: *Mizoram Millennium Souvenir,* The Millennium Souvenir Committee, Mizoram, 1989.

Das, Gurudas and Purkayastha, R. K.: *Border Trade: North-East India and Neighbouring Countries,* Akansha Publishing House, New Delhi, 2000.

Datta, P.S.: *North East as I See It,* Omsons Publications, New Delhi, 1994.

Devashish Kar: *Fundamentals of Limnology and Aquaculture Biotechnology: A Treatise on the Limnology and Fisheries of the Water Bodies in Southern Assam,* Mizoram and Tripura, Daya, 2007.

Devender Kumar Sikri: *Census of India 2001: Mizoram Administrative Atlas,* Controller of Publication, India, 2006.

Dutta, N.C.: *Politics of Identity and Nation Building in North-East India,* South Asian Press, New Delhi, 1997.

Gassah, L. S.: *Regional Political Parties in North East India,* Omsons Publications, New Delhi, 1992.

——————: *Research Priorities in North East India: With Special Reference to Mizoram,* Regency Publications, New Delhi, 2001.

——————: *Survey of Research in Political Science on North-East India 1970-1990,* Regency Publication, New Delhi, 1999.

Ghosh, S.P.: *Horticulture in North-East India,* Associated Publishing Company, New Delhi, 1984.

Goswami, B.B. Nunthra C. and Sengupta, N.N.: *People of India,* Mizoram, 1995.

Hazarika, Niru: *Profile of Youth Organisations in North East India,* V. V. Rao Institute of Micro Studies and Research, Assam, 1998.

Hooker, J.D.: *Himalayan Journals,* John Murray, London, 1854.

Jagadish Patnaik, K.: *Mizoram: Dimensions and Perspectives,* Society, Economy and Polity, Concept Pub, 2008.

John, B.: *The Voice of the North-eastern: Tribes Hills Social & Cultural Institute, Assam, Nagaland, Manipur, NEFA, Tripura,* Don Bosco Press, Shillong, 1968.

Johri, B.: *Art and Culture of North-East India*, Publications Division, New Delhi, 1998.

Joshi, H.G.: *Mizoram: Past and Present*, Mittal, 2005.

Kabra, K.C.: *Economic Growth of Mizoram: Role of Business and Industry*, Concept Pub, 2008.

Kalpana Das: *Rural Development in Mizoram: A Study of IRDP*, Mittal, 2004.

Khanna, S.K.: *Encyclopaedia of North-East India: Arunachal Pradesh, Assam, Manipur, Meghalaya, Tripura, Sikkim, Mizoram and Nagaland Tripura Sikkim*, Indian Pub, Mizoram, 1999.

Krishnaswami, A.: *The Indian Union and the States: A Study in Autonomy and integration*, London, 1964.

Kumar, B.B.: *Tensions and Conflict in Northeast India*, Cosmo Publications, New Delhi, 1995.

Kyndiah, P. R.: *Mizo Freedom Fighter*, Sanchar Publishing House, New Delhi, 1994.

——————: *Pillars of Mizo Society and Thoughts to Share*, Secretary Law and Parliamentary Affairs Department, Mizoram, 1999.

Lalhriatpuii: *Economic Participation of Women in Mizoram*, Concept Pub, Mizoram, 2010.

Lalneihzovi: *District Administration in Mizoram — A Study of the Aizawl District*, Mittal, 2006.

Lalramnghinglova, H. Bishen Singh Mahendra Pal Singh: *Ethno-Medicinal Plants of Mizoram*, 2003.

Lalthangliana, B.: *Culture and Folklore of Mizoram*, Publications Division, 2005.

Lanithanga, P.: *State of Our Union: Mizoram*, Publication Division, Government of India, New Delhi, 1997.

Lanunungsang, A.: *The Naga National Question in North-East India*, Mittal Publications, New Delhi, 2002.

Lianzela and Vanlalchhawna: *Ageing in North East India: Vol. I. Magnitude of the Problems of Elderly Persons in Mizoram*, Akansha, 2007.

Mackenzia, Alexander: *History of the Relations of the Governments with Hill Tribes of the North-East Frontier of Bengal*, Calcutta, 1884.

Mackenzie, A.: *A History of the Relation of the Government with Hill Tribes of the North-East Frontier of Bengal*, Calcutta, 1888.

——————: *The North East Frontier of India*, Mittal Publications, New Delhi, 2001.

Mali, D.D.: *International Development in North-East India*, Omson Pub., New Delhi, 1987.

Mathew, T.: *North-East*, Spectrum Publications, Gauhati, 1980.

Michell, J.F.: *Reports: Topographical, Political and Military on the North - East Frontier of India*, University of Kolkata, Kolkata, 1883.

Nag, Chitta Ranjan: *Mixo Polity and Political Modernisation*, Vikas Publishing House PVT LTD, New Delhi, 1998.

Nag, Sajal: *India and North-East India: Mind, Politics and the Process of Integration 1946-1950*, Regency Publications, New Delhi, 1998.

Neeti Mahanti: *Tribal Ethno-Botany of Mizoram*, 1994.

Nibedon, Nirmal: *North East India*, New Delhi, 1981.

——————: *Mizoram: The Dagger Brigade*, Lancers Publications, New Delhi, 1980.

——————: *North-East India: The Ethnic Explosion*, Lancers Publishers, New Delhi, 1981.

Nuh, V. K.: *Struggle for Identity in North-east India: A Theological response*, Spectrum Publications, Guwahati, 2001.

Nunthara, C.: *Mizoram: Society and Polity*, Indus, 1996.

Pakem, B.: *Insurgency in North-East India*, Om Sons Publications, New Delhi, 1997.

Phukon, Girin: *Politics of Regionalism in Northeast India*, Spectrum Publications, Guwahati, 1996.

Prasad, R.N. and Chakraborty, P.: *Administration of Justice in Mizoram*, Mittal, 2006.

Pudaite, Rochunga: *The Education of the Mizo People*, IndoBurma Pioneer Mission, Calcutta, 1963.

Querry, B.: *Studies in the History of North-east India*, MacMillan, London, 2000.

Rahman, S.A.: *The Beautiful India*, Reference Press, Mizoram, 2006.

Ravi, K.: *North-Eastern Hill University Regulation & Syllabus for Pre-University*, Shillong, 1985.

Rawat, S. K.: *Landmarks: A Study of Public Administration in Mizoram*, Aizawl, 1995.

Ray, A. C.: *States of our Union Mizoram*, Publication Division, Ministry of Information and Broadcasting, Government of India, New Delhi, 1972.

Rizvi, S.H.M. and Shibani Roy: *Kuki-Chin Tribes of Mizoram and Manipur*, B.R. Pub, 2006.

Sachdeva, Gulshan: *Economy of the North-East: Policy, Present Conditions and Future Possibilities*, Konark Publishers, Delhi, 2000.

Sapra, C.L. and Sarin, V.I.K.: *India's North-East in Flames*, New Delhi, 1980.

Sarin, V. I. K.: *India's North-East in Flames*, Vikash Publishing House, Uttar Pradesh, 1982.

Sarkar, N.: *Neolithic Celts in Arunachal Pradesh and Assam*, PINES, Arunachal Pradesh, 1993.

Sharma, T.C.: *Pre-historic Archaeology in North Eastern India: Its Problems and Prospects*, Dibrugarh University, Assam, 1974.

Singh, K. S.: *People of India: Mizoram,* Seagull Books, Calcutta, 1995.

Singh, N.P. Singh, K.P. and Singh, D.K.: *Flora of Mizoram: Ranunculaceae-Asteraceae,* Botanical Survey of India, India, 2002.

Singh, S.N.: *Mizoram: Historical, Geographical, Social, Economic, Political and Administrative,* 1994.

Sinha, A.C.: *Youth Movements in North-East India: Structural Imperatives and Aspects of Change,* Indus Publishing Company, New Delhi, 1994.

Sopitt, C.A.: *A Short Account of the Kuki-Lushai Tribes on the North-East Frontier,* Cachar, 1998.

Srivastav, Nirankar: *Survey of Research in Economics on North East India 1970-1990,* Regency Publications, New Delhi, 2000.

Syiemlieh, R. David: *Survey of Research in History on North-East India 1970-1990,* Regency Publication, New Delhi, 2000.

Tarapot, Phanjoubam: *Drug Abuse and Illicit Trafficking in North Eastern India,* Vikash Publishing House, New Delhi, 1997.

Thanga, L.B.: *The Mizos: A Study in Racial Personality,* Gauhati, 1978.

Thomas, C. Joshua: *Dimensions of Displaced People in North-East India,* Regency Publications, New Delhi, 2002.

Verghese, B.G.: *India's North East Resurgent: Ethnicity, Insurgency, Governance, and Development,* Konark Publishers, New Delhi, 1997.

Zaidi, A.: *Electoral Politics in North-East India,* Vijaya Pub., Assam, 2000.

Zairema: *God's Miracle in Mizoram,* Synod Press & Bookworm, Mizoram, 1978.

Zorema, J.: *Indirect Rule in Mizoram 1890-1954: The Bureaucracy and the Chiefs,* Mittal Pub, 2007.

Index

❑❑❑

www.ingramcontent.com/pod-product-compliance
Lightning Source LLC
Chambersburg PA
CBHW080758300326

41914CB00055B/941